Icebound Hearts

Pleasant Oaks University
Book One

A.C. MOTUGA

Copyright © 2025 A.C. MOTUGA

All rights reserved. No part of this publication may be reproduced, distributed, or transmitted in any form or by any means, including photocopying, recording, or other electronic or mechanical methods, without the prior written permission of the publisher, except in the case of brief quotations embodied in critical reviews and certain other noncommercial uses permitted by copyright law.

This book is a work of fiction. Names, characters, businesses, organizations, places, events, and incidents are products of the author's imagination or are used fictitiously. Any resemblance to actual persons, living or dead, events or locales is entirely coincidental.

Printed in the United States of America

For more information or to book an event, contact:
Amotugaauthor.com

Book design by: SimplyLuvelyArts
Cover design by: Arseda Cenollari & Farisai Makuto

ISBN Paperback: 9798310986923

First Edition: April 2025

*For the stubborn, broken souls
who swore they didn't need love—
may you find the kind that stays,
even when you try to push it away.*

AUTHOR'S NOTE

HELLO, DEAR READERS!

To ensure the best reading experience, I want to provide a list of potential triggers present in this book. While the story is primarily lighthearted, it does touch on some serious themes that may be upset- ting to certain readers. Please proceed at your discretion.

CONTENT WARNINGS:
- Absent parent
- Panic attacks
- Anxiety
- Explicit sexual content
- Alcohol consumption
- Ill relative
- Mentions of sexual assault

Your well-being is important, so please take care while reading.

PLAYLIST

Theme Song: This Is Me Trying - Taylor Swift

1. Hate The Way - G-Eazy
2. Heaven And Back - Chase Atlantic
3. Heal - Tom Odell
4. I Know Places - Taylor Swift
5. Keep Your Eyes On Me Boy - Nessa Barrett
G. Nothing's Gonna Hurt You Baby - Cigarettes After Sex
7. Boyfriend- Dove Cameron
8. Reflections- The Neighbourhood
9. Does God Cry? - Nessa Barrett
10. Your Shirt - Chelsea Cutler
11. Partition- Beyonce
12. Sports Car - Tate McRae
13. Love Looks Pretty On You - Nessa Barrett
14. Robbers - The 1975
15. You're All I Want - Cigarettes After Sex
16. Give Me Love- Ed Sheeran
17. Signs - Tate McRae
18. Salvatore -Lana Del Rae
19. Work Song - Hozier
20. Lover -Taylor Swift
21. Means I Care - Tate McRae
22. You Are In Love - Taylor Swift
23. I Wanna Be Yours - Arctic Monkeys

CHAPTER ONE

KATERINA

I never thought I'd leave Russia like this. Not with my head bowed in shame. Not with my name dragged through the mud by people who once cheered for me. Not with my dreams slipping through my fingers like ice melting under the sun. But here I am—thirty thousand feet in the air, watching Moscow disappear beneath a blanket of clouds, knowing I may never call it home again. My fingers clench the armrest as turbulence rattles the plane. My skates are resting at my feet, safely tucked in their worn-out bag. It is the only part of my past I refuse to let go of. Everything else—my country, my career, my reputation—was stripped from me when my world came crashing down. The whispers. The betrayal. The shame. I push it all down, swallowing the ache in my throat as I stare out the window.

America. A fresh start. A second chance at the dream that once felt untouchable. I don't know if I deserve it. But I do know one thing.

I'm going to take it.

When I land, my phone explodes with calls—my mother, again and again.

Ignoring her is pointless, so I give up and answer.

"I'm fine, Mom. You don't have to worry about me." I say, running a hand through my hair and letting out a frustrated sigh.

"I know you can take care of yourself, my love, but being so far away from you worries me."

I groan, rubbing my temple. My dear worries more than I do; so much for having faith in me.

"Mom, Jake is here, living minutes away, so I think I'll be fine. He is my father, even though I know you wish he never showed up. No need to worry."

Silence. Then a scoff. Shit. Why did I have to mention my father?

"Don't mention that man," she snaps, her tone sharp. "After twenty-two years, he suddenly decides to be a father and show up? Where was he all these years?"

I press my fingers into my temple, closing my eyes. My heart clenches—not for my father, but for my mother. For the pain she still carries after all these years.

"Mama, I'll be fine. I'll call you whenever I can to reassure you. Also, I start training tonight, remember? That's the biggest reason I took Jake's offer—to get my gold, especially after what happened at my qualifiers."

Silence stretches between us, but I hear her breathing on the other end—the hesitancy.

The unspoken *I don't want you near him.*

"I know, my love," she finally says. "Okay, for now, calls will have to do. FaceTime me later, please. I love you."

A small smile tugs at my lips. "I love you too, Mama. Bye."

I hang up the phone and turn toward the road. A fresh wave of unease settles in my stomach as I glance at the unfamiliar scenery outside the Uber window. I landed in Pleasant Oaks, Michigan, almost an hour ago. I'm on my way to my new home—Pleasant Oaks University. The only school in the U.S. known for producing the most figure skaters qualified for the Olympics—the elite.

After what happened at the last Olympics, my old coach had been exposed all over the internet. A single person revealed the monster behind the curtain in front of everyone. Me. The woman who broke me. My mother sued her, and when news broke about the torture she put her students through, my father—Jake fucking Hart—walked back into my life as if two decades of silence meant nothing. I was reluctant to be around him, but without him, my best friends Alexei, Alina, and I may never have had a second chance to compete for the USA and train under the best of the best.

Camilla Trusova. A legend. A three-time Olympic gold medalist in pair skating. And now, my new coach. I shift in my seat, my stomach twisting. I should be excited. I am excited. But beneath that excitement is something else— fear. This is my last shot. After what happened at the qualifiers, I have to prove I belong here.

The car slows in front of a three-story house. It's modern and clean, but something already feels off. The house doesn't look anything like how Alina described it.

"This is the house, miss," the driver says, glancing at me through the rear-view mirror.

"Thank you," I say quietly, stepping out into the cool Michigan air.

I grip the handles of my two large suitcases, slinging my backpack over my shoulder. This is all I could bring to the plane. The rest of my things should arrive in a few days. I drag my luggage up the rocky path and ring the doorbell. A few seconds later, the door swings open, and—

Oh.

Oh.

A handsome, shirtless man stands before me, leaning casually against the frame. His damp hair falls over his eyes, his abs look straight out of a fitness magazine, and his deep blue eyes glint in amusement.

"Hi. Are you lost?" he asks, his lips twitching into a smirk. I blink. "No?" I glance at the house number, and down at the paper in my hands. It's the same one.

"Is this Weblley House?" The stranger nods, his expression now matching my confusion.

"I was assigned a room here," I explain. "My name is Katerina Hart." I dig into my backpack, pull out my admissions email, and hand it to him. His brows shoot up.

"Holy shit. The school assigned you here?" He exhales a laugh, shaking his head. "Oh, sweetheart, they fucked up. This is the hockey players' house. We have an empty room, but it's meant for a hockey player—not a figure skater. Not a girl." I groan, pressing my fingers against my forehead.

"You've got to be kidding me." Crap. I have my first training session in two hours. "Fuck," I mutter. "Okay, um… Can I leave my bags here while I talk to the admissions office? I have no idea where else to put them. It's my first day in America, and this shit happens to me. I have training soon, and—oh my god—I think I'm gonna pass out."

"Yeah, of course you can. I'm sorry about this." He steps aside. "Come on in."
"I'm William Knight, by the way. But you can call me Will," he says, extending a hand. "Pleasure to meet you, even though the circumstances are... not ideal." I shake his hand.
"Katerina Petrova." His brow lifts.
"I thought your last name was Hart?" I sigh. I hate using my fathers last name.
"It's a new addition. It'll take me a while to get used to it." He nods, sensing it's not a topic I want to discuss. Will lifts my bags effortlessly, carrying them up two flights of stairs as I follow suit.
"This would've been your room, I guess." I step inside. It's spacious and modern, with a huge window overlooking the campus. A plush chaise sits in front of it, next to a sleek desk. There's a full bed, my bathroom, and—thank God—a walk-in closet. I take it all in, exhaling slowly.
"So pretty," I whisper. I hope the school will figure this out and the figure skating house has just as nice rooms.
"I'll leave you to it." Will whispers before disappearing down the hall. I unzip my suitcase, pulling out my gear. Twenty minutes later, I have on my black leggings, a fitted long-sleeve shirt, and a white puffer vest. I grab my skates, leg warmers, and water bottle before stuffing my wallet and paperwork into my gym bag. I head downstairs and nearly collide with another handsome stranger. Jesus. What is it with this house? This one is taller than Will, broader, with sharp green eyes and a serious expression. His damp hair is dark brown, curling slightly at the ends like he just stepped out of the shower. His gaze flicks over me briefly before he steps aside, letting me pass.

I mumble a quick "Sorry," but he didn't reply. He just gave me a curt nod before disappearing into the kitchen. Alright, then. Noted. I wave goodbye to Will who is laying in this huge bean bag, watching TV. "I'll let you know what they say."
"Good luck, Kat." I smile as he yells it out, raising his hand up to wave at me.
 I step outside, gripping my bag tightly. It's my first day in America, and I'm already fighting an uphill battle. Welcome to hell, Katerina. Or maybe—
 Welcome to my second chance.

CHAPTER TWO

KATERINA

"What do you mean there are no other rooms available?" My voice rises in frustration as I stare at the admissions lady, my grip tightening around the strap of my bag. She gives me a tight-lipped smile that tells me she's been dealing with complaints all day and has zero patience left. "As I said, Miss Hart, someone was supposed to assign you to the Figure Skating House, but there was a clerical error. Unfortunately, that house is at full capacity. The best we can do is have you stay in the Hockey House until the semester ends."

A headache pulses behind my temples. I pinch the bridge of my nose, inhaling slowly.

"This can't be happening."

"That's six months," I say, voice tight. "You want me to live with four hockey players for six months?" She nods, her expression full of forced sympathy. "I'm sorry, but it's either that or you defer until spring." Defer? After everything I went through to get here? After leaving Russia, uprooting my entire life, and pushing past the emotional wreckage my last coach left behind? No. That's not an option. I exhale sharply. "Fine." She slides a key across the desk. "I truly apologise for the mix-up. Here's your key and all the information you'll need." I grab it, muttering a half-hearted "Thanks" before turning on my heel and heading for the exit. The cold air bites at my cheeks as soon as I step outside. I glance at my watch and groan. The Pleasant Oaks University Ice Arena is a ten-minute walk from the admissions office, and I make the journey with quick, determined strides. Each step feels heavier than the last, and my mind is clouded with too many thoughts.

I shouldn't be this nervous; I should be excited. Instead, my stomach is in knots. Camilla Trusova is expecting me. A legend in the figure skating world. A three-time Olympic gold medalist. She doesn't take on just anyone. And yet here I am. Because of *him*. Jake Hart. My father. The thought alone sends a bitter taste to my tongue.

After all these years, the birthdays missed, the competitions he never attended—he suddenly decides to play hero. Suddenly, my dad cares about my career. I should've told him to go to hell. But Alexei convinced me otherwise.

"This is our second chance, Katerina. We'll never get another one."

So here I am, gripping my gym bag, heading toward an arena I've never skated in, about to train under a woman I worshipped my entire childhood. And if I fail?

What if I let the past creep back in? What if the ghosts of my old life resurface? No. I won't fail. I *can't*.

The moment I step inside the arena, the tension in my body loosens slightly. Bright lights cast a cool glow over the Olympic-sized rink, illuminating the pristine ice. The faint scent of minty coolant lingers in the air, mixed with the crisp sharpness of the Ice itself.

This… this is home. The distant sound of blades carving into ice echoes in the vast space. A few skaters glide across the rink, lost in their routines. Some of them landing jumps effortlessly. Others stumbling. I watch one girl attempt a triple axel, her expression fierce with concentration before she crashes onto the ice with a sharp thud. My heart clenches.

I missed this: the muscle ache, the exhaustion of perfecting a routine, and the adrenaline rush when I hit every element flawlessly. Something inside me sparks for the first time since my final competition in Russia. Not fear. Not anxiety. But determination. I drop my bag onto the bench, quickly pulling off my sneakers and lacing up my skates.

Then—loud, booming voices from the other side of the rink pull me from my thoughts. I look up, and my stomach twists in irritation—hockey players. Of course. The universe is testing my patience today. The last thing I need is a bunch of loud, obnoxious boys taking up space when I am trying to prove myself to Camilla.

"Kit-Kat!" I turn at the familiar nickname, and the tension in my shoulders eases even more. Alexei and Alina. My best friends.

I push up from the bench and throw my arms around them, squeezing tight. "Oh my God, I'm so happy to see you both," I breathe. "This stupid bad luck is following me everywhere." Alexei pulls back, brows raised. "Why aren't you at the Figure Skating House?" I groan.

"Because someone screwed up, and now I'm stuck living with four hockey players until spring semester." His jaw drops, and Alina's eyes widen.

"Can we switch spots, please?" Alexei grins. "I don't know why you're complaining because those guys are hot." I roll my eyes but chuckle, glancing toward the hockey players still practicing. I immediately spot Will—tall, athletic, and already grinning at me as he pulls off his helmet and waves. I nod in acknowledgment, offering a small smile in return.

Beside him, another player stands stiffly, still in full gear. His helmet is on, obscuring his face, but I feel his gaze on me—a strange energy zipping down my spine. Before I can linger on it, Camilla's sharp voice cuts through the air. "Gather up, everyone."

I take a deep breath and step onto the ice, the familiar sensation of my blades gliding across the surface calming me. Camilla waits for us near the boards, arms crossed, expression unreadable. "It's good to see everyone back. We also have a few new faces—some of you may already know them." Her gaze lands on Alexei, Alina, and me. "Starting today, Alexei and Katerina will train with Team USA for the qualifiers and Olympics in pairs skating. Alina will be competing in women's solo skating." A few people nod, and some murmur in acknowledgment.

Camilla gestures toward the other side of the rink. "If you've noticed the hockey players, pay them no mind." Yeah, right, easier said than done. "On Mondays, Wednesdays, and Fridays, our schedules overlap. We share the ice for one hour, but they'll be wrapping up soon." I glance back at the hockey players, and my eyes immediately land on Will before a second player catches my attention. The other guy. The one still in his helmet. The one still staring. I swallow hard and look away.

Camilla claps her hands, drawing my attention back to her.

"Now, let's get started. Alexei, Katerina—I want to see your last routine before we begin training. I need to assess where you're at and what needs improvement."

My stomach tightens. I knew this was coming, but that doesn't make it any less nerve-wracking. Alexei nudges me.

"We got this." Camilla lifts a brow. "Is that okay? Any music preferences?" Alexei nods. "Can you play I Know Places by Taylor Swift?" Camilla gives a slight nod to the sound tech.

"Alright, everyone off the ice." The skaters clear out, and even the hockey players pause to watch. I take a deep breath. I can do this. I have to do this. Alexei squeezes my hand, a silent reminder that we're in this together—the first notes of the song play, soft yet powerful. We push off. The moment my blades carve into the ice, the outside world fades. Everything else—the housing disaster, the hockey players, my father—ceases to exist. It's just me, Alexei, and the music. We move in perfect sync, and our years of partnership are shining through.

A single axel. A triple twist. It's a flawless step sequence. The final lift comes—Alexei hoists me into the air, spinning me before lowering me down gracefully. The last note plays, and we come to a smooth stop. The silence is deafening. Then—A single nod from Camilla.

"Again."

She hates it! I know it! My breath comes in slow, measured inhales as I step back into position, shaking out the tension in my arms. Alexei meets my gaze, his blue eyes sharp with focus. "You good?" he asks under his breath. I nod. "Yeah." But I don't know if that's true. The first run-through was good. Solid. But not perfect.

And Camilla expects perfection. She doesn't say it outright— she doesn't have to. Her expression, the sharp gleam in her eye, the way she simply says "Again" instead of giving praise… it's enough. The sound tech cues up the music once more. The opening notes of I Know Places hum through the speakers, sending a familiar rush of anticipation through my veins. Alexei and I push off simultaneously, our movements fluid as we transition into the opening sequence. This time, we push harder and move faster. Our steps match perfectly, the ice whispering beneath us as we carve out the routine we've spent months perfecting. The first jump approaches—a side-by-side triple Salchow. I bend my knees, launching into the rotation at the exact moment Alexei does. My body twists, my skates slicing through the air—And I land. Effortless and Smooth.

Alexei lands a second later, and we flow seamlessly into the next element. The footwork section comes next, demanding precision and synchronisation. I shift my weight, focusing on each turn, each edge, each carefully timed movement that keeps us in perfect harmony with the music. Alexei grips my waist, and I push off, soaring above the ice as he hoists me effortlessly into the air.

For a brief moment, everything disappears. It's just me, suspended in weightlessness, the cold air biting at my skin as we spin. Then, Alexei lowers me with practiced ease, and we transition straight into the final sequence, a combination spin requiring absolute control. We move as one, the world blurring until the last note plays.

We come to a controlled stop, our breathing heavy, our hearts pounding.
Silence hangs in the rink.
A few beats pass, and then a slow clap. It starts from the other side of the rink, where the hockey players still linger. My stomach twists with anxiety as my gaze flicks over. Will grins at me, giving me a thumbs up with both hands. I roll my eyes but bite back a smile. Beside him, the other one who's been watching me all morning—stands motionless, helmet still on.
Something about him unsettles me. He's quiet. Still. Like he's studying me. Before I can think too much about it, Camilla clears her throat. She steps forward, eyes scanning us critically.
"Better," she says, giving the slightest nod of approval. "But not good enough." Alexei exhales sharply beside me, but I don't let it shake me. I know Camilla. That was her version of a compliment. She turns, calling out to the rest of the skaters. "That's all for today. Be here at six a.m. sharp tomorrow. No exceptions." A collective groan echoes through the rink, but no one argues.
I skate to the boards, sliding my blade guards on before stepping off the ice. The second my feet hit solid ground, exhaustion settles in. Alexei nudges me. "We're getting drinks tonight, right?" I give him an irritated look. "You mean, you're getting drinks while I sit there and regret my life choices?"
"Exactly," Lex says, grinning. I shake my head, grabbing my bag.
"I don't know... I still have to move into hell." Alexei perks up.
"Oh, right! The Hockey House." I groan, already dreading it.

"Oh my gosh!" I exclaim. "What if we switch rooms? Please Alexei?" I beg, my eyes pleading with his. Alexei snorts, and that's when I know it won't happen.

"Malyshka, I love you, but you know me. As much as I'd love living with four sexy hockey players, I'm an OCD freak, babe. It will never work." I groan, resting my head in my hands.

"Six months, Alexei. Six months of sweaty hockey bros and their stupid protein shakes."

Alina, who's been listening quietly, suddenly smirks.

"Sweaty hot hockey bros." I sigh dramatically.

"Why is everyone acting like this is some blessing? I'd much rather be in a house full of girls who understand things like skincare and personal space." Alexei slings an arm over my shoulder, steering me toward the exit.

"It won't be that bad. Maybe you'll even have a little fun." I snort. "Doubt it." Still, as we leave the rink, a strange feeling lingers in my chest—a feeling I can't quite place. As I glance over my shoulder one last time, my eyes land on him again—the hockey player who hasn't stopped watching me, the one who hasn't said a word. Another shiver runs down my spine.

Yeah.

This is going to be hell.

CHAPTER THREE

KATERINA

Where is it? Panic flutters in my chest as I rummage through my bag, my fingers digging through layers of fabric and loose items. My breath quickens. No, no, no. It has to be here. Then, finally, my fingertips brushed against the familiar cool metal. Relief washes over me as I pull out my necklace, the delicate gold pendant catching the dim overhead lights. I clasp it around my neck, my shoulders sagging as the muscle tension eases. Grandma Anastasia gave this to me before she passed away. A tiny figure skater etched into the pendant, symbolising her unwavering belief in me. She was my biggest supporter and the reason I am where I am today. Before every practice, I make sure I'm wearing this necklace. Some might call it superstition, but it's a reminder to me—a connection to the woman who always saw my potential, even when I doubted myself. I take a deep breath, slip my headphones in, and secure my headband to keep them in place. The world outside fades, replaced by the steady rhythm of music filling my ears. Practice is gruelling, but Camilla praises Alexei and me for our performance. We ran through our routine four times, and although there's room for improvement, the fire inside me is back—the hunger, the need to be better.

Now, it's just me and the ice. The arena is empty. The fluorescent lights hum softly, casting a cool glow over the pristine ice sheet. I exhale, step onto the frozen surface, and push off. As I gather speed, my blades carve smooth lines into the ice, and the familiar adrenaline rush makes my heart race.

I move through my elements, landing a few jumps with ease. The ice welcomes me back like an old friend. But just as I gain momentum, something solid collides into me. I don't have time to react before hitting the ice, a sharp sting spreading through my right hip and shoulder. Pain lances through me as I wince, brushing the shredded ice off my leggings. "What the hell?" I mutter, disappointed at myself for falling. I look up—and my breath catches.

Dark eyes. Sharp jaw.

Raven-black hair.

The most devastatingly gorgeous guy I've ever seen stands before me, amusement dancing in his gaze. He's all lean muscle and raw intensity, displaying an almost infuriating confidence. His lips are moving, but there's no sound hitting my ears. I snap out of my daze, pulling out an earbud.

"What?"

"You should watch where you're going, Goldie." His voice is smooth, with the slightest rough edge at the end, like he's always a second away from smirking. I scowl.

"Can't you watch where you're going? I could've sliced you open with my skate blades." He crouches slightly, extending a hand toward me. "Don't worry, angel. I can handle a skate-blade." I ignore the way his lips twitch as if he finds this amusing.

"I'm not an angel," I muttered, gripping his hand. He pulls me up effortlessly, his strength sending another unwanted jolt through me. His chuckle is low, teasing.

"No? Then what should I call you?" "Nothing." I glare, pulling my hand back. "I was here first. If you don't mind, I'd like to return to my solo practice."

He doesn't move. He crosses his arms, his gaze flicking to my chest before meeting my eyes again.

"The rink's open to both of us, angel. I'm not going anywhere." My patience snaps.

"I don't care. Go practice somewhere else." His smirk deepens.

"Check the timesheet, sweetie. I have this time-slot reserved for the rest of the season. It's right here, every day, at the same time."

My jaw tightens.

"You reserved this time slot?" He nods in response. I want to scream. I need this ice time—every second counts. I huff. "Fine. Whatever. You got your way this time." I say, skating backward toward the exit. As I step off the ice, I can feel his gaze still on me, burning into my back. God, he's insufferable. And I already know—I will hate every second of knowing him, but I will enjoy seeing him. Why is it always the hot ones with a crappy attitude?

The house is quiet when I step inside. Three pairs of eyes snap at me as I approach the living room. "Kat, you're back," one of the guys says. It takes me a second to recognise him. I saw him briefly earlier—tall, dark hair, mischievous smirk. Did Will tell him my name? "I'm Roman," he says, patting his chest once, then continues, "That's Grayson." gesturing toward another guy on the couch. "And you already met Will. Our team captain, Aiden, will be here soon." Will leans back on the couch, eyes still on his game. "So? What'd they say?" I sigh, dropping my bag.

"Looks like you guys are stuck with me for six months. They said I could stay here or defer a semester, and that's not happening." Will grins.

"Hell yeah! We need a girl around here—one that isn't Roman's latest mistake."

"Booty call," Roman corrects.

"Oh," Roman adds. "Someone delivered your stuff earlier. We put everything in your room. I hope you don't mind." My mouth parts slightly in surprise. "You did what?" Will shrugs. "It was mostly Roman. He got excited about a girl moving in." I shake my head, a small smile tugging at my lips. "Thanks, guys. I appreciate it."

Three hours later, my room is finally starting to feel like *mine*.

I have hung my clothes, made my bed, and added the perfect softness to my mattress topper. My bookshelves and trophy shelves are missing, but I'll get to that later. My phone rings, and I reach towards my nightstand, grabbing it.

Jake.

I hesitate before answering, putting in my headphones. "Hey, Jake," I say, hoping the call ends quickly.

"Hi, Kat. Are you okay?" I sigh, rubbing my temple.
"Yeah. Why?" My brows dip in confusion. Does he already know about the housing situation?
"I heard about the housing situation. It's unacceptable. I was going to come down tomorrow, talk to the Dean, maybe get you your place—"
"No." My voice is firm. How did he find out so soon? Is he going to be breathing down my neck the whole semester?
"Please, don't. I just unpacked, and I'm not moving again. Plus, having a little male influence in my life is refreshing, considering I haven't had any all my life." The silence stretches between us before he exhales.
"Are you sure, Katerina?" I know he is trying, but knowing my every move and not giving me space will not fix our relationship.
"I'm sure." A knock at my door pulls my attention. "Hold on," I say before opening it.
Will stands there, arms crossed. "Hey, uh… there's a guy outside. Says he's delivering a car." A sinking feeling settles in my stomach. I mute Jake before storming outside. I feel my blood boil when I see the sleek black Jeep parked in our driveway.
I quickly unmute the phone, "Are you serious? What the fuck, Jake? I told you not to throw money at me! You weren't there for twenty-one years, and now you think you can buy me?" I abruptly end the call before he can respond.
The delivery guy clears his throat and steps forward with a clipboard. "Miss, I need you to sign so I can drop off the car." I drag a hand down my face. "Can you take it back?" My voice is softer now, and exhaustion is creeping in. "I'm sorry, but it's been paid off already."

Of course, it has. I huff out a breath, sign the damn papers, and watch as the delivery guy sets the keys on top of the paperwork he laid on the hood of the car before driving away. Silence lingers as I go back inside, the boys watching me with varying degrees of concern. Well—three of them.

Standing there, leaning against the door, is the guy from the rink. What is he doing here?

Roman is the first to speak, walking over with a glass of water and handing it to me, "You okay?" I nod, taking a sip. "Just frustrated. I can't believe my dad would do this shit." Roman observes me.

"Touchy subject?" I nod, swirling the water in my cup. "Very."

He hesitates before offering, "Well, if you need someone to talk to, me and the guys are here for you."

A deep, familiar chuckle comes from behind me. I whirl around—and of course, it's him.

"You," I breathe, staring at him in disbelief. The smirk on his face is infuriating.

Oh my god.

Is he my fourth roommate?

This cannot be happening.

The jerk leans casually against the doorframe, arms crossed over his chest. His dark eyes flick over me, and that infuriating smirk tugs at his lips. "You seem surprised, angel face." I blink, my brain short-circuiting. "You live here?" I ask, pointing around the house.

"Clearly." His voice is smooth, dripping with amusement. "Try to keep up." I open my mouth, then quickly shut it. Of course, he lives here. Of course, the cocky, ice-stealing, smirking jerk is my fourth roommate. The universe must genuinely hate me.

Roman clears his throat behind me, watching the scene unfold like prime-time entertainment.

"Sooo... I take it you two know each other?" I let out a sharp laugh. "Unfortunately. We met right before he kicked me off the rink." My eyes catch a muscle twitch in his arm, and I hover over it, noticing how defined and strong they are.

"Whoa, whoa." Roman's brows shoot up. "Aiden, tell me you didn't." Aiden. That's his name. The Jerk feels more fitting, but I won't fault his parents for that. Aiden just shrugs. "She was in my time slot." I glare at him. "Anyone can use the rink, asshole. You don't fucking own it." Roman whistles while Will and Grayson chuckle. Aiden's eyes darken slightly, but the corner of his mouth quirks up.

"I own it when I reserve it, Goldie." I scoff, brushing past him and storming inside the house. I can hear him chuckling behind me, his voice carrying easily. "This is gonna be fun."

I head straight to my room, my blood still simmering. Of all the hockey players I could've been forced to live with, it had to be him. He's such an arrogant ass. And worst of all, I find him unbelievably hot anyway. The way his muscles tensed when he leaned against the doorway, and his tattoos curled around his biceps—ugh. Why did he have to look like that? I groan, flopping onto my bed pressing my hands to my burning face. This is going to be the longest six months. A sudden knock at my door causes me to jolt up.

"Go away," I call. The door swings open anyway—because, apparently, boundaries are just a suggestion in this house. To my relief, it's Roman, not Aiden. Not that I wanted it to be Aiden.

Roman holds up his hands in surrender. "Whoa, not the enemy. Just came to check in." I sigh, relaxing my

shoulders. "Sorry. I just- this day has been a lot."
Roman nods, stepping inside and leaning against my
desk. "Yeah, I can tell. You wanna talk about it?" I
hesitate, then exhale.

"It's my dad, Jake. He-" I pause, searching for the right
words, "he wasn't in my life until recently, and now
he's trying to throw money at me. Like that'll magically
fix everything." Roman tilts his head. "The car
outside?" I nod. "I didn't ask for it. I don't *want* it. But
he thinks expensive gifts make up for years of not being
my father." Roman stays quiet for a moment, then
shrugs. "You could sell it."
I blink. "What?" He grins. "Sell it. Donate the money.
Or keep it for yourself. If he wants to play the 'rich,
guilty dad' card, at least *you* should benefit." I snort.
"That's actually... not the worst idea." Roman taps the
side of his temple. "Genius, I know." I shake my head,
smiling slightly. Roman's easygoing, playful energy is
precisely what I needed after the nightmare of a day.
"You know," he says, crossing his arms, "Aiden's not
that bad." I scoff. "He *is* that bad." Roman chuckles.
"Nah, he's just... rough around the edges. Give it time.
You might like him." I arch a brow. "Doubt it." That is
what I say, but I mean when hell freezes over.
"We'll see, Kit-Kat," he smirks. I grin at the nickname,
pointing at him. "You heard my friends calling me that
at the rink, didn't you?" Roman shakes his head in
denial as he grins at me, "What? I just made that up
right now." I laugh at his sarcasm, feeling better after
talking to him. I think Roman and I will be good
friends.
"But since Aiden kicked you off the ice earlier, I might
have a way to fix that." I raise a brow, intrigued. "Go
on."

"He gets that extra hour because he volunteers to teach kids to skate at six a.m. They're looking for more volunteers; if you sign up, he has to share the rink with you. He can't kick you out." Aw, the asshole has a heart. A slow grin spreads across my face. "Roman, you just earned mega brownie points."

With that, Roman heads for the door, throwing me a wink before disappearing into the hallway. I exhale, flopping back onto my bed. Aiden. Jake. This ridiculous housing situation. I just wanted ice time, not a damn soap opera. I close my eyes, forcing myself to breathe deeply. Tomorrow, I'll wake up. I'll skate. I'll focus. And I'll prove to Jake, Aiden, and myself that nothing will stand in my way. Not even a cocky, insufferable hockey captain with a face that could ruin lives.

CHAPTER FOUR

KATERINA

After an hour of relentless begging, charming smiles, and shameless ass-kissing, Mrs. Richards finally caved. Barely. She wasn't thrilled with my persistence, but after I dramatically explained how desperately I needed the extra ice time, she sighed, rubbing her temples like I was responsible for her impending migraine.

"Fine," she said, exasperated. "You can start tomorrow. 8 AM sharp. And before you ask, you cannot pick a different partner." And that's how I set myself up to be assisting Aiden fucking Knight. I tried pleading again, but Mrs. Richards's look made me snap my mouth shut. Beggars can't be choosers. At least I had secured the ice tonight. And the best part? I was about to ruin Aiden's little private practice session.

Smirking to myself, I make my way toward the rink, anticipation buzzing under my skin. Oh, he was not going to like this. I spend time lacing up my skates, ensuring each loop is snug. Tonight, I've opted for a sleek black bodysuit, the long sleeves hugging my arms like a second layer of skin. My high ponytail is tight, and my headband keeps my headphones secure. When my skates touch the ice, I toss my skate guards onto the bench and exhale deeply. The world fades when I push off, gliding effortlessly across the rink. Dark Paradise by Lana Del Rey floods my ears, drowning out everything—every thought, frustration, and lingering bitterness toward my father, my situation, and Aiden. Here on the ice, I'm weightless. Untouchable. I lose myself in my routine, executing a series of quad jumps, feeling the sharp bite of the cold air against my skin. Each successful landing sends a rush of satisfaction through me. The rink belongs to me in these moments—until I slam hard into a solid, warm chest. Two strong hands grip my waist, steadying me before I can fall over. My breath hitches as I lift my gaze and lock eyes with Aiden. Fuck.

I barely register Lana, still crooning in my ears as I stare up at him. Were his eyes this pretty yesterday, or did I bump my head somewhere? The world blurs, my heart pounding far too loudly in my chest. Aiden frowns, his lips moving, but I can't hear him over the music. He snaps his fingers before my face, dragging me back to reality.

Annoyed, I reach under my headband and yank out an earbud. "What?"

Aiden sighs, his hands on my waist lingering a second too long before he finally lets go.

"Angel Face," he starts, exasperation clear in his tone. "I thought we talked about this yesterday. This is my ice time. It's booked for me. Not you—me."

I smirk, knowing exactly how much this is about to piss him off. "Well, now it's my ice time, too."

His frown deepens. "What the hell does that mean?" Aiden asks, confused. "Your dear friend Roman gave me some stellar advice yesterday," I say, folding my arms over my chest. "So I chatted with Mrs. Richards, and guess what?"

His jaw ticks, and he clearly understands where this is going. "What?"

"I'm the newest junior coach," I exclaim with a grin. I watch as he processes my words, his shoulders rising and falling with a deep, frustrated breath. His jaw clenches once, then unclenches.

"Oh, and the best part?" I lean in slightly, enjoying the way his dark eyes narrow. "We have to teach together." Aiden exhales harshly through his nose. "You're kidding." I grin harder.

"Nope. And before you even think about going to Mrs. Richards to get reassigned, don't bother. I already tried, and she shut me down." He turns his face away, clearly attempting to keep himself from saying something he'll regret. I can't help but admire the sharp line of his jaw, the way his black fitted shirt hugs his every muscle, the flex of his forearms as he crosses them over his broad chest—

"Fine," he finally says. "We'll share the rink. The left side is mine. I'll put a cone in the middle, and you better not fucking cross it." I raise my hands in surrender. "Sure, Aiden. Whatever you say."

His scowl deepens. "It's Knight to you." I roll my eyes, sliding my earbuds back in as I skate away. I'm midway through my jump sequence, practicing my

quad toe when my skate catches at the wrong angle. The impact is immediate. I slam hard onto the ice, pain exploding in my right shoulder as I land.
Fuck.
I hiss, flexing my arm. A sharp, familiar pain shoots through me. Damn it. I should have booked my physical therapy appointment days ago.
Before I can fully process the pain, a pair of hockey skates stop in front of me.
I look up. Aiden.
Concern flickers in his dark eyes. Is that a genuine concern, or am I hallucinating?
I tap my earbuds, silencing the music. "What?" I ask.
"Are you okay?" His voice is gruff, but I catch the slightest hint of worry underneath.
I hesitate for a split second before taking his outstretched hand, but the moment I move, another sharp twinge shoots through my shoulder, causing me to wince. Aiden notices as his gaze flickers to my shoulder, then back to my eyes. "You're hurt," he states. I force myself to straighten, shaking my head. "I'm fine. I don't need your help."
I skate away, snatching my skate guards from the bench, yanking off my skates, and storming out of the rink before he can say anything else.

Sitting in the Jeep, my father gifted me. I attempt to Facetime Alina. The second her face appears on my screen. I feel my entire body relax.
"Malyshka, I miss you," she coos dramatically. I grin.
"Come over? Bring Alexei, too? I need my friends, or I

will lose my mind surrounded by four hockey bro roommates all night."

Alina nods, turning to whisper something to someone beside her. "Can Maddie come? I want you to meet her," she asks.

"Of course, the more the merrier!" I say, rubbing my throbbing shoulder. "Alexei's grabbing groceries now. Dinner and a movie?" she asks.

"Yes, I'll prepare drinks," Alina squeals. |I love you!" She yells, and I laugh. "See you soon."

After hanging up, I shoot a quick text to the guys. Don't even get me started on the name. Will thought it was funny, but It's not.

Hockey House + Ice Princess

Ice Princess

> Hey guys, just a heads-up—some of my friends are coming over. We're making dinner, playing board games, and drinking. You're welcome to join.

Roman

> Is your friend going to be there? The one you were talking to at the rink.

I roll my eyes. Typical.

Ice Princess

> "Yes, she will. Also, my skating partner Alexei is very into hockey players."

William added Aiden to the chat, and I froze, staring at the notification.

William

> Kat invited her friends over for game night. Are you joining?

My heart flips when I see the three dots pop up. I briefly hover over his contact before saving it under *Grumpy Hockey Player*. My phone pings and a new message appears.

Grumpy Hockey Player

> Sure.

What? I blink at the screen. Fuck. I was so sure he was going to say no.
I pull into the driveway, the evening sky darkening, and switch off the engine. My fingers are stiff from gripping the steering wheel, and my thoughts are a mess. I need this night to unwind—my body is sore from practice, and my mind is stuck on Aiden. There's no escaping it: he has invaded my thoughts, and as much as I try to push him out, he lingers. With a sigh, I grab the bags from the backseat and make my way to the front door, unlocking it with a slight twist. The familiar scent of the house greets me, but it doesn't feel like home tonight. It feels like I'm standing at the edge of something, unsure if I'm ready to dive in.
 "Hey!" Will's voice pulls me out of my thoughts as I enter the kitchen. He and Roman are leaning against the counter, focusing on me as I walk in. Roman shoots me a grin, his usual teasing smile plastered across his face.
"I got it," Will says, reaching out to grab the grocery bags from my hands. He lifts a large bottle of tequila from the bag and holds it up like a trophy. "Is this what I think it is?" I nod, trying to focus on the task ahead and distract myself from the racing thoughts about the man who is probably upstairs right now.
"Yep, that's the one," I say, glancing around for the rest of the ingredients and hoisting the last bag on top of the

counter. "I'm making my signature cocktail. That's why I bought this drink dispenser." Roman raises an eyebrow and gives me an exaggerated, approving nod. "Impressive. But I'm watching you, Kat. Don't mess it up." I laugh softly, the sound feeling more and more genuine as I begin to pull out the oranges, cutting them into thin, delicate slices. The scent of citrus hits my senses, and I let it ground me. I grab a couple of strands of rosemary, their fragrant needles giving off a refreshing smell as I drop them into the dispenser. The pomegranate seeds and cranberries follow right after. Lastly, I add the tequila— the entire bottle—feeling the weight of its contents pouring out. It's not just the alcohol I need to focus on tonight. It's the whole night. I need to loosen up, not think about practice, and ignore Aiden's presence.

"Jesus, that looks so good," Will says, licking his lips as he leans over to get a closer look.

"You can have some," I reply, glancing at him. "Just don't open the new bottle. That's for the Jenga shot game." They exchange puzzled glances.

"Jenga?" Will asks, his tone mocking. "We're playing Jenga?" He cracks a grin, clearly intrigued. "Yeah, drinking Jenga. At the last Olympics, Alina and I got bored in our hotel room, so we devised our version. It's a lot more fun than you'd think," I smirk, imagining the chaos that will follow. Roman claps his hands together. "Fuck yeah. Now I'm excited."

"Alright, alright, save some energy," I tease, shaking my head as I finish stirring the concoction and adding the ice. This is precisely what I need tonight—some chaos and fun. "What are we eating for dinner?" Graysen's voice cuts through the buzz of conversation, his tone light and casual as he walks into the kitchen, looking around with an appreciative glance.

"Homemade pizza," I reply, setting the cocktail dispenser aside. "Alexei and the others should be here soon." Greysen rubs his hands together, a smile creeping across his face.

The doorbell rings just as I finish the dough, and Will and Roman both jump to their feet, practically knocking each other out of the way as they rush to answer it. I can already feel the energy in the house shifting. Everyone is here to have a good time, and I'm determined to make sure that happens, even if thoughts of a certain someone and when he'll be joining us keep trying to invade.

"Wait—what?"

Roman's voice carries from the front door with a surprised laugh. I look up from the kitchen counter to find Roman standing in the doorway, staring at the brunette woman on the front step.

"Maddie?" Roman asks, his voice tinged with disbelief. "What the fuck are you doing here?" "Hello, brother dearest," Maddie says, her voice light and playful. "I was invited, so here I am." I blink, caught off guard by the sudden revelation. Will looks equally stunned.

"She's your sister?" Will asks, his tone full of genuine surprise. Roman glances from Maddie to Will, then back to Maddie, before giving a slow nod.

"Yeah, she is."

Wait, what? "How do you not know she is his sister? I ask, confused. "My sister lived with our grandparents most of her teenage years. The guys never met her." I give Roman a nod. It makes sense now.

Roman shoots Will a suspicious look. "Wait, is she the brunette you talked to me about earlier today?" Roman asks, narrowing his eyes at Will. Will's face instantly flushes a deep red.

"What? No," Will replies, his voice awkward and strained. "I wasn't—" Roman leans in and whispers something in Will's ear, and I see Will gulp, clearly taken aback by whatever Roman just said or threatened. I can't help but smirk at the awkward energy in the room, mainly since it doesn't involve me for once, as Roman excuses himself to help Alina, who just walked up with a bag that is slipping off her shoulder. The sight of Alina's flushed cheeks only makes me love her more—she has no poker face.

"Come on in, guys," I say, trying to ease the tension. "It's freezing outside." Alexei follows behind them, looking around the house with curiosity. "This place is nice, love," he comments, a playful grin tugging at his lips. "It needs a bit of a feminine touch," I say, rolling my eyes. "But I'm working on it." Alexei chuckles and then nods toward the living room. I notice Greysen is now back in the living room, his attention fixed on his video game.

"Bestie, kto on?" Alexei asks in Russian, his eyes narrowing mischievously. "Who is he?" I give Alexei an amused smile, glancing toward Graysen. "Hockey player." I lean in closer. "I don't know if he's gay, though," I whisper. Alexei smirks, his gaze moving up and down Graysen's frame. "I'll find out." He answers in Russian. Before I can stop myself, I toss a cranberry at Alexei, hitting him square in the face. "Nice aim, Kat," he says, wiping his face, a playful glint in his eyes.

The night continues, the banter flowing effortlessly between us as we prepare the pizzas, dividing ourselves into groups to make it smoother. Ever the strategist, Alexei calls dibs on Graysen being his partner, which has both of them laughing as they begin to spread sauce and cheese over the dough. Roman hasn't left Alina's

side since she arrived, flirting with her shamelessly. Meanwhile, Will is doing his best to make small talk with Maddie, although he keeps glancing over at Roman, who hasn't taken his eyes off either of them. Maddie, though—she's a gem. The second Alina introduced us, and the conversation came quickly, as if we had known each other forever. I can tell Roman has a soft spot for her, and it makes the whole night feel lighter. The door swings open, and there he is.
Aiden.
His gaze flicks to me as he walks past me and into the living room; for a brief second, everything else blurs—like the entire world just paused. My heart leaps, thudding wildly in my chest, betraying me. Damn it.
"Ale, are you okay?" Alina's voice pulls me back, soft but knowing. She follows my line of sight toward the living room, and when she glances back at me, a smirk spreads across her face.
I swallow hard, forcing my expression into something neutral. "Yeah. I'm fine." Will raises an eyebrow, unconvinced. "Why are you calling her Ale?" he asks Alina.
Alina shrugs, still grinning. "Kat's middle name is Alexandra. Ale is my nickname for her. We're Ali and Ale. And no, you can't call us by those names; only Ale and I can." I shoot her a mock glare but can't help the small smile that tugs at my lips. Before I can respond, Graysen's voice cuts through the air.
"Knight." I turn just in time to see Aiden approaching the kitchen. The space suddenly feels smaller. The air is sharper. I hate how aware I am of him, how I can feel his presence before seeing him. The scent of pine and bergamot surrounds me as he stops behind me, his height making him tower over me. His movements are effortless as he leans slightly to the left, pushing his

arms over the counter, over my arms, over me, before stretching my slab of dough between his hands, the muscles in his forearms flexing.

The muscles in my jaw clenched. I swallow. Focus. It's just pizza dough. Get a grip, Kat.

"You're struggling." He states his voice is low, smug. I roll my eyes, gripping the counter's edge to ground myself. "Thanks for stating the obvious cap, everyone has a partner, and I suck at this," I mutter.

Aiden chuckles as he drags the dough I was working on, bringing it closer to himself before flashing me a smirk. I scream in my head.

I hate him so much.

His hands work the dough with a practiced ease, large and veiny, making the motion look natural. I catch myself staring and snap out of it, my face heating. The knot in my stomach tightens. I need a distraction. Now. Without thinking, I grab a shot glass, fill it to the brim, and knock it back in one go. The burn does little to settle me. "Are you okay?" Alina's voice is quieter now, laced with curiosity. I nod, though my eyes betray me, flickering back to Aiden. He's talking to Roman now, laughing at something.

Why does he have to look like that when he laughs? Why does it make something in my chest squeeze?

"Oh my god," Alina whispers, inching closer with a knowing grin. "You like him." I nearly choke on my drink.

"No, I don't." The denial comes too fast, too forced. Alina raises an eyebrow, waiting. I exhale sharply, dropping my head back in frustration. "I mean... yeah, my body is attracted to him, but he's an asshole." Her smirk deepens.

"Sure, Ale. Whatever you say." I shoot her a glare, but it holds no real heat.

"Sometimes it's okay to think about something other than figure skating," she says, more serious this time. I frown, resisting the urge to shut down the conversation entirely. Her words settle uncomfortably in my chest. I risk another glance at Aiden—just in time for him to look at me. For a split second, our eyes meet. Something shifts. Just a crack. Just enough to feel it. I break eye contact first.

"Okay, let's focus," I whisper to Alina, forcing lightness into my tone. "Pizza time." Alina lets it go, but I know what she's thinking. She always sees more than I want her to. I push it aside and move back to the dough that Aiden has finished kneading, but the tightness in my stomach lingers. Across the room, Roman gravitates back toward Alina like he can't help himself. The way he looks at her—there's something there, something I don't think even he realises. And maybe that's why I suddenly feel this strange, quiet jealousy. Seeing them potentially falling for one another doesn't make me want someone. It just reminds me that I don't have someone.

I sit down on the stool next to Aiden's before I can overthink it, glancing at him. "I think your best friend likes my best friend." He smirks. That's exactly what I was just thinking.

"Seems like it." His voice is quieter now. "I wish I'd been here to see Will's face when he realised the girl he's crushing on is Roman's sister." I burst out laughing at the thought. Will the ever-so-serious one being blindsided by the reality of Maddie? Yeah. That was good.

Aiden chuckles along with me, his eyes lingering on mine. And then he smiles. Not his usual cocky smirk. A real smile. The kind that softens his expression makes

him look different—more open and human. The kind that makes my stomach feel like it's doing backflips. Shit.
Are we bonding? Ugh. Why does it feel like that? Before I can spiral any further, Aiden speaks again, breaking the moment. "Okay, pick your toppings. Half of the pizza's yours, and half is mine." He drops pepperoni onto his side, covering it with cheese. How original. I roll my eyes but focus on my half, carefully choosing each ingredient. Anything to not think about the way my body is reacting to him. The pizzas are in the oven five minutes later, and the kitchen smells incredible.
"Jenga time, bitches!" Alexei yells from the living room. I shake off the tension in my chest and follow the others to the game. We gather around the small table, our makeshift arena for the evening. Alexei sits to my right, Aiden to my left.
Too close. I can feel the heat of his proximity, the occasional brush of his leg against mine. But I don't move away. Not yet. Alexei pulls the first block.
"Rock, paper, scissors, shot with the person on your right." He reads aloud before he turns to Greysen, who smirks, accepting the challenge. "Rock, paper, scissors, shot!" Alexei calls out, and Greysen holds up the paper while Alexei shows scissors. Greysen groans. "Drink up, pretty boy," Alexei yells.
Greyson sips his cocktail, and Alexei smirks, effortlessly placing the block on top of the stack.
"My turn," I mutter, shifting to my knees. I pull out a block and flip it over. I glance at Aiden, a challenge flashing in my eyes. "Do your best impression of the person to your left," I announce. Aiden groans, dropping his head into his hand like the universe has personally wronged him. I giggle and stand up, clearing

my throat dramatically. Then, with exaggerated confidence, I deepen my voice, puff out my chest, and lean forward.

"Angel Face. I told you, this is my rink. Only I can skate after hours. It's booked by me, not you, so leave." Laughter erupts around me, and I soak it in, grinning. But when I glance at Aiden, he's not rolling his eyes or looking annoyed.

He's just staring at me.

His lips curl into a slow, knowing smile. His dark eyes stay locked on mine, something unreadable flickering beneath the amusement.

"Cute, Ale," he murmurs mockingly, using the nickname that only Alina ever calls me. The way he says it—soft, teasing, intimate—sends an unexpected shiver down my spine. I can feel the warmth spreading through my body, my cheeks heating against my will. I need to move. Step back. Create distance. But his smile. That damn smile—it's too much.

"Hey, find your own nickname," Alina interjects with a playful pout. "That one's mine."

Aiden just shrugs, but his eyes don't leave mine. I sit back down, feeling the weight of something unspoken settle between us. It lingers, stretching between us like a taut wire, buzzing, waiting. Aiden pulls out a block next. The tower wobbles slightly as he flips it over. His brow furrows before he reads the challenge aloud.

"Play tag. Loser has to finish their drink." His gaze snaps to mine, his lips tilting into something smug, something dangerous. I raise a brow, smirking back at him. "Angel Face, are you ready to lose?" His smirk deepens.

"Hell no. I'm good at tag." I push to my feet, adrenaline already coursing through me. The playful spark in my chest ignites.

"I'll have mercy and give you a five-second head start," Aiden says, his voice dripping with challenge. I don't wait. I bolt. I take the stairs two at a time, my heart pounding against my ribs. My laughter rings through the house as I slip into the supply closet, pressing my back against the door. I hold my breath, so Aiden doesn't hear me. He's close. I can hear his footsteps approaching, his movements carefully calculated. Then, I make a break for it. I burst from the closet, dashing toward the bathroom, but he's already seen me. The chase is on.

"There's nowhere to hide, Angel," he calls, voice full of amusement. I laugh, but it dies in my throat when two strong hands grip my waist. I barely have time to react before I'm being lifted clean off the ground, my world tilting as Aiden throws me effortlessly over his shoulder.

"Got you, loser," he taunts, his grip firm, unrelenting. A nervous giggle escapes me—half from the tequila, half from the sheer ridiculousness of the moment. Then, my hair tie slips out.

My long waves cascade down, falling around us as I dangle over his shoulder. I feel the shift immediately—his grip tightening, his steps faltering slightly. When he finally puts me down, I push the hair out of my face, trying to regain some sense of normalcy. But Aiden is still watching me. His eyes darken, flickering with something I can't name. His fingers reach out, brushing a few strands of hair from my face. He doesn't pull away immediately. His touch lingers. And suddenly, I can't breathe.

"You should let your hair down more," he says, voice barely above a whisper. I swallow. Hard. My pulse hammers so loudly I swear he can hear it. I force a slight shrug, trying to play it off.

"Yeah, maybe." Then I turn and head back toward the living room before I do something stupid.

When I sit down, Roman's smirk is already waiting for me.

"Who won?" he asks, eyes darting between me and Aiden. I grab my drink, downing a large sip before answering. "Mister Perfect." Roman's brows lift slightly, but he lets it go. Aiden takes his seat next to me again, but something has shifted. He doesn't engage with the game as much. He doesn't make a show of teasing me like he had before his turn.

His focus stays on me.

And I can feel it, that silent, suffocating weight of his attention. I know he's watching me even when he's not speaking or even when someone else is laughing. I shouldn't be enjoying this, but I do. And that's what terrifies me the most.

The night continues—laughter, inside jokes, easy conversation, and pizzas.

But for me, none of it registers. Because even as we settle in to watch White Chicks, even as the movie plays in the background and the others joke and drink, I can't focus.

CHAPTER FIVE

KATERINA

The tension in this house is suffocating. It started over something stupid—a hoodie left in the common area. But with four overgrown hockey players and me, a figure skater who wasn't even supposed to be here in the first place, nothing ever stays small for long.
"You don't just leave your shit lying around!" Aiden snaps, holding up the hoodie like it personally offended him. His dark eyes narrow, shoulders tight with

irritation. I cross my arms, refusing to let him intimidate me.

"Oh, I'm sorry. Did I break one of your sacred house rules? Maybe I should write that one down." My voice drips with sarcasm because if I don't meet him with defiance, I'll end up swallowing his hostility like a bitter pill. His jaw tightens.

"This isn't funny, Hart. You keep acting like you own the place." I scoff. "Trust me, if I had any choice, I wouldn't be living with a bunch of hockey Neanderthals. But thanks to your school's incompetence, I'm here. So deal with it." His expression flickers—just for a second—but I see it. Something unreadable. Then, just as quickly, it hardens again.

"You don't belong here." That one hits a little too hard, but I won't let him see it. I tilt my chin up.

"And yet, here I am. Must suck for you."

"Yeah, it does." His words are sharp like he wants me to bleed. "I don't have time to babysit a princess who thinks she can skate through life on pity." Anger blazes through me, hotter than any humiliation.

"Pity?" I step closer, getting right in his face. "You think I got here on pity? I had to claw my way back after somebody ripped everything from me. Unlike you, I wasn't handed my spot on a silver platter." His eyes darken, his nostrils flaring.

"You don't know shit about me," he replies.

"And I don't want to." I push past him, shoulder-checking him harder than necessary. "Stay out of my way, Knight." I don't wait for his response before storming off. I don't care what he has to say. I don't care about anything other than proving to him, to everyone, that I belong here.

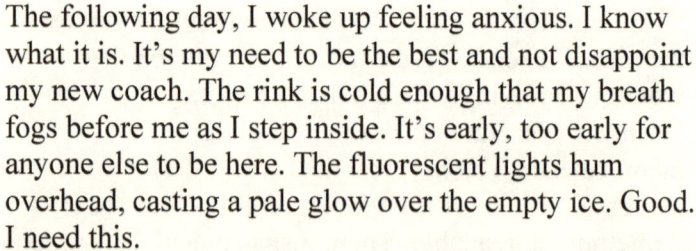

The following day, I woke up feeling anxious. I know what it is. It's my need to be the best and not disappoint my new coach. The rink is cold enough that my breath fogs before me as I step inside. It's early, too early for anyone else to be here. The fluorescent lights hum overhead, casting a pale glow over the empty ice. Good. I need this.
I need the ice, the control, the quiet focus of skating that drowns out everything else. The second I lace up my skates and step onto the frozen surface, the world fades away. The tension in my chest eases, replaced by the rhythm of my movements. But, of course, nothing in my life is ever that simple. Aiden is already here. I hear him before I see him—the sharp scrape of his blades cutting into the ice, the unmistakable rhythm of an athlete who knows exactly what he's doing. When I look up, he's gliding effortlessly across the rink, his movements fluid and powerful. Damn it. If I didn't hate him so much, I might admit he's a damn good skater. But I do hate him, so I won't.
I push forward, skating onto the ice, pretending he doesn't exist. Maybe he'll do the same if I ignore him—no such luck.
"You lost?" he calls out, his voice carrying across the empty rink. I grit my teeth, matching his glare.
"No. I'm right where I'm supposed to be." He skates closer, his presence suffocating.
"You just can't help yourself, can you?"

"What the hell is that supposed to mean?" I reply.
"You want me to snap at you." His voice is lower now, more dangerous. "And you want me to hate you!" I don't flinch.
"I don't give a damn what you feel about me." He laughs humourlessly, skating backward, his movements infuriatingly smooth. "Keep telling yourself that, Angel Face." My fists clench as I watch him glide away effortlessly like none of this affects him. But I know better. He hates me. And I hate him right back.
Or at least, I want to.

The tension from the morning lingers long after I leave the rink. Even back at the house, I can feel Aiden's presence like an electric charge in the air. I try to avoid him, but that's nearly impossible with four hockey players crammed into one space. I'm in the kitchen, stirring sugar into my tea, when I hear footsteps behind me.
"Still sulking?" I don't have to turn around to know it's him. His low and edged, amused voice makes my blood boil. I take a slow sip of my tea before answering.
"Still talking?" He exhales sharply, stepping closer. I can feel the warmth of his body just behind me.
"You're exhausting," he adds.
"So are you." I snap back, turning around, and for a second, we're too close. I can see the flecks of gold in his dark eyes, the faint crease between his brows. His expression is unreadable, but there's something there—something I don't understand or want to understand. But I feel this deep need to.
He shakes his head, stepping back first.

"You should watch yourself, Hart."
"Or what?" His lips curve slightly, but there's no humour in it.
"You might find out." He leaves before I can respond, disappearing down the hall and leaving me frustrated and confused.
I hate him.
I hate him and his stupid smirk.

CHAPTER SIX

KATERINA

The following morning, I had one goal: to avoid Aiden Knight at all costs. After last night's argument, I need space. It's time to let the anger simmer down before I do something reckless, like throw one of his stupid hockey sticks out the window. My knuckles are still sore from how tightly I clenched my fists when stormed out of the rink. Even now, lying in bed, I can feel the remnants of frustration curling in my stomach, threatening to boil over.

A sharp knock on my door nearly sends me leaping out of my skin.

"Kat, you alive?" Roman's voice filters through the wood door. I groan, rolling onto my stomach. "Unfortunately."

"Good. Because Will made pancakes, and if you don't hurry, I'll eat your share." That gets me moving. I

shuffle out of my room and into the kitchen, where the rich scent of coffee greets me. Roman is leaning against the counter, scrolling through his phone, while Will flips pancakes at the stove like some domestic god.
"Morning, Kit-Kat," Roman greets without looking up. "Rough night?"
"You have no idea." I grab a mug and pour myself coffee, inhaling the warmth before taking a slow sip. The caffeine hits like a lifeline. Will eyes me and pushes a plate of pancakes in my direction.
"You and Aiden gonna murder each other soon, or should we start placing bets?" I groan.
"I'm trying to ignore him."
Roman snorts. "Good luck with that. You two have this… thing." I glare at him. "There is no thing."
"There's totally a thing," he replies.
"Shut up and eat your pancakes." Before he can retort, the front door swings open, heavy footsteps echo through the hallway, and Aiden appears.
His damp hair curls slightly from his morning workout, sticking to his forehead. He's wearing a hoodie and sweats, his gym bag slung over his shoulder. Our eyes lock for half a second. Just long enough to feel the static between us. It's just long enough to remind me why I hate him. Aiden says nothing. He just grabs a protein shake from the fridge and disappears upstairs.
I exhale slowly, pretending that interaction didn't shake me. But Roman notices. "Oh, yeah," he muses.
"Definitely a thing." I chuck my napkin at his head, but he manages to catch it, his smirk unwavering.

After breakfast, Alexei picks me up for practice, and I'm over the moon that we are about to train with Camilla. Until practice starts.
It's brutal.
Camilla has us running our routine over and over again. Each time, she points out something that needs fixing—my landing is a fraction off, my hold with Alexei isn't tight enough, and my expression isn't emotive enough. By the fifth run-through, I'm sweating and biting back the urge to scream. Coach's voice cuts through the silence like a blade.
"Again, Katerina. You're being sloppy today," she calls, her sharp tone echoing off the walls. My body feels like it's made of lead, weighed down by the exhaustion that clings to every muscle. We've been practicing since six in the morning, and it's almost noon. The first qualifier is next Friday, and Coach has been pushing us to the limit. Alexei, too, looks like he's running on fumes. Every time Alexei lifts me, his arms shake, and I can feel the tremor in his grip. It's only a matter of time before he collapses, but he keeps pushing forward.
"Both of you need to be in exceptional sync," Coach barks. "It may be just the first qualifier, but you must show them why you're the best at what you do." I know she's right. I want to be the best. But all I can think about right now is food, sleep, and the dull ache that's settled deep in my bones. I glance at Alexei and see the same exhaustion in his eyes.

"Again," Camilla says, tapping her pen against her clipboard. Alexei groans under his breath. "She's trying to kill us."

"She's succeeding," I mutter, shaking my arms before stepping back into position.

We go again, and this time, it's sharper. Stronger. I push through my exhaustion, channeling every ounce of frustration into my movements. Every jump, every spin—perfect. When we finish, Camilla finally nods in approval. "Better, that's enough for today. Alina, it's your turn. Alexei, Kat, take a break." I nod at our coach as I make my way towards the exit. I practically collapse onto the bench as I unlace my skates. My entire body aches; I only want a hot shower and sleep for the next twelve hours.

"Oh my god, this bitch is trying to fucking murder us," Alexei mutters, collapsing beside me. I laugh softly, throwing my head back.

"She is, isn't she? But I like her. She knows what we need to work on and doesn't make us starve ourselves."

Alexei glances toward the rink, where Alina is practicing her quads.

"Are you okay?" He asks, his tone softer now, laced with concern. I pause, then nod, placing my hand on his. "I'm alright. I think. I'm just tired."

Alexei doesn't ask questions, thankfully. He's a great friend like that—one who listens without prying, accepting my answers for what they are.

"What's up with Alina and that creepy guy?" Alexei asks, shaking his head.

I laugh softly. "You mean Roman? The scary-looking tattooed guy who's obsessed with her?"

"Yeah, him." Alexei's voice is a mix of disbelief and humour.

"She was chewing him out the other day," I say, smirking. "That guy is crazy."

"Crazy for her," Alexei adds, laughing. I nod, my smile softening.

"Definitely." We watch Alina finish her routine, and when Coach gives us the all-clear, we head out to the parking lot.

"Guys, Roman invited us to their first hockey game of the season this Friday," Alina says, slowing her pace.

"Did Roman invite you, and you just don't want to go alone?" Alexei teases.

Alina glances down at her feet, then looks up at us, nodding slowly.

"He intimidates the shit out of me, but I want to go. I've never been to a hockey game." I glance at Alexei, who rolls his eyes but nods in agreement.

"Yeah, babe, we'll go with you." Alina squeals, wrapping her arms around us in a tight hug.

Alexei plops down next to me, nudging my shoulder. "Drink tonight?" I shake my head. "Too tired."

"Come on, Kit-Kat. One drink. You need to unwind." Alina says, wrapping her arms around my left one. I hesitate. Maybe a drink wouldn't be the worst idea: anything to take my mind off skating and my ongoing war with Aiden.

"Fine," I sigh.

"One drink." Alexei grins and Alina claps in excitement.

"That's my girl." Alexei says wrapping his arms around my shoulder, as we walk out of the rink.

The bar is packed. Loud music. Laughter. The scent of alcohol was thick in the air. I lean against the counter, waiting for our drinks, when a voice behind me sends a shiver down my spine.

"Didn't take you for the drinking type, Angel Face." I don't even have to turn around. I already know who the voice belongs to. My body is always aware of his presence. I blame him for his stupid looks.

Aiden.

I scowl as I twist to face him. He's standing there, drink in hand, looking like he owns the damn place. His dark eyes flick over me, amusement dancing in them.

"I didn't take you for the talking type," I shoot back.

Aiden smirks. "That's funny, considering how much you enjoy arguing with me."

I grip my glass tighter. "Trust me, I don't enjoy anything about you." He leans in slightly, his voice dropping just enough to make my pulse stutter.

"Then why are you so obsessed with proving me wrong?"

I open my mouth, ready to rip into him, but Alexei appears out of nowhere, throwing an arm around my shoulders.

"Problem here?" Aiden's expression cools.

"No problem." He downs the rest of his drink and walks away without another word. Alexei watches him go before returning to me.

"You really know how to pick 'em." I groan.

"I hate him." I say shooting glares at Aidens back.

Alina just grins. "Keep telling yourself that."

When I get home, the exhaustion hits me like a wave. I wince as I walk upstairs, each step sending a pulse of pain through my body. I step into the bathroom turning on the shower. The hot water feels like heaven against my skin, but I know it won't ease the ache in my bones. After drying off and slipping into my pyjamas, I stand in front of the mirror and freeze. A dark purple bruise stretches across my thigh, stark against my skin. I turn around, and sure enough, there's another bruise on my injured shoulder.

"Fuck," I mutter under my breath. I sigh, walking downstairs to grab some ice. As I reach the kitchen, I freeze when I see Aiden grabbing water from the fridge. My heart skips a beat, and the air feels thicker with each passing second.

"Hey," he says, stepping aside to make room for me. I grab the ice and turn to face him. His gaze lingers on my thigh, his expression darkening.

"Jesus, Katerina, that's huge." His words make my heart race, and I realise I don't like how his eyes are fixed on me. I shift uncomfortably.

"It's fine," I say quickly. "Practice was harsh today. I'm exhausted." Aiden steps closer, his concern evident.

"Yeah, but you don't see me getting bruises like that and I play hockey, a violent sport." His fingers graze my bruise, and I wince—not because it hurts, but because the touch of his hand sends a fire through me.

"Can you stop pretending like you care?" I snap, turning to face him.

"Sorry," he mutters, pulling his hand back, but the damage is done. I turn away, trying to steady my breathing, but it feels like everything is spiralling out of control.

"We have our first qualifier in two weeks," I say, trying to change the subject. "I have to be perfect." Aiden's

eyes never leave me as I speak; his presence is so intense that it feels consuming. "I heard your game is this Friday," I continue, trying to shake off the tension.
"Yeah," he responds, his voice distant. "Roman said you're coming with your friends." I nod.
"Yeah, we'll be there."
"Well, I guess I'll see you there." He says, turning to leave. As he walks away, I feel the familiar tug in my chest—the one that tells me this thing between us is something.
Stop it, heart. I'm tired of your bullshit around this guy. I force myself to breathe, but the feeling lingers.

CHAPTER SEVEN

AIDEN

It's Game day here at Pleasant Oaks University, and let me tell you, everyone loves us. Returning after last year's brutal season feels like the first inhale of spring air.

I step onto the ice, my skates biting into the surface, the cold air filling my lungs. The energy in the arena crackles like a live wire, thousands of voices blending into a low, humming roar. It's the season's first game, and the expectations are higher than they've ever been. I skate towards the centre of the rink, stick tapping against the boards as the rest of the team gathers. Roman's already bouncing on his toes, practically vibrating with excitement, while Will and Grayson are locked in their usual pre-game routine of staring at the other team like they're about to eat them alive. Good. We need that intensity. I take a breath, steadying myself before I speak.

"Listen up," I start, my voice cutting through the noise. "We've trained for this. We know what we're capable of. We don't second-guess, we don't hesitate, and we don't let the opposing team dictate our pace. We play our game. Hard, fast, and relentless."

Roman lets out a sharp "Hell yeah," and a few other guys nod, cracking their knuckles or bouncing on their skates.

I scan the room, ensuring every pair of my teammates' eyes are on me before continuing.

"They think they're better than us. They think they can out-skate us, out-hit us, outwork us. Let's show them exactly how wrong they are." The guys murmur their agreement, the tension building and I clench my jaw, feeling the familiar burn of adrenaline creeping up my spine.

"And one more thing." My grip on my stick tightens. "We fight for each other. No matter what happens out there, we have each other's backs." A chorus of agreement rumbles through the team, and I nod. "Let's fucking go." The team erupts, sticks tapping against the ice, the boards rattling as we break apart. My heart pounds as I skate toward the bench, my focus locked in. Nothing else matters but this game until I see her.

She's sitting in the stands, right beside Alina, arms crossed, one leg draped over the other like she's utterly unbothered by the chaos around her. Her usual sharp glare is on me, lips slightly pursed in what I'm sure is an attempt to look unimpressed. But it's her pose that gets me. That signature figure skater stance—back straight, head high, the kind of posture that screams discipline. Grace. Poise. Even sitting down, she looks like she owns the damn place.

I feel my irritation spike. I don't know why I feel so surprised. I knew she'd be here. Of course, she's watching. I don't know why it bugs me so much, but it does. Maybe it's because I know she doesn't care about hockey. Perhaps because I know she's probably critiquing everything, ready to throw some smart-ass comment my way later. Or maybe because I can't stop looking at her. Panic crashes over me at the thought of losing focus and ruining this game because I keep looking at Kat. The buzzer sounds, snapping me out of it, and I force my gaze back onto the ice. I shake my head, rolling out my shoulders. Focus, Knight.

The puck drops, and we're off.

The first period is brutal. The Bears come at us hard, trying to set the tone early. It's fast, physical, and precisely the kind of game I live for. I throw a hit along the boards, dig deep into the corners, and force their star forward to turn over the puck. By the time the second period rolls around, we're tied two-two. Sweat drips down my neck as I skate to the bench, gripping my stick as I catch my breath.

I glance up at the stands again. Kat's still watching. Still perched in that annoyingly perfect pose, still with that same expression—bored, like she expected more from us.

Jesus Christ. Right on cue, she lifts a brow as if daring me to impress her.

Oh, it's on.

I shake off my exhaustion and hop over the boards, my focus sharper than before. The moment I hit the

ice, I chase down the puck, weaving through defenders like they're standing still. My teammates adjust, moving into position, and just as I fake a pass to Roman, I pull the puck back and rip a shot top shelf. The red light flashes, and the crowd erupts in cheers. For some stupid reason, I look back up at Kat.
She's clapping, but it's slow. Almost as if she is mocking me. I narrow my eyes and she smirks back at me.
I swear to God, she's going to be the death of me.
 By the time the game ends, we're walking away with a 5-3 win, and the adrenaline is still burning through my veins. I should be feeling good, riding the high of the victory, but all I can think about is the inevitable conversation waiting for me the second I step off the ice.
And sure enough, there she is, leaning against the tunnel wall, arms still crossed, looking way too entertained for my liking.
 "Not bad, Knight," she muses, tilting her head. "Didn't completely embarrass yourself."
I scoff, pulling off my gloves. "Oh yeah? Better than your pirouettes?" She glares at me, pushing off the wall.
"It's no triple axel, but I guess it was fine."
I take a step closer, heat still pulsing through me. "You watched the whole game, Angel Face. Clearly, you were interested." Her lips curve upward, but there's a challenge in her eyes.
 "Oh, I was watching. Studying, really." She taps a finger against her chin. "And I noticed something interesting."
"Yeah? What's that?"

She leans in slightly, and for half a second, I think she's going to say something profound. Instead, she smirks. "You play recklessly when you're mad."
I blink. "What?"
"That second-period goal? You only went for it because I pissed you off." She lifts a shoulder. "It's cute, really. Like a little puppy trying to impress its owner."
I let out a sharp laugh. "You're out of your damn mind." She pats my chest like I'm some kind of pet, and I hate how much I enjoy it.
"It's okay, Knight. I get it. I'm motivational."
I grab her wrist before she can pull away, holding it just tight enough for her to stop and look up at me. The teasing in her expression falters just slightly, just enough for me to see it.
She feels it, too. The tension. The pull. The way this fire between us is only growing hotter every time we push against it. I lower my voice.
"You think you get in my head that easily?" Her breath hitches, but she doesn't back down.
"I know I do." I lean in just a little, my grip still firm.
"Careful, Angel Face. You might not like what happens if you keep playing this game with me." Her lips part slightly, and for a second, something unreadable flashes in her expression. Then she snatches her wrist back and steps away.
"We'll see, Knight," she says, turning on her heel. "We'll see."
I watch her go, my pulse still racing. She's going to drive me insane.
And I might let her.

CHAPTER EIGHT

KATERINA

Classes at Pleasant Oaks University are about what I expected—a mix of overachievers, sleep-deprived athletes, and students who are here because their parents have too much money and not enough supervision. I fall into the first two categories.

I sit in the back of my Statistics class, my notebook open, but my mind isn't on standard deviations or probability distributions. Instead, I'm replaying last night's game in my head.

More specifically, how Aiden looked at me when I teased him afterward. His hand around my wrist, his voice dropping to that low, almost dangerous tone. The way I felt breathless for half a second.

I shake the thought away, tapping my pen against my notebook.

Focus, Kat.

The professor drones on, and I do my best to pay attention, but my brain keeps drifting. The problem isn't just Aiden— it's everything: the pressure of training, school, and trying to prove myself in a country that still doesn't feel like home. A folded note lands on my desk, breaking me from my thoughts. I glance up, catching Alina's amused expression from two rows ahead. I unfold the note, recognising her neat cursive immediately.

You're spacing out again. If this is about Aiden, blink twice. I roll my eyes but can't fight the small smile pulling at my lips. I quickly scribble back.

It's about how I'm going to kill you for that comment. I flick the note toward her, and she catches it effortlessly, giving me a knowing smirk before returning to the lecture. After class, we walk toward the main quad, the crisp fall air nipping at our skin. Roman and Alexei are waiting for us near the campus library coffee shop. Roman is leaning lazily against the counter while Alexei complains about the lack of decent Russian tea options.

"Just admit you like coffee," Roman teases, sipping his iced latte.

Alexei glares. "I will not. Coffee is bitter and depressing. Like your soul."

Roman grins. "My soul is delightful. Just ask Alina."

Alina, who had been in the middle of checking her phone, looks up, her cheeks slightly pink.

"Why me?"

Roman shrugs. "You seem to enjoy my company more than most."

Alexei fake coughs. "Understatement." Alina glares at him, but I don't miss how her fingers tighten around her coffee cup. I exchange a quick look with Alexei. He notices it, too.

Roman and Alina are a thing. Or at least, they want to be a thing.

They just don't know it yet.

I tuck that information away for later as we leave the coffee shop, heading toward the library's double doors to get some studying in before training. We find a quiet table in the back, books and laptops spreading out as we settle in. Everything is fine.

Until the devil himself walks in. He spots us almost immediately, his dark eyes locking onto mine for a split second before he looks away. He's with Will and Grayson; all three still carry that post-game energy.

Will says something that makes Grayson laugh, but Aiden just nods, his expression unreadable.

I force myself to focus on my work, but it's impossible. Not when he's so close.

And then, because the universe loves testing me, he walks over.

"You're in my seat, Angel Face," he says, standing across from me.

I look up, arching a brow. "Oh? I wasn't aware you had a reserved throne in the library."

Roman snorts. Alexei hides his grin behind his laptop.

Aiden sighs like I'm exhausting him. "You always have to be difficult, don't you?"

"It's one of my best qualities."

Alina looks between us, eyes wide with amusement, but stays silent. I swear I hear Roman mutter, "Here we go again." Aiden doesn't move. He just stands there, waiting. I should tell him to find another seat, but I won't give him the satisfaction of thinking he's getting under my skin.

So, I move.

Slowly. Casually. Like I want to.

I grab my coffee, stand, and slide into the seat beside Alexei, stretching my legs out as if I hadn't just ceded my spot to the enemy. Aiden smirks.

"See? That wasn't so hard." I roll my eyes and turn back to my notes. For the next hour, I pretend he's not sitting across from me, but it's impossible. Every time I glance up, he's already looking at me. Every time I shift in my seat, I feel his gaze flicker to the movement. And worst of all?

I like it.

And I hate that I like it.

When we finally leave the library, Alina falls into step beside me, nudging my arm. "That was fun to watch."

"You need a new definition of fun," I grumble, but Ali grins.

"You like fighting with him."

I scoff. "I do not."

"You do. And he likes it too."

I shake my head, but I don't argue further. Because deep down, I know she's right.

I don't know if I want this tension between me and Aiden to stop. When I think about what it would be like if he ignored me completely, not acknowledging me at all, I almost miss him. What does it say about me if I would rather argue with this man than not get the chance to interact at all?

Later that night, after training, we all end up back at the Hockey House. Someone suggested a movie night, and before I knew it, I was curled up on the couch next to Alexei, Roman, and Alina, sitting suspiciously close on the other side of the room, and Aiden stretched out in the armchair across from me.

The lights are dim, and the movie plays in the background, but I can't focus. Not when Aiden keeps looking at me. Not when I keep looking back.

Roman suddenly stretches, throwing an arm over Alina's shoulders like it's the most natural thing in the world. She stiffens at first, then relaxes, leaning slightly into him. I smirk, whispering to Alexei, "Took him long enough." Alexei chuckles.

"Five Bucks says she pretends to be annoyed but secretly loves it," I add with a smirk. Confident. I know Ali will push him away.

"Deal," Alexei says, shaking my hand. The movie ends, and as people start filtering upstairs, I grab my empty cup and head to the kitchen. Aiden is already there, leaning against the counter. We stare at each other for a long moment, the weight of everything unsaid hanging between us. I roll my eyes, turning away toward the sink. I rinse my cup, focusing too hard on the swirling water, but Aiden's presence lingers behind me, feeling like a gravitational pull. Alexei walks into the kitchen with a confident smile on his face.

"Did you notice who's happily sitting with an arm over their shoulder?"

My train of thought disappears when I hear Roman's voice from the living room. "Hey, Alexei, how much does Kat owe us for losing that bet?"

I freeze. Roman makes his way into the kitchen, going straight for the fridge.

Aiden raises an eyebrow. "Bet?" I slowly turn around, shooting daggers at Alexei, who looks like he'd melt into the floor instead. Roman, on the other hand, has no such survival instincts.

"Yeah, the bet on whether Alina would let Roman put his arm around her," Alexei mutters, rubbing the back of his neck. Aiden looks from me to Alexei, amused.
"And what does that have to do with Kat?"
"Oh, she was so confident Alina would shove him away," Alexei supplies, clearly ready to die on this hill. Aiden grins, and I immediately regret everything.
"Wait. Did you just lose a bet? You?"
I cross my arms. "It was a miscalculation." Roman cackles as he closes the fridge shut, water in his right hand. "She was so sure. So smug."
I glare at him. "Traitor." Aiden leans against the counter, smug.
"I don't think I've ever seen you be wrong before, Angel Face. This is a historic moment."
"You realise you're setting yourself up for an 'I told you so' in the future, right?" I say sweetly. His smirk deepens.
"Are you implying that there's something for you to be right about? Interesting."
I make a frustrated noise, pushing past him toward the doorway. But before I leave, I throw back, "Fine. Laugh it up. But when Alina and Roman get together, I expect interest in those five bucks. Remember that bet."
I snap at Alexei, who's already pulling out his phone with a sigh.
"Yeah, yeah. I'll Venmo you." I give all of them the middle finger as I exit the room and go upstairs.
Roman, still grinning, calls after me, "Make sure you don't lose any other bets, Kat. Wouldn't want to ruin that winning record of yours."
Aiden chuckles behind me, and I don't have to look to know this is far from over.
I have a feeling he will enjoy holding this one over my head.

CHAPTER NINE

KATERINA

The way Aiden looks at me sets me on edge. Not in the way that makes me want to run. No, it's the kind of tension that coils in my stomach, the kind that makes me feel restless like I need to prove something to him—to myself. And I hate that. I hate that he gets under my skin like this.

I also hate that I keep catching myself staring at his hands. It's stupid, really. But there's something about the way he grips his hockey stick, the way his fingers flex, his veins standing out against his skin—it's distracting.

And distraction is dangerous.

Because I have enough on my plate without getting tangled up in Aiden Knight, I shove the thought away as I step into the lecture hall for Biology. Alina's sitting in the second row, flipping through her notebook. I slide into the seat beside her and drop my bag onto the desk.

She glances up, smiling. "You look—" She pauses, eyes narrowing. "Oh my god. You're flustered." I scoff. "I am not flustered." She leans in, voices low.

"Did something happen with him?" I know who she's referring to. Why would she think anything could happen between Aiden and me? We both hate each other. "No."

A pause.

"Did you want something to happen with him?" I shoot her a glare. "Alina."

She smirks but doesn't push for now. Before she can interrogate me further, Roman and Alexei drop into the seats behind us. Roman looks annoyingly smug as if he knows something I don't.

I sigh. "What?"

Roman grins. "Nothing."

"Liar."

Alexei rests his chin on his hand, watching the exchange with mild amusement. "He's just excited that Alina didn't push him away last night."

Alina turns bright red. "I—I was tired."

Roman smirks. "Of course you were." I exchange a knowing look with Alexei. They're so obvious. But before I can tease them, my body tenses.

Aiden walks in with Will and Grayson, looking effortlessly confident, like he owns the room. He spots me almost immediately, his lips twitching like he's waiting for me to react. I don't give him the satisfaction.

I turn back to my notes, determined to ignore him. It doesn't work.

Because instead of sitting in his usual seat, he slides into the empty one next to me. I try to snap at him or say something snarky, but my brain is in a haze from his presence. He carries a scent that lingers- clean, rich, and undeniably intoxicating, a mix of crisp cedar-wood and warm amber clings to his skin, softened by the faintest trace of vanilla and citrus. I can't help but breath him in. Why is he sitting next to me? Alina's eyes widen. Roman's eyebrows shoot up. Alexei whistles under his breath. And Aiden? The cocky bastard just leans back in his chair like this is normal. "Comfortable?" I mutter. "Very." I grip my pen tighter. I hate him.

Class starts, and I do my best to focus, but it's impossible with Aiden sitting so close. He's too big, too warm, too there. At one point, he stretches his arm out along the back of my chair. Not touching me, but close enough that I feel the heat of him.

I don't react.

I won't give him the satisfaction.

I take my time flipping through my notes, tapping my pen against the desk with deliberate precision. I make a show of leaning forward, blocking his view of my page, knowing full well that he wasn't even looking at my notes in the first place. Aiden doesn't move his arm. If anything, I think he leans in a little closer. I clench my jaw and focus on the professor, deep into a lecture about mental resilience in athletes. Fitting. I could use some of that right now.

Alina nudges me under the desk, her phone screen angled toward me.

Do we need a distraction? Blink twice.

I resist the urge to roll my eyes. Instead, I type back: I will murder you.

She just smirks.

Aiden shifts beside me, tapping his pen lazily against his notebook. He's not even pretending to take notes.
"You're not even listening," I whisper.
"Neither are you," he murmurs back.
I grit my teeth. "Unlike you, I need to pass this class."
His lips twitch. "Don't flatter yourself. I already passed Biology last semester."
I whip my head toward him. "Then why are you here?"
He leans in just a fraction, voices low and smug.
"Thought it'd be fun." I stare at him, my pulse pounding in my ears. He's here just to mess with me and to get under my skin. I should ignore him. I should rise above it.
Instead, I shift in my seat ever so slightly, angling my body so his arm, still draped lazily over the back of my chair, brushes against my shoulder.
Aiden stills.
I don't look at him. I keep my gaze fixed ahead, but I can feel the tension radiating off him.
Good.
Two can play this game.

After class, I don't wait around. I shove my notebook into my bag and bolt toward the door, ignoring the amused glances from Alina and Roman. I make it halfway down the hall before a voice stops me.
"Running away, Angel Face?"
I spin around, scowling. "Stop calling me that." Aiden grins like he enjoys pissing me off. Which he does.
"Can't take the heat?" he taunts, stepping closer. "I don't feel like dealing with your inflated ego today."

"You sure about that?" He raises a brow, eyes flicking down
to my lips. The air between us tightens, charged. I should walk away.

I don't.

Instead, I cross my arms. "You think I'd fall for this?"

His grin deepens. "Oh, I know you will." The absolute audacity of this man.

I open my mouth to fire back, but before I can, Roman and Alexei stroll up, clearly entertained.

"What's this?" Roman muses, eyeing the tension between us. "Another lovers' quarrel?"

I groan. "Not even close."

Aiden just smirks. "Yet."

I'm going to kill him. Alexei sighs. "Can you two just kiss and get it over with? The sexual tension is unbearable." I whip around. "Alexei."

"What? It's true."

Aiden laughs. "He's got a point. You clearly find me attractive."

I shove past them, ignoring the way my skin feels hot. "You're all insufferable."

Aiden calls after me, "You love it."

I flip him off without looking back.

By the time training rolls around, I've convinced myself I'm over it.

It's fine. Everything is fine. We're running drills, the sound of skates cutting through the ice sharp in the otherwise quiet rink. I focus on my movements, the rhythm of my strides, the familiar comfort of being here, where nothing else matters.

And then Aiden skates up next to me. I sigh. "Do you ever go away?"
"Nope."
I roll my eyes and push ahead, but he matches my pace effortlessly.
"Let's make it interesting," he says.
I glance at him warily. "What?"
"A race. You and me. One lap, full speed." I snort. "I'd win."
He smirks. "Prove it."
It's stupid. I know it's ridiculous. But Aiden challenges me, and I can never back down from a challenge.
"Fine," I say.
We line up at the edge of the rink. Alina, Roman, and Alexei catch on quickly, skating to the boards to watch. Roman whistles. "This should be good."
The coach hasn't arrived yet, so we won't get yelled at for goofing off. Grayson skates over, a knowing smile on his face. "On my count," he says.
Aiden and I crouch low, ready.
"Three… two… one… go!"
I shoot forward, pushing hard, my skates cutting deep into the ice. I don't look at Aiden. I focus on the rhythm of my strides, the way the cold air stings against my skin. Halfway through, we're neck and neck. I grit my teeth and push harder, determination burning in my veins.
Out of nowhere, Aiden bumps into me.
It's subtle. Just enough to throw me off balance. I stumble, my skate catching the ice, and suddenly I'm falling. I brace for impact, but an arm catches me before I hit the ice. Aiden.
We crash together, skidding across the ice in a tangled mess of limbs until we finally land, Aiden underneath me like a warm, padded mattress of muscle.

For a second, I don't move. Aiden cheated.
"You cheated!"
Aiden grins up at me, flat on his back, still holding onto me. "No idea what you're talking about." I shove his arm away, sitting up. "You bumped me!"
"It's called strategy, Angel Face." I glare. "It's called being an asshole." He just smirks. "Same thing."
Alina skates over, trying and failing to hold back laughter. "Wow, that was… something."
Roman claps his hands. "I'm giving that a solid nine for the fall alone." I groan, shoving myself up. Aiden follows, brushing ice off his jersey.
I narrow my eyes at him. "I want a rematch." He winks. "Whenever you want, Angel Face."
I whip off my glove and chuck it at him. He ducks, laughing.
I officially hate him.

CHAPTER TEN

KATERINA

I am going to kill him. Not just yell at him. Not just throw something at him. Kill him. Because Aiden Knight has spent the past two days making my life a living hell.
Ever since our little race, he's made it his mission to push each one of my buttons. And he's enjoying it. It started small—stealing my seat in the library, purposely walking in front of me in the dining hall so I have to stop short, bumping my elbow just enough to mess up my notes in class. Annoying, but nothing I couldn't handle.

Then he escalated. He changed my phone background to a photo of himself smirking, which he somehow got past my passcode (Roman was the traitor, I know it). He 'accidentally' knocked my gym bag over at practice, sending my neatly packed belongings everywhere. And the worst offense?

He took my coffee.

I had set it down for one second before practice, and when I turned back? It was gone. I found him on the ice, casually sipping from my cup like he owned the damn thing.

"You don't even like iced caramel lattes," I had snapped at him. He had the audacity to take another sip and smirk. "I do now!"

I swear I almost lunged at him right then and there. So now, as I sit in the living room of the Hockey House, flipping through my notes, I am actively plotting his demise. Roman and Will are playing FIFA on the couch, Alina is curled up with a book, and Alexei is texting someone suspiciously fast. I barely glance up when I hear the front door open. But the moment Aiden steps inside, I feel it. It's like my body has developed a sixth sense for detecting his presence. He makes a beeline for the fridge, grabbing a water bottle before he finally notices me. His smirk is already forming. I brace myself.

"Hart," he greets, leaning against the counter like he's casually here and not about to make my life harder.

I don't look up. "Knight."

There's a beat of silence before he speaks again. "You look tense. Thinking about me?"

I slam my book shut. "Oh, constantly. In fact, I was just imagining all the ways I could get away with murder."

He grins.

"You'd miss me."

I scoff. "Like a migraine." Aiden pushes off the counter and walks over, plopping down in the armchair across from me. He stretches out, looking obnoxiously relaxed.

"You're fun when you're mad, you know that?" I grip my pen tighter. "And you're infuriating when you exist. We all have our talents."

Roman, who has been listening with way too much amusement, leans over to Will. "Tension. So much tension." Will nods.

"They need to make out already."

Alina nearly chokes on her drink. Maddie just smirks, looking entirely unsurprised.

I glare at them. "Both of you—shut up." Aiden, of course, is grinning ear to ear.

"Hear that? Even our friends see it."

"There is nothing to see."

"Mmm." He tilts his head. "You sure?"

I swear my face is on fire.

Before I can throw something at him, Aiden's phone buzzes, and as he glances at it, his smirk fades slightly. Aiden stands up and, without another word, disappears upstairs.

We all blink in surprise. Roman is the first to break the silence.

"Well, that was weird."

Alina frowns. "That was not normal for him." I chew the inside of my cheek, my irritation momentarily forgotten. Aiden looked off. Not like his usual smug self.

I tell myself I don't care. I do. But later that night, I found out that's a lie.

I'm heading to my room when I hear muffled voices coming from Aiden's room, his door slightly ajar. I don't mean to eavesdrop. I don't.

But then I hear the frustration in his voice, and my feet stop moving.
"I know, Dad. I'm handling it." A pause. Then, sharper, "No, I don't need you to—just forget it."
Silence.
I hear a thud—something hitting the wall, followed by a heavy exhale. I don't know what possesses me to knock, but I do. After a beat of silence, Aiden opens the door.
"What."
I push the door open and lean against the frame. "Your charming personality is shining through right now."
Aiden sits on the edge of his bed, running a hand through his hair. His phone is face down on the nightstand like he wants to hide it.
His eyes flick to me, and for once, there's no smugness, no teasing. Just… something raw.
I shift, suddenly unsure why I even came here. "You okay?" His brows furrowed like he wasn't expecting that question. "What do you care?" I shrug.
"I don't. But I'd rather not get caught in the crossfire if you're about to go on a rampage."
Aiden exhales, rubbing his face. "It's nothing. Just my dad being his usual self."
I hesitate, then step inside. "Want me to slash his tires? I have connections." That earns me a chuckle. It's a small one, but still. "Tempting."
Silence stretches between us. It's… different. Not tense. Just there.
Then Aiden shakes his head as if snapping out of it. His usual smirk starts creeping back. "Wow. You almost sounded concerned for a second there." I groan. "Forget it. I regret everything."
I turn to leave, but before I reach the door, he calls my name. I glance back, eyebrows raised. "What?" I ask.

He rubs the back of his neck, looking almost awkward.
"I, uh… I got something for you."
I blink. "What?"
He gets up, walks to his desk, and grabs a small paper bag. Then he hands it to me.
I stare at him. "Is this a prank? Is something going to explode?"
He rolls his eyes. "Just open it."
I do as he says, but I'm still wary.
It's a coffee. My coffee. Iced caramel latte, just the way I order it. I look up at him, suspicious. "You stole my coffee, and now you're giving me another one?" He shrugs, stuffing his hands in his pockets.
"Figured I owed you." I don't know what to say to that. Because of this? This was weird. Aiden Knight doesn't do nice things. He steals my coffee.

He messes with me, but this was sweet, and that might be the most infuriating thing he's ever done.

CHAPTER ELEVEN

AIDEN

Practice is brutal. My head is a fucking mess. I skate harder, pushing my body until my muscles scream, but nothing quiets the storm brewing inside me. Not the cold bite of the rink air, not the satisfying scrape of my blades against the ice—nothing. Because no matter how fast I skate or how many pucks I shoot into the net, I can't outrun reality.

I can't change that my baby sister, Sophia, is sick. I can't fix her disease with a well-placed check or a fucking hat trick. And I sure as hell can't make my dad see that hockey is the only thing keeping me sane right now. His words from last night still echo in my head:

"She will never get better, Aiden. Instead of spending every minute with her, you should focus on your degree. This hockey crap needs to stop. Sophia will die. I refuse to spend time with someone who will not be part of our lives in a few years."

I'd taken the phone away from my ear before he could hear me slam my fist into the wall. Like, I don't know there is a chance she will die. She's still waiting for a bone marrow match.

I think about it every second of every goddamn day.

I grit my teeth and wind up for another slap-shot. The puck hits the top corner of the net so hard that it rattles, but it doesn't feel like enough. Nothing feels like enough.

"Alright, that's enough, Knight."

I glance up, my grip tightening on my stick. Will stands at the boards, arms crossed, watching me like a ticking bomb. Not a lot of people know, but Will is my fraternal twin. We don't have the best relationship because of our father. While growing up, he took Will everywhere, leaving me and Sophia behind like we didn't matter. I don't hold it against Will. We just don't have the same connection I have with Soph.

"Not done," I mutter.

"Yes, you fucking are." His voice is firm, and I know that look on his face—it's the same one he's had since we were kids. The don't be an idiot, Aiden look. I exhale sharply and skate toward him, tapping my stick against the ice before hopping over the boards.

"What do you want?"

Will hands me a water bottle. "For you to get your shit together before you self-destruct."

I roll my eyes but take the bottle anyway. "I'm fine."

He gives me a deadpan stare.

"Right. That's why you're acting like a damn psycho on the ice." I don't respond. Because if I do, I might say what's running through my head. Whenever I lace up my skates, I feel like I can breathe again. If I stop moving and pushing, I'll have to sit with the fear that we won't find a match for Sophia in time. That she'll—No. I won't go there.

Will observes me like he can hear the thoughts I'm trying to suppress. Then, in a rare moment of softness, he claps a hand on my shoulder.

"Look, I get it. You don't have to talk about it, but you don't have to keep pretending you're indestructible." I huff out a breath, shaking my head.

"No offence, but I don't need a heart-to-heart right now."

"Yeah, I figured," Will says dryly. Then he smirks. "Maybe you need something else. Something infuriating."

I frown. "The hell are you—" Before I can finish, someone crashes into me from behind, nearly knocking me off balance.

"What the—"

"Watch where you're going, Asshole." I know that voice. I hate that voice. That's a lie, I don't.

I turn around, and there she is. Standing on the ice with her hands on her hips, looking damn beautiful, Goldie sneers up at me like I'm the problem.

My right eye twitches. "You literally ran into me." She shrugs, entirely unbothered. "You were in my way." I stare at her, then glance at Will, who looks way too entertained by this.

"You brought her here?" I demand. Will lifts a shoulder.

"Figured you could use a distraction." Kat tilts her head, all fake innocence.

"Don't tell me I make you lose focus, Knight." I exhale the frustration through my nose.

"You are a distraction." Her lips curve into a slow, taunting smile.

"Then I must be doing something right." Will is outright laughing now, and I swear to God, I'm going to kill him. Kat skates backward, her movements effortless. "What's the matter? Not used to someone being better on the ice than you?" I let out a sharp laugh.

"Better? Sweetheart, did you forget who won the other night? You twirl for a living. I fight." Kat gasps dramatically.

"Oh, no. The big, bad hockey player thinks he's tougher than me. I'm so scared." I smirk, enjoying the back-and-forth with her.

"You should be."

"Try me, Knight." She pushes off, gliding down the ice, and something about the challenge in her voice makes my blood heat. Fine. I skate after her, closing the distance in seconds, but she's already spinning into a perfect turn, barely out of reach. I lunge. She dodges. It's infuriating. It's exhilarating. And the worst part? I'm enjoying it. We keep this up for a few more minutes—her teasing, me chasing, neither of us backing down. Will and Roman are watching from the boards, probably placing bets on who will snap first. Finally, Kat slows down, stopping near the centre of the rink. She's breathing fast, and her cheeks are flushed from the cold. I skate up to her, close enough that our blades nearly touch.

"You always this annoying?" She smirks, eyes gleaming at my question.

"Only around people who deserve it." I shake my head, but I don't move away. I should step back, but I don't.

I can't. Her expression shifts slightly as if she just realised how close we actually are. Her breath comes out in a small puff of air, and I catch the faintest hint of vanilla and something sweeter—caramel, probably from her coffee addiction. I don't know why I noticed that. Or why I don't hate it. Kat opens her mouth, probably to throw another insult my way, but before she can, I mutter,

"You ever shut up?" She tilts her head, considering. Then she grins.

"Make me." I exhale sharply, shaking my head, and a smile threatening to reach my lips.

"You're impossible." She grins and winks at me. "And yet, here you are."

Before I can respond—before I can do something stupid like admit she's in my head—she skates off, leaving me standing there. Will skates up next to me, smirking.

"Feeling better?" I snap, glaring at him.

"Shut the fuck up." He just laughs, skating away. I stand there for a second longer, watching Kat as she spins effortlessly, her movements fluid and precise.

And despite everything—despite the weight on my shoulders, the stress, the exhaustion—I realise something.

Will was right. I do feel better, and maybe I don't hate her, but I like her presence.

The rest of the day is a blur: training, arguments with Dad, and trying to stay sane in a house full of idiots. I should be getting some sleep, but instead, I do what I always do—claim my usual spot on the couch, flip through channels, and ignore the fact that Kat herself is sitting just a few feet away from me.

"Aiden, do you want to play?" Roman asks. I nod, stand up, and sit beside him in our giant beanbag. I grab one of Roman's remotes and start picking my team, but I still feel her. Lately, I feel her everywhere. I think about her during school, practice, and at home. She has invaded my head, and I can't stop thinking about Katerina Hart.

She has Maddie on the loudspeaker, talking animatedly about figure skating. She says people don't take it seriously enough and should be considered one of the most challenging sports.

I smirk to myself. She's so passionate about it, so utterly Kat,

that I almost let it slide. Almost.

"Figure skating isn't a real sport, Kat." I don't even look up when I say this. I just toss it out there like it's a fact, waiting for the inevitable explosion. Roman snaps his head towards mine, eyes wide in disbelief at what I said.

"Excuse me?" I finally glance at her. She's staring at me, the phone still pressed to her ear, looking like she's torn between ending the call or strangling me. I shrug.

"It's performance. Not a sport." Something shifts in her expression. It's subtle, but I see it—the moment I hit a nerve.

Kat hangs up without another word and stands up. She marches towards me and plants herself directly before me, blocking my view of the TV.

"Say that again." I raise an eyebrow, amused. She's pissed. Really pissed.

"Fuck man, You did this to yourself," Rome says, patting my back as he stands up to leave. I didn't want to argue with her, but I couldn't help it. I like seeing her angry, mainly when that anger is directed towards me. Which means I can't stop now. I lean back, stretching my arms over the back of the couch.

"It's a hobby. Not a sport." Her hands ball into fists at her sides. And fuck me, she's cute when she's mad.

"You think just because your sport revolves around shoving
people into walls, it makes it harder than mine? You don't know a damn thing about what I do." I smirk.

"I know you get judged on how pretty you look." The throw pillow hits me square in the face. I catch it, laughing. "Touch a nerve, Hart?" She glares.

"If you think it's so easy, why don't you try landing a quadruple jump?" I lean forward, resting my elbows on my knees.

"Why don't you try taking a hit on the ice and still finishing the game?" Her eyes narrow. "Oh, I'm sorry. Did I sign up to get slammed into a wall for fun? No, I have actual skills."

I chuckle. "Skills? Please. You twirl around in sequins and call it work." The second pillow comes flying at me before I can duck. This time, it hits. I wipe a hand down my face, grinning.

"Resorting to violence, Angel Face?" She throws her hands up.

"You are insufferable!"

"And you love it." Kat groans, spinning on her heel and storming off, mumbling something under her breath. But I don't miss the way her pulse jumps at her throat. The way her ears flush pink.

I don't miss the fact that, even as she leaves, she doesn't want to.

And fuck, neither do I.

CHAPTER TWELVE

KATERINA

I can't breathe. I don't know what triggered it or pulled me under, but the air is thick and pressing down on my lungs, and my fingers tremble as I dig them into the couch cushion.

"I love you, but you can't be pushing yourself that hard," my mom says, her voice tinged with concern on the other side of the phone.

"It's starting again, Mom. I don't know what to do." My voice cracks, and I can hear the helplessness creeping in. I look at myself in the mirror, but I only see a reflection of Max standing behind me with a creepy smile. The tiredness in my eyes is only matched by the exhaustion in my body.

'You are so weak, Katerina. Only made to please me.'

'I'm the strong one. You are nothing.'

I shake my head, forcing the thoughts back. "Get out of my head, Max. Get the fuck out of my head." I slap my temple, the sting doing little to ward off the wave of anger and fear. Tears roll down my face, a mixture of frustration and sorrow.

"Get out. Get the fuck out of my head. Not again." I shout it, but the words are useless. I throw my phone towards the mirror, watching it crash against the glass, shattering it everywhere. I slowly back up against the wall, feeling its coldness seep into my bones.

"Please, just leave me alone," I whisper, my voice shaking as I curl into myself, pressing my knees to my chest. It's not real. I know it's not real. But my mind doesn't care. Suddenly, I'm no longer in the hockey house. I'm back there. Back in that dark, empty hospital room. Back with him.

Max's voice slithers into my ear like poison.

'You don't think you can do this without me?' His grip tightens on my wrist. *'Don't act like you don't want it, Kat.'*

My body rigidifies, and my breathing becomes shallow. As the walls close in, my vision tunnels, and my thoughts turn against me.

You let it happen.

You froze.

You should have fought harder.

I gasp for air, but I can't get enough, my chest tightening, my heartbeat hammering in my ears. Someone calls my name, but it's muffled, distant—like I'm underwater. A hand touches my arm, and I flinch back violently, scrambling away.

"Kat! Hey. It's me." The voice is familiar.
Safe. Alina. I blink hard, trying to shake the phantom hands off me, focusing on now—not then. I'm in the living room. Not in that hospital room. Not with Him. Alina is kneeling in front of me, her hands up in surrender, her brown eyes wide with worry. "Breathe with me, okay? In for four, out for four."
I shake my head, gripping my arms.
"I—I can't—"
"Yes, you can," she says, firmer now. "You're safe, Kat. You're safe."
"Ali, it's happening again. Why the fuck is it happening again?" I whisper, the panic clawing at my throat. Alina doesn't hesitate. She sits next to me and pulls me into her arms, holding me tightly as I sob.
"I know, baby girl. I'm sorry." She whispers, the warmth of her embrace grounding me, if only for a moment. Roman and Aiden stand at the door, unsure whether to come in, but Aiden's gaze burns through the side of my face, a heat that doesn't feel like pity but something more complicated.
I squeeze my eyes shut, trying to focus on the rise and fall of her breathing, trying to drown out his voice, but the panic is still clawing at my ribs.
Alina glances at her phone, swearing under her breath.
"Shit. I have to be at work in ten minutes." I nod rapidly despite my hands still shaking and my thoughts still spiralling.
"I'm fine. Go."
"You are not fine," she argues, hesitating as she scans my face full of concern.
"I'll stay with her." Both of us freeze. Slowly, I look up. Aiden stands in the doorway, arms crossed, brow furrowed. His usual smirk is nowhere to be found.
Alina hesitates, glancing between us.

"Are you sure?" Aiden nods, his eyes not leaving mine. "Go. I got her." Alina kisses the top of my head before rubbing my arm.

"I'll drop you off," Roman tells her, and she nods in response, casting a glance towards me. Alina squeezes my knee gently before grabbing her bag and heading for the door, giving Aiden one last look that says, don't screw this up.

I sit stiffly, staring at the floor, trying to pretend that my entire

body isn't still trembling. Aiden doesn't move at first and doesn't say anything. He just watches me, his dark eyes unreadable.

"You wanna tell me what that was?" he finally asks. I shake my head quickly. "No." He exhales sharply but doesn't argue. Instead, he moves towards the couch across from mine and—much to my surprise—sits on the floor beside it, his back resting against the cushions. We sit in silence for a minute. Two.

"I used to get them, too," Aiden says quietly. "Panic attacks." I glance at him, startled. He keeps his gaze fixed on the ceiling,

his jaw tight. "After my mom left, I couldn't sleep for shit. I couldn't breathe, sometimes. It got worse when a family member got sick." I swallow hard, my heartbeat still uneven.

"How did you make it stop?" He lets out a humourless chuckle.

"I didn't. Not really." He taps his fingers against his knee. "But I figured out how to shut up the voice in my head when it got too loud." I stare at him, my throat tightening. "How?" Aiden shifts, finally looking at me. "Distraction." I blink. "What kind of distraction?" The smirk makes a slow return. "Annoying the hell out of you usually works."

I groan. "Of course it does." His lips twitch up, but it doesn't last long.

"Look, Kat, I'm not good at the whole... talking thing. But if you need something to keep your mind from going there again, I can be obnoxious enough to help with that." I huff out something between a laugh and a sigh.

"You're already obnoxious."

"Exactly." He smirks. "I'm doing you a favour just by existing."

I roll my eyes, but the panic is finally loosening its grip, the phantom weight of Max's hands fading. Aiden watches me closely, his smirk fading just a little.

"You don't have to tell me what happened," he says, voice quieter now. "But if you ever do... I'll listen." Something in my chest tightens.

"Everyone knows what happened, Aiden. It was all over the news." I whisper, looking away, focusing on the steady rise and fall of my breathing. Aiden's voice brings me back.

"I don't know what happened," he says, his brow furrowed in confusion. My head snaps to his. I search his eyes for any sign of falsehood, but there's only honesty.

"You really don't?" I ask, my voice almost incredulous. Aiden shakes his head, and I nod, feeling the weight of my unspoken truths settle in my chest.

"Promise me you won't look me up," I say, my voice barely above a whisper. "I'll tell you what happened, but I want to be the one to tell you, not the articles and their lies." Aiden's lips curl into a small smile, and he lifts his pinky, his eyes locking with mine.

"Pinky promise?" He asks, a teasing glint in his gaze. I laugh softly, nodding as I wrap my pinky around his. It's absurdly comforting—this small, innocent gesture.

And for a moment, I don't feel the world's weight on my shoulders.

"Thanks," I murmur. Aiden nods like it's no big deal as if he didn't just do something that no one else has been able to. For the first time in a long time, the voice in my head is silent.

"Hey," I say, breaking the silence. "Can you please grab my phone? I threw it while talking to my mom, and she's probably really worried." Aiden stands up, walking over to the sink. He picks up my phone, its cracked screen still showing the thirty missed calls from my mom.

"I'll be outside if you need me," Aiden says, his voice barely audible. I nod, answering my mom's incoming call. As he walks out, my eyes follow his retreating figure, my heart thumping in my chest.

CHAPTER THIRTEEN

KATERINA

The house is alive with energy. Music pounds through the walls, the bass vibrating in my chest as the heat from too many bodies in one space thickens the air. The smell of cheap beer and sweat lingers, mixed with the faint scent of cologne and perfume. This is a typical college party. I should be enjoying myself. Alina had made a whole speech about how we deserved this night after the week we'd had. And she wasn't wrong. Classes were exhausting, training was brutal, and I needed something to relieve stress. But then Aiden walked in.

He's hard to miss, standing near the kitchen, laughing at something Will said, his usual effortless confidence on display. The black t-shirt he's wearing clings to his arms, and his hair is messy, like he's been running his fingers through it. He doesn't look like he belongs in the middle of a rowdy, sweaty crowd.

He looks like he owns the damn place. I don't realise I've been staring until Alina nudges me with her hip.

"You're glaring." I snap my eyes back to her.

"I am not." She raises an eyebrow.

"Right. You're sending mental daggers in his direction because you like him so much." I scoff, crossing my arms.

"He's just annoying."

"Uh-huh," Alina smirks, taking a sip of her drink. "So that's why you haven't stopped looking at him?"

"I haven't—"

"Kat," she cuts me off. "Just admit he gets under your skin and move on. Or, I don't know, do something about it?" I scoff.

"Like what? Strangle him?" Alina winks.

"Or kiss him. Same energy." I nearly choke on my drink.

"Absolutely not." Alina laughs, and I groan, deciding I need another drink before this conversation worsens. I approach the kitchen, pushing past a group of overly excited frat guys, when someone steps into my path.

"Kat?" I blink, momentarily caught off guard.

"Logan?" Logan Matthews. Hockey player. Junior. Blonde, tall, and annoyingly charming. We have a class together, and he's pretty easy to talk to. He flashes me a smile, his gaze dipping briefly over my outfit before returning to my eyes.

"Didn't expect to see you here," I smirk, leaning against the counter. "I do have a social life, you know." He chuckles.

"Could've fooled me. All I ever see you do is skate."

"And yet," I say, tilting my head, "You still watch."

Logan grins, his fingers tapping against his cup.

"Guilty." It's an easy conversation. He's flirting, and I could flirt back. I should flirt back. But I find myself not wanting to. I feel Aiden before I see him. He moves into the space next to me, his presence an uninvited weight in the air. I refuse to acknowledge him, but Logan does, offering a casual nod.

"Knight." Aiden nods back, his expression unreadable. Then, as if I'm not standing right here, he leans against the counter and casually takes a sip from his drink, eyes scanning the party like he has nowhere else to be. Annoyance flares in my chest.

I turn back to Logan, offering my most charming smile. "So, Logan, what's your major again?"

"Business," he says, returning my smile. "Thinking about sports management, actually."

"Oh," I hum. "So you plan on working with athletes instead of just being one?" Logan smirks.

"Exactly." Before he can say more, Aiden snorts under his breath. Not loud. Not obvious. But pointed at Logan.

I whip around to face him. "Something funny, Knight?" He lifts a shoulder, taking another sip.

"Just wondering how long you were going to pretend to be interested in that conversation."

My blood boils. Logan chuckles, glancing between Aiden and me, sensing the shift in tension. "I'll let you two figure out your thing."

I glare at him. "We don't have a thing." Logan winks. "Sure you don't." As he disappears into the crowd, I whip back to Aiden.

"What the hell is your problem?" He shrugs.

"No problem." I cross my arms, irritated at the man before me.

"You just had to interrupt, didn't you?"

"I didn't interrupt. I just spoke facts."

I groan, exasperated. "You are impossible." Aiden smirks, his gaze dropping briefly to my lips before flicking back up. "You're still standing here. Aren't you?" I don't get a chance to respond because someone from the living room yells,
 "TRUTH OR DARE!"
I exhale sharply. "Nope. Not happening."
Alina suddenly appears, grabbing my wrist. "Oh, it's happening."
Before I can fight it, I'm dragged into the circle forming in the centre of the room. Aiden follows, of course, settling into a spot across from me, stretching his arms over the back of the couch like he has all the time in the world.
The game starts mild. Embarrassing dares, a few tame truths. Then it's Alina's turn.
"Truth or dare?" Roman asks, grinning. Alina narrows her eyes. "Dare." Roman smirks. "Kiss someone in this circle."
My eyes snap to Alina, who—without hesitation—grabs Roman's shirt and pulls him in, pressing a quick, confident kiss to his lips. The room erupts in cheers and whistles, but I barely register it because she just did that.
Roman looks stunned, but his hand lingers at her waist for just a second too long before she pulls away, shrugging like it was no big deal.
I knew it.
Next, someone dares Will to shotgun a beer in under five seconds, which he does embarrassingly fast.
"Aiden."
I snap my gaze at him. He looks too calm, sipping his drink like none matters. "Truth or dare?" He smirks. "Dare." The girl smiles, biting her bottom lip as she flutters her eyes at him. My stomach does this

uncomfortable flip, but I ignore it. "Kiss someone you'd never expect to kiss." The tension in the air thickens. My stomach twists violently, and my heart starts thumping out of my chest. Aiden's gaze immediately flicks to me. I hold my breath. He watches me for a beat—one, two, three seconds—then smirks and leans toward the girl who dared him, pressing a brief, easy kiss to her lips instead.

I don't know why I feel relief. Or maybe it's disappointment. I don't know. All I know is I take a long sip of my drink, ignoring how my pulse is suddenly too fast and how Aiden's eyes linger on mine like he knows that affected me.

It's like he's waiting for something. A reaction.

I refuse to give it to him.

I refuse to give him anything. So, I keep my expression blank, sip my drink, and pretend my stomach isn't in knots. That I don't care that Aiden just kissed some random girl instead of— No. Doesn't matter.

Alina nudges my knee under the table, eyes filled with something between amusement and suspicion. I warn her with a look, but she grins and leans back against the couch, far too entertained.

The game moves on, but the energy has shifted. Aiden's attention isn't fully on the dares anymore. Now and then, I catch him watching me. Not obviously. Just… aware. I hate that I notice, and I hate that it makes me feel something. When it's my turn, I don't even hesitate. "Dare."

The guy across from me—some senior I don't know—grins. "I dare you to do a body shot." The room bursts into cheers, and my stomach twists again—but this time for a completely different reason.

Before I can even think about backing out, Alina claps her hands. "Ooooh, now this is about to get interesting."

I glare at her before looking at the guy. "Off of who?" His grin widens, and he gestures vaguely around the circle. "Your choice." I can feel Aiden's gaze on me; our eyes meet, but I refuse to pick him even though I wouldn't mind dragging my tongue up those abs of his. I can hate him and still want to fuck him, but I know better.

Instead, I scan the group to decide the least humiliating choice.

Before I can choose, Logan leans forward, flashing an easy smirk. "I volunteer as tribute." The group cheers louder, and I force a smile. Logan is harmless. This means nothing. And if Aiden gets annoyed— Well, that's just a bonus.

Logan leans back, resting against the couch with his shirt slightly lifted, waiting. Someone hands me a salt shaker, and I move without thinking, dragging my tongue across his skin before sprinkling the salt. Cheers erupt, and I barely hear them over the pounding in my ears. I grab the lime, hold it between my lips, and throw back the shot. As soon as the tequila burns down my throat, Logan leans in, taking the lime from my mouth with his own. It's over in seconds, but the crowd eats it up, whistling and laughing. I sit back, heart hammering against my ribs, and glance at Aiden for a second. Just long enough to see his jaw tighten, his grip flex against his glass. He's not smiling anymore. Interesting. The game continues, but I'm done.

"I need another drink," Alina smirks.

"Oh sure, now you need one."

I ignore her and head for the kitchen. The party is still strong, with bodies moving in a blur of laughter and music. After that dare, I should feel lighter, victorious, or smug. Instead, I feel restless. As I pour another drink, I feel someone step up beside me.

"You have a habit of showing off, Hart." I don't have to look to know who it is. I take my time stirring my drink before turning my head slightly.

"Funny, I was thinking the same about you." Aiden doesn't respond immediately; he just watches me. His dark eyes are unreadable, but there's something there—something charged.

"You didn't have to do that," he says, voice lower now. I feign innocence.

"Do what?" I ask, pretending not to know what he is talking about.

His lips press into a line. "You know what."

I sip my drink, shrugging. "It was just a game." A muscle in his jaw ticks.

"Right." We stand in tense silence, the party still raging around us. Then, he leans in slightly, his breath warm against my ear. "Next time you want my attention, you don't have to go through someone else." A shiver runs down my spine, but I cover it with a scoff.

"Your attention? You think too highly of yourself." He smirks, finally stepping back.

"Maybe. But you did look at me first."

"So did you!" I counter, raising my voice. Aiden nods, pressing his lips together.

"Yes, I did. The dare said kiss someone I'd never expect to kiss." He takes a couple of steps towards me, lowering his head, cold lips grazing the top of my ear. "I very much so expect to kiss you." My heart plummets at his words, but before I can argue, he disappears into the crowd.

I let out a slow breath, my grip tightening around my cup.

Infuriating.

Absolutely infuriating.

And yet, I know exactly who I'll think about when I sleep tonight.

CHAPTER FOURTEEN

KATERINA

The following morning comes too fast.
My alarm blares, and I slap my phone, turning the alarm off groaning as sunlight spills through the blinds. I roll out of bed, my head only slightly pounding. It could've been worse. Alina is already up when I shuffle into the kitchen. She leans against the counter, scrolling through her phone, sipping coffee like the image of ease.

She glances up. "Morning, sunshine," I grunt, grabbing a mug and pouring myself coffee. "Don't start." She grins.
"Start what? Talking about the fact that Aiden was practically eye-fucking you all night?" I freeze mid-sip.
"He was not."

She shrugs, unbothered. "Maybe not in an obvious way, but I noticed," I scowl, sinking into a chair.

"It was just the game. He was being his usual arrogant, annoying self. Nothing new."

Alina hums in amusement. "Sure, Kat. Whatever helps you sleep at night."

Before I can argue, my phone buzzes on the table. I unlock it to see a message from the devil himself.

Grumpy Hockey Player

> *Class today. One hour. Don't be late.*

I glare at the screen like it personally offended me. "Unbelievable."

Alina peeks over. "Oooh, texting already? Cute." I shove my phone into my hoodie pocket. "It's not cute. It's torture."

She grins. "Same thing."

An hour later, I'm lacing up my skates, my irritation growing when I spot Aiden already on the ice, casually stretching like he didn't spend last night making my life difficult. He looks up as I step onto the rink, smirking.

"You're late."

I scowl. "By one minute."

"Still late." He twirls his stick. "Gonna make me regret having you teach with me?"

I tighten my ponytail, rolling my shoulders back. "You will regret it."

His grin is slow, teasing as he says. "Prove it."

As the kids pile in, we're off, pushing each other, challenging, bickering, pretending that there isn't something lingering between us that neither of us is ready to name.

"Thanks for the class, Ms. Hart!" One of my little skaters grins as she glides toward the bench, her cheeks pink from the cold. I nod, waving at her.

"See you on Monday!" She gives me a bright smile before disappearing toward the exit. I should consider my next lesson plan or focus on the lingering warmth from teaching. But my mind keeps drifting back to him. To the way he looked at me before storming off. I swallow hard, my eyes flickering to the exit where Aiden had disappeared minutes ago. He's mad at the whole body shot thing. I know he is. And the worst part? I don't even know if I want to fix it.

"Malyshka, are you ready?" The familiar voice makes me freeze. I whip my head to the right, convinced I'm imagining things. But no—standing by the rink's entrance, beaming at me like I just won an Olympic gold medal, is my mother. A sharp breath escapes me before a wide smile spreads across my face.

Mama.

Without a second thought, I skate toward her, stepping off the ice and pulling her into a tight hug. I don't care that I forgot to put my skate-guards on. But, of course, my mother does.

"Your skates, baby," she scolds, her strong Russian accent making the words sharper. "You will ruin them. Put your guards on." I smile at her, already grabbing the blade covers from my bag. "I missed you so much, Mama." She cups my cheek as I stand up correctly, her blue eyes shining warmly. "I missed you too, Malyshka."

For the first time since I set foot at Pleasant Oaks University, I can breathe. All because of her. The moment is perfect—until I feel eyes on me. I look up, my breath catching in my throat. Across the rink, just before the exit, stands Aiden. His deep brown eyes pierce through me, unreadable yet heavy with something I can't name. My heart clenches. I should look away, but the intensity of his stare keeps me locked in place. Something electric hums in the space between us.

Then, as suddenly as he appeared, he was gone. I exhale slowly,
my chest tightening.

"Alexei is excited to see me, and I can't wait to meet your roommates," my mother says, unaware of my spiralling thoughts. My stomach drops. Right. I haven't told her.

"About that…" I purse my lips, suddenly fascinated by my skate guards. I take a deep breath, then blurt it out in one breath:

"Theadmissionsofficemadeamistakeandinsteadoflivinga tthesatinghouse,ilivewithfourhockeyplayers."

My mother stares at me dumbfounded. "What?" I sigh, inhaling sharply before repeating, "The admissions office made a mistake, and instead of living at the skating house, I live with four hockey players." Her mouth parts slightly, but nothing comes out.

"Boys?" she finally asks, her voice pensive.

I nod, bracing myself. "Yes, but they're great. Like older brothers—mostly. They take care of me." She doesn't look convinced. I scramble.

"You'll meet them tonight for dinner! I'll make sure they're all there." That seems to do it. Her lips twitch, then curve into a small smile. "I would love that." I exhale, relieved, wrapping my arm around hers as we head toward the exit.

Pulling out my phone, I quickly text the group chat.

Hockey House + Ice Princess

Ice Princess

> *Hey guys, my mom is here and wants to have dinner with you at six p.m. Please don't be late.*

William

> *When you say mother, do you mean MOTHER or stepmother?*

I chuckle, sending back a reply.

Ice Princess

> *MOTHER, Will! As in Anya Petrova. The woman who gave birth to me.*

"Are you texting them?" My mom raises an amused eyebrow.
I nod. "Just letting them know they can't skip dinner."
She laughs softly. My phone pings again.

Roman

> *Are we about to try Russian food from the queen herself?*

Graysen

> *I will be there, hands down.*

William

> *OMFG, I'm about to meet the legend herself.*

I roll my eyes, but before I can put my phone away, another message pops up.

Grumpy Hockey Player
> I'll be there.

Three simple words. My pulse stutters.
"Are you okay? You're breathing weird." My mom studies me, concern laced in her voice. I force a casual smile. "Yeah, just excited for dinner." Liar.
No one knows me better than my mother, so I avoid her gaze.
"Let's grab some ingredients so I can cook," she says, connecting her phone to my car's Bluetooth. The moment she starts playing Russian music, nostalgia hits me like a freight train. I missed her. I missed this.

When dinner rolls around, the entire house is buzzing with energy.
The girls and Alexei arrive first, eager to help with the meal. The boys arrive exactly at six—loud, chaotic, and ready to meet my mother.
"Honey, I'm home!" Will announces dramatically, stepping into the kitchen like he owns the place. I grin, but my smile falters the second I meet Aiden's gaze. He's unreadable, his expression carefully blank. But the tension crackles in the air between us, thick and undeniable. The guys introduce themselves one by one, earning hugs from my mother. But something shifts when Aiden steps forward.
"Hello, ma'am. I'm Aiden." His voice is calm and polite, but his eyes flick to me for half a second. My mom smiles, wrapping him in a hug.

"Nice to meet you, Aiden. You seem like a quiet one. Let me guess, you keep them in check, don't you?"
He laughs slightly. "I try. It's your daughter who keeps us in check." I blink. What? Since when do I keep him in check?
My mother raises an eyebrow, looking between us. Suspicious.
Then, before I can react, Aiden moves toward me—and in a swift motion, he crouches slightly and wraps his arms around my lower back.
My heart stops. Why is he hugging me?
"Angel face," he murmurs, his voice low and hoarse.
I freeze. Then, like a reflex, I wrap my arms around his shoulders. My fingers press against warm muscle, and his scent—a mix of clean soap and something undeniably Aiden—invades my senses.
I breathe him in, my eyes fluttering shut for just a second. Why do I like this?
Aiden, let's go first and takes a step back. The loss of his warmth makes my skin prickle. I meet his gaze, my heart hammering, and he smirks at me.
Asshole.
This is a game. He knew the hug would throw me off. Fuck him. He nods at me once before heading toward the kitchen.
I barely have time to process it before I hear my mother
clearing her throat. I turn slowly.
She's standing there, arms crossed, eyebrows raised.
"Just roommates, right?" I gulp. "Of course." She does not look convinced at all.
When we all sit in the living room, my mom announces dinner is ready. We approach the dining table, but Will flashes right by me and into my seat. Will grins at me while I shoot daggers at him. I glare at him again,

taking the only seat available with a sigh. I was supposed to sit by Maddie, but someone almost glued himself to the chair… cough…cough…. Will, forcing me to sit next to Aiden.

I feel sick. Not because the food isn't incredible—it is. But because every time Aiden moves, his thigh brushes mine. I can't focus. I can't breathe.

I hear Aiden scoff, and I bring my attention to him. "Problem?"

He shrugs. "Your mom was saying she loves your new coach. I was just thinking it's insane that your coach has you training six hours a day on top of everything else." My mother's head snaps toward me.

"Malyshka, is that true?" I murder Aiden with my eyes. He just smirks, taking another bite of his food. Oh, he's dead.

Tonight.

I don't care if my mother is here. Aiden Knight is going to suffer. I don't care that we're in the middle of dinner. The second I can get him alone, it's over for him. I glare daggers at him as I force a tight smile toward my mom, who is observing me, her fork hovering mid-air.

"Malyshka," she says slowly, "are you pushing yourself too hard?" I shake my head immediately. "No, Mama, I—"

"She is," Aiden interrupts, casually sipping from his water like he didn't just throw me under the bus.

I snap my gaze back to him. "Aiden." He raises an eyebrow, feigning innocence. "What? It's true. You're covered in bruises half the time, and let's not forget that time you nearly collapsed after practice." I kick him under the table. He barely flinches, but his lips twitch like he's trying to hold back a laugh. Bastard. My mother's gaze sharpens.

"What do you mean collapsed?" Damn it. I shoot Aiden another warning look, but he's enjoying this way too much.

"It was nothing," I say quickly. "I was just exhausted that day." My mom sets down her fork.

"Katerina, I raised you better than to push yourself to the point of collapse." I grit my teeth, resisting the urge to throttle the smug man

sitting next to me. "It was one time, Mama. I was fine." "Barely," Aiden mutters.

I snap my head toward him. "Do you have a death wish?" I yell. He smirks, leaning in just slightly. "Just stating facts, Angel Face." I hate that my stomach flips. I hate everything about him. Before I can tell him exactly how much I loathe his existence,

my mom sighs and shakes her head.

"You are just like your father. Stubborn, reckless—" My chest tightens. She doesn't mean to bring him up. I know that. But still. I force a smile and reach for my drink. "You say that like it's a bad thing." She sighs, clearly not convinced, but thankfully, Grayson saves me.

"So, Anya," he says, turning to my mom, "What do you think of us so far? We're not completely terrible, right?" she eyes them all thoughtfully, but her expression is warm.

"You seem like an outstanding group of boys. I was worried when I first heard Katerina was living with hockey players, but now I see I have nothing to worry about."

Roman grins. "We protect our own."

"Damn right we do," Will adds, nudging me with his elbow. I roll my eyes, but my heart swells. My mom smiles. "Then I'm happy." After dinner, we all help

clean up. My mom insists on doing the dishes, but I convince her to let me handle it. Or at least, I try to. "You are my guest," I say, practically pushing her toward the living room. She gives me a look. "You are my daughter."
"And?"
"And I will always be the mother. So sit." I groan but don't fight her. The others are already in the living room, lounging around as Will, Roman, and Grayson argue about some hockey stat that no one cares about. Aiden is nowhere to be found.
Coward. As I look around, I spot him near the back porch, standing just outside the open door. His arms are crossed, the cold night air ruffling his dark hair slightly. I shouldn't go to him. I should stay inside, drink tea with my mom, and not acknowledge him. But, of course, I'm an idiot.
I step outside, the chill biting at my skin. "You're avoiding me." Aiden doesn't turn around to face me. "Wouldn't dream of it."
"You threw me under the bus." He finally glances at me, that infuriating smirk still in place. "You mean I told the truth?" I scoff. "You didn't have to say it like that. My mom already worries enough."

"She should." I freeze. His tone is different now—quieter, less teasing. He exhales, running a hand through his hair.

"Kat, you push yourself harder than anyone I know. And yeah, I admire the hell out of you for it, but…" He pauses, his jaw clenching. "You also don't know when to stop."
"I can't afford to stop." His gaze snaps to mine, something dark flickering in his expression. "That's bullshit." I narrow my eyes. "Excuse me?"
He steps closer, heat rolling off him despite the cold.

"Kat, I get it. I do. You want to prove yourself. You want to be the best. But pushing yourself until you're barely standing? That's not strength. That's self-destruction." I stiffen, the words hitting too close. "I'm fine," I say, forcing the words out. He lets out a dry laugh. "Bullshit." I grit my teeth. "You're so dramatic." "And you're so stubborn."

I huff, crossing my arms tighter around myself. "Why do you even care?" Silence. I sigh as Aiden presses his lips together, looking at me as if I'm important to him. "Because it's you." My breath catches. He looks at me, really looks at me, and I feel like the world tilts slightly. Aiden has always had this effect on me—this unfair ability to pull me into his gravity, to make my heart hammer in my chest even when I don't want it to.

He steps closer, his voice lower now. "You drive me insane, Kat. And you're reckless as hell. But I…" He exhales sharply as if he doesn't know how to express his thoughts. "I just—"

Before he can finish, the door swings open. "Kat!" Will's voice rings through the night. "Your mom wants to know where the tea is." I jump back like I just got caught doing something illegal. Aiden's jaw tightens. I clear my throat. "Uh—second cabinet to the right of the stove!" Will nods before disappearing back inside. The second the door closes, the tension between Aiden and me snaps back into place.

I shift on my feet. "I should—"

"Yeah," Aiden mutters, dragging a hand through his hair.

"Go." I hesitate for half a second longer before turning on my heel and heading inside. But even as I walk away, I still feel his stare burning into my back.

CHAPTER FIFTEEN

KATERINA

The drive to my qualifier is three hours long. Three long, excruciating hours in a car with Aiden, Roman, and Alina—while my mother? She's getting a ride with my father. That was a plot twist I wasn't prepared for. I ask my mom, horrified, as she casually puts her suitcase in the trunk of my father's car.

"You two are riding together?" I ask my mom, horrified, as she casually puts her suitcase in the trunk of my father's car.

"Yes, Katerina," she says, amused by my panic. "He offered. It's been years—we can be civil."

Civil? My parents? In a confined space for three hours? This had disaster written all over it. But before I could argue, Aiden yanks open the passenger door of our car and turns to me.

"You're sitting in the back," Aiden says casually, and I scowl.

"Says who?" I can't sit in the back. I'm a passenger princess—always have been—and that will not change today.

"Says the driver."

I cross my arms over my chest in denial. "I should drive." Aiden lets out a dry laugh. "You? Drive my car?" Roman whistles under his breath.

"Don't even dream about it, Kat. Aiden doesn't let anyone touch his car." I smirked at the piece of information I had just been given, plotting my next move. Alina, already buckled in the backseat, grins like this is the best entertainment she's ever witnessed.

"Kat, just get in. We don't have all day." I let out a long-suffering sigh before dramatically throwing myself into the backseat. Aiden smirks like he won, which only fuels my irritation. The second he turns on the engine, I reach for the aux cord. Aiden snatches it first. My eyes narrow.

"Give it."

Aidens grin widenes. "Not a chance." I lunge for it, but he dodges me effortlessly, plugging his phone in before I can react. The second the first heavy rock riff fills the car, I gasp in outrage.

"Absolutely not," I say, immediately reaching to unplug it. Aiden grabs my wrist mid-air, his grip firm but warm. His stupid smirk deepens.

"You got a problem with real music, Angel Face?" I yank my hand free and glare at him. "This isn't music. This is just noise."

Roman snorts. "She's got a point." Aiden shoots him a glare, not believing Roman just agreed with me over him. "You're dead to me, Rome."

I lean forward, dramatically resting my chin on Aiden's shoulder to annoy him. "If I must be stuck in this car with you, we are listening to Taylor Swift." Aiden visibly tenses at my proximity before tilting his head slightly, eyes meeting mine briefly in the mirror. "You're actually serious," he says, like he can't believe it, I'm being serious. "Dead serious." He laughs, shaking his head as he focuses back on the road. "Not happening." I pout. "I thought you were all about protecting my fragile figure-skating soul?" His lips twitch up in amusement. "Not when it comes to my speakers." Alina grins, enjoying every second of our banter.

 "I don't know, Aiden. 'The Archer' would really fit the mood right now." Roman nods at Ali's words. "She has a point. That song goes hard." Aiden groans, rubbing a hand down his face. "I hate all of you," "You'll survive." I snap back. But then he does something unexpected. Instead of fighting back, he scrolls through his phone, clicks on a song, and lets it play.

The second I hear the first note of 'Cruel Summer,' I gasp dramatically.

"You did not just put on Taylor Swift." Aiden shrugs, completely indifferent.

"Figured I'd give you your moment." I stared at him, suspicious. "You're trying to get on my good side, aren't you?" He grins, eyes flicking to me in the mirror. "Maybe." Something about the way he says it sends a shiver up my spine.

I should have let it go, ignore the way my stomach twists stupidly. But because I never know when to back down, I tease. "So you do like Taylor Swift,"

Aiden scoffs. "Let's not get carried away, Angel Face." Roman grins.

"It's too late. You let her win." Aiden shakes his head, but I don't miss the way his fingers tap lightly against the steering wheel to the beat. Alina elbows me.
"I think we just converted him." I lean back against my seat, satisfied. "This is officially the best road trip ever." Aiden rolls his eyes, but there was something softer in his expression. Something that makes my heart beat a little too fast.
Damn him.

The ice is my sanctuary. No matter how loud the arena gets or how the energy buzzes in the air like static, the moment my skates touch the ice, everything else fades. The world beyond this rink doesn't exist. It's just me, Alexei, and the routine we've practiced a thousand times. I breathe in and out to centre myself. We've trained for this. There is no room for hesitation. Alexei meets my gaze, squeezing my hand before the music starts.

"Showtime, Malyshka." The music swells, and we move in perfect sync. Every jump, every lift, every step sequence flows seamlessly. Months of skating together have made us a single entity on the ice, a machine built for precision. A triple twist—flawless. A side-by-side triple axel—perfectly timed. As we hit our final lift, I soar above Alexei, suspended in the air for a breathless moment before he lowers me effortlessly. The final note of our program echoes through the rink as we glide into our finishing pose, my chest heaving as the roar of the crowd explodes around us.

We did it. Alexei's arms wrap around me as we spin in place, his laugh ringing through the arena. "That was perfection, Katerina!" My heart pounds against my ribs, adrenaline coursing through my veins. As we skate off, the cameras flash, and I glance up at the scoreboard. The numbers appear in rapid succession—
First place. Gold.

The emotions hit all at once—relief, pride, and something deeper, something that made my throat tighten. I made it back—after everything that was stolen from me. Alina is waiting for us, still breathless from her performance.

"You did it!" she beams, tackling me into a hug.

"We both did it," I yell in excitement, wrapping my arms around her in a tight hug. Her scores were posted minutes ago—she secured gold in women's singles, her jumps impeccable, her artistry untouchable. We're going to the next round of qualifiers together.

A slow, mocking clap echoes through the air, slicing through my moment of triumph like a knife.

I don't need to turn around to know who it is. Maxim Serkov. The name alone makes my stomach churn. After everything he did to me. After the news broke out, I have no idea how he was able to compete today. Daddy must've paid big money to make it happen.

"You looked stiff out there, Katerina," Max muses, a smirk tugging at his lips. "But then again, you always did choke under pressure." The rage that coils in my chest is instant, but Alexei's grip on my wrist steadies me.

"Leave, Serkov," Alexei says coldly, stepping slightly in front of me.

Max's new partner lingers awkwardly behind him, clearly uncomfortable. She has the same haunted look I used to have, the same stiffness in her shoulders. Our old coach probably trains her, too. Max scoffs, his gaze flicking back to me. "You think you deserved this win? After what happened last time?" His lips curl in disgust. "After you humiliated yourself?"

The air in my lungs turns to ice. I know exactly what he's referencing. The fall. The injury. The nightmares. The night he tried to take more than just my career. Max leans in slightly, his voice just low enough that only I hear. "I bet you still think about it."

A fresh wave of nausea grips me. My fingers curl into fists, nails digging into my palms. I won't break. I won't let him see me break. But before I can say anything, a blur of motion flashes past me; a sickening crack echoes through the air. Max stumbles back, blood trickling from his lip, eyes wide in shock. Aiden stands in front of me, fist still clenched, breathing hard. His expression is unreadable, but his eyes burn with a fury that sends a shiver down my spine.

"Say one more word to her," Aiden growls, his voice dangerously low. "I dare you." The entire rink falls into stunned silence. People are staring, whispers spreading like wildfire. Max wipes the blood from his lip, glaring at Aiden.

"You just made a mistake."

"I'll live." Aiden chimes in, grinning at Max like a maniac. Security is already moving toward us, and coaches are yelling, but Aiden doesn't move. He just stands there before me, daring Max to try something else. Max sneers at both of us. "She doesn't need you to protect her."

Aiden doesn't flinch. "She doesn't need me to, but I'm going to anyway." My breath catches in my throat as Max scoffs before security steps between them, ushering him away.

The moment he's gone, Aiden turns to me, eyes scanning my face. His jaw is tight, his hands flexing at his sides as if fighting the urge to hit something again. "You okay?" he asks quietly. I should be angry. I should scold him for causing a scene. For making this about him. But all I can do is stare at him, my heart racing, my body still on high alert. Because for the first time in a long time, I feel safe. All because of Aiden, and I don't know what to do with that. Instead of answering, I exhale slowly, nodding once.

Aiden studies me for a beat longer before nodding, too. He doesn't say anything else, doesn't press, just stands beside me. The moment we leave the rink, the air outside is sharp and cold, but it does nothing to cool the adrenaline still thrumming through my veins. The chaos from inside the arena still lingers—whispers, shocked faces, coaches scrambling to do damage control. But all I can focus on is the six four pure muscle, grumpy hockey player. How did he go from tormenting me to protecting me? He's walking ahead of me, hands in his pockets, jaw tight. His knuckles are still red from the punch he landed on Max, and I should be lecturing him for it. I should be angry that he just got himself into unnecessary trouble.

But I'm not. Because when Max leaned in and whispered those words, when he tried to drag me back into the past I've been fighting to escape, Aiden was there. No hesitation. No questions. Just action. And I don't know what to do with that.

"You didn't have to do that," I say finally, my voice breaking the tense silence between us.

Aiden stops walking but doesn't turn around. "Yeah, I did." I exhale, stepping up beside him. "Now you're going to have to deal with whatever fallout comes from punching him in the face."

"Worth it," Aiden adds, slowly turning around to look at me. I shake my head, crossing my arms.
"You can't just go around throwing punches every time someone says something you don't like." He finally looks at me, dark eyes unreadable. "You really think that was about me?" I don't answer. I don't have to. Because deep down, I knew it wasn't about him. It was about me. About what Max did— about what he almost did. Aiden saw it in my face. He knew. And that's what terrifies me most of all. He takes a slow breath, his hands flexing at his sides like he wants to say more but doesn't know how.
Instead, he just mutters, "Let's get out of here," and starts walking again. I follow, my emotions tangled into a knot so tight I don't know how to unravel them.

Back at the hotel, the celebration is in full swing. Alexei is basking in the win, holding court in the centre of the room, while Alina is practically glowing, still riding the high of her gold medal. Drinks are flowing, music is blasting, and the weight of competition isn't pressing down on us for once. But I can't relax. Not completely. I keep glancing at Aiden, who's sitting in the corner, beer in hand, talking to Will and Roman like nothing happened earlier. As if he didn't just throw a punch that has probably already made the rounds on social media. Alina plops down beside me, nudging my arm.
 "You okay?" I force a smile.
"Yeah. Just tired." She hums knowingly, her gaze flicking toward Aiden before returning to me. "So,

when will you admit that you're into him?" I nearly choke on my drink.

"Excuse me?" Alina grins, completely unbothered. "Oh, come on, Kat. It's painfully obvious. The way you two bicker, the way he watches you like he's waiting for you to throw the first punch—" I groan.

"That's just Aiden. He's annoying. He gets on my nerves on purpose." "Mmm," Alina muses. "And yet, you haven't stopped staring at him all night." I open my mouth to argue, but—damn it—she's right. Before she can say anything else, Aiden makes his way towards us,

"Are you okay?" Aiden asks, his voice gentle. Alina leaves, making her way towards Roman, sending an I told you, so look behind her shoulders.

I nod, swallowing hard. "Yeah." A beat of silence stretches between us before he mutters, "If he tries anything again, I will hit him harder." A laugh escapes me before I can stop it. "Violence isn't always the answer, you know." Aiden smirks.

"Worked pretty well today."

The buzz from our victory still lingers, but the weight of everything else threatens to crush it. Even as the celebration rages on around me, laughter and music filling the air, I can't stop thinking about him. The way he looked at me, the smugness in his voice, the reminder of everything I've worked so damn hard to bury. And then there's Aiden. He's been watching me all night. Not obviously, not in a way that screams concern, but in that way, he does when he thinks I won't notice. Like he's waiting for me to crack, I won't. I refuse. But as the night drags on, I feel my grip slipping.

"You need to breathe," Alexei murmurs beside me, his voice low enough that only I can hear. I force a small smile. "I am breathing."

He raises his left eyebrow, unconvinced. "You're also gripping your drink like you're about to throw it at someone." I glance down at my hand. He's right. My knuckles are white against the plastic cup; my fingers curled so tightly around it that it might shatter if I squeeze harder. I exhale sharply and loosen my grip. Alexei studies me for a moment before tilting his head toward the door.

"Let's get out of here for a minute." I blink at him. "What?" He shrugs. "Let's go get some fresh air. You need it." I hesitate, glancing around the room. Alina is caught up in a conversation with Roman, and Will is in mid-argument with Grayson about some play from the last hockey game. Aiden…Aiden is still watching me. I need space.

"Fine," I mutter, letting Alexei guide me toward the exit. The night air is sharp against my skin, a welcome contrast to the heat of the party. I inhale deeply, filling my lungs with crisp, cool air, trying to ground myself. We walk silently for a few minutes, the crunch of gravel beneath our feet the only sound. It's peaceful. Calming. And then Alexei sighs.

"You're thinking about him." I stiffen because he is right. Max has total control of my mind right now.

"I don't know what you're talking about." He gives me a look that says, 'I know you're bullshitting me.'

"You do." I swallow hard, shoving my hands into the pockets of my jacket.

"It doesn't matter."

"It does matter, Kat. He's still getting in your head." I shake my head, jaw tightening. "No, he's not." Alexei stops walking, turning to face me fully.

"Then why are we out here instead of celebrating?" I don't have an answer to that. Because the truth is, Max is in my head. Not just because of the past but because he's here. No matter how many gold medals I win or how many times I prove that I don't need him, he still has the power to unnerve me. And I hate it.

I swallow the lump in my throat, forcing a tight smile. "I'm fine, Lex."

His gaze lingers on me, searching for something, but eventually, he sighs. "If you say so." We walk a little longer before heading back inside. The party is still going strong, but my mood hasn't shifted. If anything, I feel heavier.

And then I see Aiden. Why is he everywhere I am?

He's leaning against the wall, arms crossed, brows drawn together as he watches me. I don't know what expression I have on my face, but whatever it is, it makes him push off the wall and start walking toward me. Alexei pats my shoulder. "I'll leave you to it."

"Lex—"

But he's already gone. Traitor.

Aiden stops before me, and for a moment, neither of us speaks. The air between us is thick, the noise from the party fading into the background.

"You good?" he asks finally. I huff out a mocking laugh. "Why do you keep asking me that?" He shrugs. "Maybe because you look about two seconds away from snapping." I cross my arms. "And if I was?" Aiden tilts his head.

"Then I'd be here to ensure you don't do something stupid."

"Like what?"

"Like convincing yourself that that guy still has any power over you." I inhale sharply, my nails digging into my palms.

"I don't—" Aiden steps closer, close enough that I have to tilt my head up to meet his gaze. "Yes, you do. And I get it. But you don't have to." My throat tightens. "I don't need you to fight my battles, Aiden."

"I know," Aiden answers, his voice steady. "But that doesn't mean I won't." I hate that my heart stumbles at his words.

"Why? You hate me," I say, scratching the tip of my nose unconsciously. I stop, staring at my hand. I'm nervous. I only do that when I'm nervous. Around Aiden? Oh my god! Alina was right. When Aiden doesn't answer, I look away, swallowing hard.

"I just want to move on." He nods and exhales, running a hand through his hair. "Then let me help." I glance back up at him, searching his face. "Why?" I ask again, needing an answer. An explanation as to why he cares. His jaw flexes like he's debating how much to say or not to say.

"Because I don't hate you, Angel face, and I don't like seeing you like this." My breath catches.

Because that's not teasing, that's not banter. That's real.

CHAPTER SIXTEEN

KATERINA

It's official—I hate how much I think about him. Ever since yesterday, Aiden has been living rent-free in my head, and I want to evict him. Immediately.

I don't care about him, or how he looked at me after the qualifier, or that there was something in his eyes last night that wasn't the usual cocky arrogance. I shouldn't care. But then I walked into the kitchen this morning, and there he was—half-asleep, shirtless, standing in front of the fridge glaring as if it had personally offended him. I should've turned around and left. I should have. Instead, I opened my stupid mouth.

"Rough night, Knight?" He groans, rubbing a hand down his face before shooting me a glare.

"Do you wake up actively looking for ways to annoy me?" I smirk, loving how this is getting to him.

"Oh, absolutely, it's the best part of my day." He exhaled sharply, grabbing the milk carton and chugging straight from it like a Neanderthal. I wrinkled my nose. "You live with other people, you animal." He wipes his mouth with the back of his hand, looking at me entirely too amused.

"You wanna share a glass, Hart?" I almost throw my coffee at him. Instead, I grab a banana off the counter and launch it at his head. He catches it without even looking.

Of course, he does. "Impressive aim, Angel Face," he muses, peeling the banana calmly. Like he wasn't the most infuriating person to exist. I scowl.

"I hope you choke on it." Aiden grins around his first bite. "You'd miss me too much, baby." The word of endearment makes me pause. Why do I like it?

Before I can respond—before I can come up with a perfect, cutting remark—Roman and Will walk in, immediately sensing the energy in the room. Roman smirked.

"Are we flirting? Or fighting?"

"Both," Will said without hesitation as he continued to eat his cereal.

I throw my hands in the air in defeat. "I hate all of you." Aidens smirk grows, shoving the rest of the banana in his mouth before winking at me. Winking.

I storm out of the kitchen, yelling curse words at the boys before I commit a crime.

By the time I get to class, I've almost managed to shake off my irritation. Almost.

But, of course, the universe isn't on my side today because the only empty seat in our biology class is next to him. Aiden looks up as I approach, a slow, taunting grin spreading across his face.

"Missed me already?" I plop into the seat, dropping my bag onto the desk with a little too much force.

"Don't flatter yourself." He leans back, arms crossing over his chest, with a smile on his face. "You're the one who sat here, Hart." He chimes in, his stupid boyish grin making him look handsome.

"It was either this or sitting next to the guy who chews his gum like a goat. Aiden chuckles. "Wow. I feel so special." I roll my eyes, pulling out my notebook, determined to ignore him for the rest of class. I can do this.

Except I can't because halfway through the lecture, I feel something brush against my foot. I freeze. It happens again—a slight, deliberate nudge against my ankle. I don't react. I won't react—another nudge. I exhale slowly, keeping my gaze trained on the professor. He wants me to respond.

Fine. I shift slightly and—without warning—kick his shin under the desk. Aiden lets out a quiet grunt, shooting me a glare while I smile sweetly at the board. He leans closer and whispers in my ear.

"You're evil." I scribble something in my notes, feigning innocence.

"I have no idea what you're talking about." His knee presses against mine, just for a second, just enough to send an annoying zing of awareness through me. I stiffen, refusing to move first. It's a standoff neither of us wants to lose.

By the time class ends, my heart is pounding, and my head is a mess. I practically shove my notebook into my bag, ready to bolt—But Aiden is faster. He blocks my exit with a lazy smirk. "What's your hurry, Angel Face?" I scowl. "Move."
"Say, please." I push past him without a word, pretending that my pulse isn't out of control. He follows me out into the hallway like he enjoys making my life difficult.
"Admit it," he says, walking beside me. "You like bickering with me." I stop abruptly, turning to face him.
"You are relentless."
"And you love it." Before I can respond, Alina and Alexei appear, breaking the
Moment. Alina glances between us, smirking. "What did I miss?" I groan. "Nothing."
Alexei snickers. "Nothing? Because it looks like something." Aiden stretches like he has all the time in the world.
"She just can't stop thinking about me." I glare at him. "You stole my coffee this morning."
Alina gasps cause she knows. She knows how I am about my coffee,
"Again? Aiden, that's practically a declaration of war." Aiden shrugs, entirely unrepentant. "She deserved it."
"HOW?" I ask raising my hands up in a question.
"For existing." He winks at me, and my stomach erupts in butterflies. Stupid hormones.

Alexei and Alina laugh as I march away, ignoring their teasing. But I do hear Alexei mutter, "They should just make out already." I roll my eyes, making my way towards the library. I sit in a corner, my books all sprawled out, as I do my homework when the walls start to ripple. The pages blur, words turning into insects crawling across the paper and into my arms. My throat tightens, my pulse skipping painfully.

'Katerina. Being alone always makes you think of me.'

I shake my head to clear my mind, Max's voice echoing in my head. My fingers tremble as I grab my phone, and half of me is unsure who I'm about to text. But my brain knows before my heart catches up.

Angel Face

Are you at the rink?

The reply comes almost instantly.
Grumpy Hockey Player

Yeah. Why?

I stare at the screen, debating how much to say.

Angel Face

Can you come get me? It's happening again.

Three dots. They disappear. Then reappear.
Grumpy Hockey Player

Where are you?

Angel Face

Library. Second floor. Back corner.

I expect him to ask questions, to demand answers, to gloat. But all he sends is three words.

Grumpy Hockey player

On my way.

I try to take deep breaths to get rid of Max's voice by thinking about anything else, but nothing is working. I hear loud footsteps approaching, and then I see Aiden.

He finds me with my head between my knees, hidden behind a row of books. The second I see him, I want to cry. Not because I'm happy to see him—because I'm not—but because it means I don't have to hold myself together anymore.

"Breathe," he says softly, crouching next to me. "We've done this before, remember?" I nod, tears burning at the edges of my eyes. His hand hovers near my back—not touching, but close enough that I can feel the heat of his hand. It should make my skin crawl. Instead, it anchors me.

"Four in," he says, voice steady. "Hold it and four out." We breathe together. When my hands stopped shaking, I realised I was clutching his hand pretty hard. I let go like it burns, face hot with embarrassment.

"Sorry," I mutter.

"I've had worse," Aiden says, shrugging like it's nothing. I believe him.

"Thank you," I say, but the words feel awkward, like trying to speak a foreign language. "You can hate me again tomorrow," he says. "But for today, I'm not going anywhere."

And the worst part? I believe him.

Aiden doesn't speak. He just sits there, one leg stretched out, the other bouncing restlessly like he's still trying to burn off some leftover energy from practice. The only sound is my breathing—uneven but not terrifying —and the faint ticking of my clock. It's almost unbearable, the silence.

"You can go," I say, even though I don't want him to. "I'm fine now." He gives me a look. The kind that says you're full of shit, and I hate that it makes me want to curl in on myself.

"I'll leave when I believe that."

"You're not my babysitter." I snap.

"Yeah, you keep saying that, yet here I am."

My cheeks heat, not from attraction—God no—but from sheer humiliation. He's seeing me like this. Sweaty. Shaking. Half out of my mind. I can practically hear the stories he'll tell in the locker room tomorrow. Except…he doesn't seem like he's planning to tell anyone. There's no teasing grin, no obnoxious joke about 'crazy Kat.' If anything, he just looks tired. Not bored-tired, but something else. A kind of tired, I recognise. He's been here before. The realisation punches me so hard in the chest that I almost forget to breathe again.

"Do you—" My voice snags in my throat. "Do you still get panic attacks?"

He blinks, caught off guard. "What?"

"Nothing." I backpedal fast, hating how my voice trembles. "Forget, I asked." Aiden's quiet for a long moment, his jaw working like he's trying to decide something. Then, to my surprise, he nods. "Yeah."

"Yeah?"

"Yeah." He shrugs like it's not a big deal like we're discussing whether or not it might rain tomorrow. "I get them sometimes. Not often. But enough."

I should be relieved, knowing he gets it. But somehow, it just makes me feel exposed—like he knows exactly what's in my head like he's been here long enough to read me better than I want to be read.

"Great," I say, voice dripping sarcasm. "Bonding moment complete. You can leave now."

"Nope."

He leans back into the bookshelves behind him, making himself way too comfortable in a public library. "You just admitted you're not fine, and now you think I'm leaving you alone with that mess in your head? Try again." I grab the nearest object—a book—and chuck it at his stupid face. He catches it quickly like it's a puck. Of course, he does. "I hate you," I mutter.
"No, you don't." he grins at me.
  As soon as I feel good enough to walk, Aiden drives us home. I sigh in contempt when I see my bed, jumping in it and closing my eyes.
The thing about panic attacks is that after they're over, they leave you feeling like you got run over by a truck. My limbs feel leaden, my brain fogged, and every sound is too sharp. If I look too closely, the shadows are still there, twitching at the edges of my vision like a glitch in reality. I open my eyes and lay back against my headboard, staring at the ceiling. The cracks have stopped breathing, at least. That's progress. "You want water or something?" Aiden asks, his voice softer now.
"No."
"Food?"
"Why are you still here?" He doesn't answer right away. When he does, his voice is quieter than I've ever heard it.
"Because you need me." That shuts me up.
"Yeah, I do," I admit because I have no idea what else to say. Aiden spins in my chair as he leans his head back, staring at the ceiling with a grin.
  I must fall asleep at some point because the next time I open my eyes, the room is drenched in early morning light. My head feels heavy, and my body feels sore, like I ran ten miles in my sleep.
  The chair is empty. For a second, I think I imagined the whole thing. Maybe Aiden was just another

hallucination, some twisted projection of my fried brain. But then I spot something—on my desk, right next to my lamp. A Gatorade bottle and a granola bar. Both are unopened, clearly left there on purpose. I pick up the bottle, and a crumpled piece of paper is under it. There's writing scrawled across in thick black Sharpie.

Hydrate, dumbass.

I snort, then immediately feel guilty for finding it funny. I should be mad that he stayed, furious that he saw me like that, but I don't —not at all. Alina was right. I do like him.

CHAPTER SEVENTEEN

AIDEN

I woke up feeling like someone had snuck into my room overnight and stomped all over my chest. Not physically—no, I would've noticed that. It was emotional damage. My brain felt overloaded, my heart a little too aware of its own beating, and every time I so much as thought about Kat, my stomach twisted like I'd swallowed a live snake.

I groaned and flopped back onto my pillow. Last night had been… intense. I wasn't exactly the guy people went to for comfort. Sarcasm? Absolutely. Witty insults? All day. But soft reassurances and steady hands? That was new territory. And yet, when Kat had broken down, something in me had just—clicked. Like

I was supposed to be there and keep her steady while her world tilted. And I had, which was terrifying.

Because now, in the cold light of day, I couldn't stop thinking about it. The way she'd leaned into me. The way her breath hitched. The way I'd wanted to press my chin to the top of her head and tell her that she was okay and that I wouldn't let anything happen to her. I was officially losing my mind.

A sharp knock on my door yanked me out of my downward spiral.

"Aiden," came a familiar voice that haunted my mind day and night. "Are you alive in there, or did your ego finally crush you under its massive weight?"

Ah, there she was. My blood pressure was back to normal. I swung my legs over the side of the bed and opened the door, only to find Kat standing there with a single eyebrow arched and a smirk on her lips.

"Good morning to you, too, sunshine," I say, rubbing the back of my neck. "I'd invite you in, but I wouldn't want to expose you to the sheer devastation of my morning hair."

Kat doesn't even blink. "I've seen worse." I squinted, jealousy creeping in.

"Have you?" She shrugs. "I had a figure skating partner for years. There were some dark times."

The teasing was familiar and safe, like slipping into a favourite old hoodie. It was our thing. We bickered. We argued. It was a battle of wits where no one really won, but neither of us ever wanted to stop. It was easy. It was fun. And yet, standing here, watching her smirk at me, I couldn't ignore the fact that something had changed.

She was still Kat—sharp, quick, and endlessly infuriating—but now I also knew the softness underneath. The vulnerability. The way her voice cracked when she was scared, the way she clung to me like I was the only solid thing in the room. I was so screwed.

"What are you doing here?" I ask, mainly to keep myself from thinking too hard. Kat rolls her eyes. "Wow. Rude. Maybe I came to check on you. Ever think of that?" I blinked.

"No."

She sighs dramatically. "Typical. Anyway, since I'm clearly wasting my concern, let's get to the real reason I'm here. I need a ride to the store. Alina has my car, and I'm craving junk food." I raised an eyebrow. "And what makes you think I'm your personal chauffeur?"

"Well," she said, tilting her head, "for one, I asked nicely."

"No, you didn't."

"For two," she continues as if I hadn't spoken, "you owe me after last night." I frown.

"Wait—how do I owe you? I was the one who—" She cuts me off with a wave of her hand.

"Emotional labor, Aiden. You made me have feelings, and now I have to balance that out by buying junk food. I can't do that without a ride. So, really, this is your fault." I stare at her in disbelief. "That is the most ridiculous thing I've ever heard," I say, walking towards the dresser.

Kat grins. "And yet, here you are, grabbing your keys." I look down at the keys in my right hand and groan... Damn it. She's right.

Fifteen minutes later, we were in my car, windows down, music playing at a low volume so we could still talk. Kat had her feet propped up on the dashboard despite my half-hearted protests, and every now and then, she'd turn her head just enough that I could catch the faintest trace of a smile on her lips. It was distracting.

"So," she says, flipping down the sun visor and checking her reflection, "are we going to talk about it?" I tense, refusing to look at her.
"Talk about what?" She shoots me a look. "Come on, Aiden. Last night." I grip the steering wheel a little tighter.
"What about it?" Kat lets out a sigh and turns to face me fully. "Look, I just… I wanted to say thanks. You didn't have to stay with me, but you did. And you didn't make it weird. So. Yeah. Thanks."

For once in my life, my brain short-circuited. I am so used to our conversations being battles, volleys of sarcasm and wit, that hearing her say something real—something soft—makes me forget how to respond. "You don't have to thank me," I say finally, keeping my eyes on the road. "I wanted to." The second the words leave my mouth, I regret them. They feel too honest, too raw, like I'd accidentally left a window open and let something vulnerable slip through.

Kat is quiet for a moment. "Well," she says at last, "if it makes you feel better, I still think you're a pain in the ass." Relief washes over me, and I let out a breath I hadn't realised I was holding. "Good. I'd be worried if you didn't."

She smirked, and just like that, we were back to normal. Or at least, as normal as we could be with this new thing buzzing between us—this awareness that hadn't been there before. I don't know what it means. I don't know what to do with it. But as we pulled into the store parking lot, and Kat shot me one last playful glare before hopping out of the car, I knew one thing for sure.
I like her.
And that is a problem.

CHAPTER EIGHTEEN

KATERINA

It's been five days since Aiden and I went on our little store trip, and things have been somewhat normal. We are still bickering, but I've been spending more time with my friends. Tonight, the boys have a game, and we are all going. My mom is still in town, so she decided to stop by for the game. The energy in the arena is electric. The air crackles with excitement, the crowd's roar vibrating through the walls as fans chant and stomp their feet. It's the biggest game of the season—Pleasant Oaks versus Westbridge University.

The rivalry is brutal. The tension is thick, and I am not okay.
I tug at the oversized jersey swallowing me whole, shifting uncomfortably as I try to ignore the way his name and number are plastered across my back.
Aiden Knight. 10. I'd fought it. Hard.

"It's a new tradition," Alina had said, twirling in Roman's jersey like she was thriving in this. "We will be wearing their numbers. Maddie's in Will's, I'm in Roman's, and even Alexei is wearing Grayson's." Sure enough, Alexei had smirked and thrown an arm around Grayson, who looked way too smug about the whole thing. I had tried everything to get out of it. But Alina smirked, held up Aiden's jersey, and said, "Wear it, or I will tell him you begged to have his number."

So here I am, in the stands, drowning in Knight's name while he storms onto the ice like he owns it. My mom laughed when she saw me. When I told her I was forced into wearing it, she simply said, "The Kat, I know, wouldn't do anything she didn't want to do." To which I had nothing to say back. She knows me better than anyone else. The crowd erupts, chanting Aiden's name as the team skates out.

Alina nudges me. "You look way too tense for someone who's supposed to be having fun."
I glare at her. "I hate that I got stuck with his number." She smirks, shaking her head at me and says, "You love it." I refuse to dignify that comment with a response because deep down, I know Ali is right.

Westbridge plays dirty. From the first drop of the puck, it's clear they aren't here to win clean. They slash at sticks, shove harder than necessary, and go for cheap hits when they think the refs aren't looking. It's dangerous, messy, and Aiden is thriving in it. He moves with complete confidence like every shift is his personal battleground. He's aggressive, relentless, and entirely in control—but it doesn't stop me from tensing every time he throws himself into a collision. Every time his body slams into the boards, I feel it in my chest.

By the second period, Pleasant Oaks is up by two goals. The crowd is losing it, the energy in the arena reaching a fever pitch. But I can't stop watching him. A Westbridge player—number 27—skates up behind Aiden
after the whistle and slams him into the boards. It's a cheap, dirty shot. Aiden's body whips forward, his head snapping dangerously close to the glass. My stomach drops. But Aiden doesn't hesitate. His gloves hit the ice.

"Oh, shit," Alexei mutters. "Here we go." Before the refs can react, Aiden is on him. Fists fly. The entire arena erupts, the crowd screaming as chaos explodes on the ice. Aiden lands a solid right hook to number 27's face. Then another. The refs scramble to break them apart, but Aiden isn't letting go. I jump to my feet, my pulse racing. You absolute idiot.

When they finally drag Aiden off, he skates to the penalty box, blood dripping from his lip, chest heaving. And all I can do is clench my fists and breathe through the frustration. Pleasant Oaks wins, but I can't bring myself to celebrate appropriately. Because now I have to deal with him.

We wait outside the locker room, the air still buzzing with post-game adrenaline. Alina and Maddie chat excitedly, but I stand there, arms crossed, foot tapping. The second Aiden emerges, hair damp, a fresh bruise blooming on his cheekbone, he spots me immediately. And, of course, he smirks.

"You looked good in my jersey, Angel Face." I glare at Aiden, angry that he just fought someone and now is openly flirting with me.

"You looked stupid getting into that fight." His smirk deepens.

"Oh, so you were watching." I step closer, jaw tight.

"What the hell were you thinking? You could've gotten hurt. You could've gotten suspended." The amusement flickers, but he holds my gaze. "He took a cheap shot."

"That's hockey, Aiden! You don't have to fight every guy who pisses you off!"

His eyes darken, the space between us shrinking. "You think I was just pissed off?" His voice drops lower now, something dangerous curling beneath it. I freeze. That wasn't just about the hit. It was about me. Number 27 said something about me to provoke Aiden.

"He said something?" I whisper. Aiden nods, clenching his jaw. My heart thuds violently, but before I can react, a new voice cuts through the air.

"So, this is what you do?" I whip around. My mother stands there, arms crossed, eyebrows raised. Aiden's shoulders stiffen.

"Oh my god," I whisper, ,squeezing my eyes shut. My mom tilts her head at Aiden. "You fight on the ice, and then you flirt with my daughter?" Alina chokes on her drink. Aiden runs a hand down his face, exhaling. "Not flirting, ma'am. Just—talking." My mother hums, unconvinced.

And then she smiles. "I liked that punch you threw," she says simply. "Good form." Aiden blinks. "Uh. Thanks?" I groan. This cannot be my life. Alina is shaking with laughter at this point.

Roman claps Aiden on the back. "Looks like you've got Anya's approval, bud." I spin around, pointing at them. "You are all the worst."

My mother just shrugs, glancing back at Aiden. "Next time, aim for the ribs. It'll slow them down." Aiden grins at the comment, and I want the earth to swallow me whole. Roman howls with laughter. "She's giving him pointers?!" I rub my temples. "I can't believe this is happening." My mother waves me off. "You worry too much, Katerina. Let the boys have their game."

Aiden leans in, his voice low in my ear. "See? Even your mom thinks I did the right thing." I turn sharply, my face so close to his that I can see the cut on his lips up close.

"You are—" I inhale sharply. "Unbelievable." Aiden's smirk softens just slightly. Like he sees something I don't even want to admit.

"Maybe," he says.

"We're getting drinks," Alexei calls. "You coming?" I step back, pulse still racing. "Yeah," I say quickly. "I'll be there."

Aiden watches me, something unreadable flashing in his eyes. Then he leans in again, just enough to make my breath hitch. "We're not done here, Hart."
He whispers, walking past me and disappearing into the crowd—my pulse pounds. No, we're definitely not done here.

CHAPTER NINETEEN

KATERINA

I hear Maddie's voice, high-pitched with excitement, as she says how amazing I would look with my hair down for tonight's party. It was supposed to be just drinks until Roman had the idea to throw a house party. Maddie has been at it for the last twenty minutes, trying to convince me to ditch my bun and let my hair fall loose, but my decision is final.
"I hear you, Maddie. I want to party, too, but my hair stays up," I sigh, crossing my arms, "It'll get so hot, and I'll probably get a heat stroke if I leave it down." Maddie bursts out laughing, shaking her head.
She's relentless.
 "Come on, Kat. Picture this, red corset with black low-rise jeans and high heels. All the guys will drool when they see you." I snort, covering my mouth, trying to stifle the laugh.

The mental image is too ridiculous. "I love you, but I'm not wearing heels," I say, my gaze drifting to Alina, who's glaring at me with mock annoyance.
"What? It's a house party." She raises an eyebrow, not buying my excuse. "Exactly! It's a house party at your house. If your feet start hurting, hurt here, and put on your sneakers. Easy." I groan, grabbing a pillow and slamming my face into it, hoping the pillow can block out the noise of their arguments.

"Fine, give me the damn clothes," I huff annoyed, grabbing the clothes and shoes from Maddie.
"Finally! Two hours later." Alexei says with exaggerated
surrender, standing up and clapping his hands. I glare at him as I grab a pillow and throw it toward his head, but he ducks, and it hits my door instead.
"I'm doing your hair and makeup," Alina announces excitedly, clapping her hands.
"Sure," I say, walking toward my vanity and sitting down. There's no point arguing now. They've worn me down.

An hour and a half later, I'm staring at my reflection, not recognising the person in the mirror. Alina worked her magic, and my makeup was simple but striking—a smoky eye, red lipstick that matches my outfit, and my hair cascading in loose curls down my back. The corset pulls my waist in, making me feel like I'm suffocating, but it looks damn good. I take in the final details, scanning myself in the full-length mirror. "Oh, shit." My voice is barely a whisper, stunned by the transformation. "You look beautiful, Kat," Alina says, her voice filled with approval as she steps back to survey the finished product. I turn sideways and gaze at my exposed skin, a couple of inches between the jeans and my corset. I grin, but that grin disappears when my eyes land on my ass.

"No. I'm changing my pants," I say, walking towards my closet. Alina grabs my shoulders, spinning me around to face her. "No, you're not. Yes, your ass looks big, but that's because you've got hips and an ass to die for. Stop being insecure. You look terrific, Kat. We will dance, we'll get drunk, and we're going to have fun tonight, okay?" Her voice is insistent, and the firm shake of my shoulders reminds me that I'm not backing out now. I gulp, nerves creeping up on me. I'm used to jeans and a T-shirt, not… this.

"Okay, one more shot and let's go," I say, my voice shaky but determined. A night of fun is what I need, after all. I pour us another shot, and we take it in unison. The warm burn of tequila traveling down my throat, fuelling my boldness.

"Let's go get laid!" Alexei yells, making us all laugh.

We walk out of my room, and I can smell the alcohol and smoke thick in the air. The music is loud, the energy electric. The party has already escalated, the living room is packed with strangers. I scan the crowd, instantly noticing Will. He's talking to a group of people, but his eyes light up when they land on me. He grins and walks over, giving me a hug.

"Will, where's the bar?" I ask, crossing my arms leaning on my right hip. "I need to get fucked up if I'm going to be in these clothes all night." Will doesn't answer at first. His gaze flickers behind me, and I know exactly who he is looking at. I snap my fingers in front of his face to get his attention.

"Shit, sorry, roomie. She looks gorgeous," he mutters, almost to himself, before blinking and focusing on me. I roll my eyes and grin at his comment.

"Yeah, so stop being a little bitch, who's scared of Roman, and go talk to Maddie," I tease, nudging him in the ribs.

"The bar is in the kitchen," Will chuckles, his voice trailing as he eyes my friends, "Greysen will give you drinks from an untouched bottle." I hug him goodbye before making my way back to my girls.

"Let's dance first," Alexei declares, grabbing me by the wrist and pulling me into the living room, which has now transformed into a makeshift dance floor. The guys moved the couches to the side, clearing out space.

A loud thrum of Beyoncé's "Partition" blares from the speakers and Alexei squeals as if he's just been handed the best Christmas present. I'm not much of a dancer, but tonight feels different. Tequila has already loosened me up, and the music is calling me. My hips move with the beat, my body loosening up as I feel the rhythm. Alina and Maddie join us, and the four of us grind to the music. It feels freeing. I let go of everything—the nerves, the awkwardness—and just lose myself in the movement.

I try not to. I really do. But I can't help myself. My eyes look for him, searching the room while I dance until they land on his honey-colored eyes. Aiden is across the room, surrounded by his teammates, his usual cocky smirk in place. His hair is still slightly damp from his post-game shower, and his jaw is bruised from the fight, making him look more infuriatingly attractive. I should look away. I should. But I don't. Because the second I glance back at him, his gaze locks onto mine, dark and unreadable. The tension from earlier still lingers between us, heavy and charged.

Before I can process it, a hand touches my waist, and I turn to see Logan grinning down at me.

"There she is," he says, leaning in slightly. "Didn't get a chance to tell you earlier, but you looked damn good in Knight's jersey tonight."

I roll my eyes. "I did not wear it by choice." He chuckles, his grip on my waist tightening just a little. "Could've fooled me. Looked natural on you." I open my
mouth to fire back a response, but someone's chest makes contact with my back. My heart starts racing. Aiden.

The energy shifts, the air in the room growing thick as his eyes lock on Logan's hand on my waist.

Oh.

Oh.

"Matthews," Aiden drawls, stepping into our space like he
owns it. "Didn't realise you were still hanging around," Logan smirks at Aiden. "What can I say? Hart's good company." A muscle in Aiden's jaw ticks.

"Yeah? Funny, I don't remember her needing your company." Logan lifts his hands in mock surrender. "Relax, man. Didn't know she was claimed."

"She's not," Aiden snaps. "But she's also not interested." I narrow my eyes. "Excuse you?"

Aiden doesn't even glance at me. His focus is entirely on Logan, his body tense, his stance firm, like he's daring him to push further. Logan looks between us, realisation dawning in on his expression. Then he smirks. "Got it." He pats my arm. "See you around, Kat." And then he's gone, leaving behind a very pissed-off Aiden and an even more pissed-off me.

I whirl on him. "What the hell was that?"

Aiden just shrugs, completely unapologetic. "You looked uncomfortable. I handled it."

I scoff. "Handled it? You scared him off like some territorial caveman."
"Maybe if he had better instincts, he would've left on his own."

My fingers twitch around my drink, tempted to throw it at him. "I don't need you to fight my battles, Knight." His gaze sharpens, something dark flashing in his eyes. "Yeah? Then why didn't you push him off sooner?" I freeze, my breath catching in my throat. Because I don't have an answer. Because the truth is, I wanted a reaction.

Aiden steps closer, the heat from his body radiating into mine.

"Go ahead, Goldie," he murmurs, his voice low and dangerous. "Tell me you didn't want me to step in."
"Tell me you weren't waiting for it." I don't like how well he knows me. I hate that he's right.
"Alina, let's go play Drinking Jenga," I yell, trying to escape the conversation. Aiden scoffs walking away.,

Alina and I quickly stop at the restroom before we start playing. As we make our way toward the group, my stomach twists. I spot Roman and then Aiden as he sits next to his best friend, who looks more annoyed than interested in the game. But it's too late to back out now. Alina claims her spot next to Roman, and I reluctantly sit beside Aiden. His presence is suffocating. The smell of his cologne fills my nostrils, and I can feel the tension between us simmering. I clench my hands on my lap, trying to ignore the way my heart skips a beat at every accidental brush of our bodies. The game begins, and of course, Alina picks first. She smirks at me, pulling a Jenga piece and flipping it over.
"Make out with the hottest person in the room," she reads, her eyes immediately flicking toward Roman.

But I know her better than that. She walks past him, right toward me, and without warning, she grabs my face in her hands and pulls me in for a kiss.

The room explodes in groans and cheers as our lips meet, a quick but intense kiss. We both pull away, laughing at the shock on Roman's face. "That was the hottest thing I've ever seen," Roman says, his eyes wide with surprise. I sit back down, my pulse still racing. Aiden shifts and his thigh grazes mine. I let out a small gasp at the contact, and my eyes widen.
Fuck. He did not hear that.
"Your turn, Cap," Roman says, nodding at Aiden as the latter sighs. Aiden reaches over and pulls a wood piece, flipping it over to read.
"I'll just drink," he says nonchalantly, grabbing his cup, but Roman doesn't let him off the hook that easily as he grabs his wood piece and reads it.
"Get a lap dance from the person on your left," Roman announces, eyes glinting with mischief. My heart stops, and for a moment, I think I'm going to choke on my own breath. I glance at Aiden, trying to gauge his reaction.

"What? Are you scared of a lap dance?" I ask, a teasing smile forming on my lips, even though inside, I'm shaking. "No, I just didn't want to make you uncomfortable," Aiden replies, his tone defensive, though there's a flicker of something darker in his eyes. I stand up, my pulse pounding, fighting the rush of nerves. "Grab a chair," I order, my voice much bolder than I feel. Aiden hesitates but eventually gets to his feet and grabs a chair from the corner. He sits down, and the room goes silent, all eyes on me. Roman queues up "Partition," and the beat drops.

I strut over to Aiden, my hips swaying to the rhythm. His eyes widen, and I can see the shock in them as I move closer. The crowd's energy grows louder, but it feels like it's just the two of us now. My hands move over my body slowly, teasingly. I stand between his legs and Aiden gulps. Without thinking, I lower myself, my hips grinding down and back up in time with the music. Aiden's hands grip the chair, and his knuckles are white as he tries to control his reaction.

Feeling bold, I straddle Aiden's lap and run my hands through his hair as i move my body against his. I could feel my heart racing with excitement, but I also felt something else right under my core poking at me enough to know he wants me. Aiden wraps his hands around my ass to bring me closer, and I swear my heart gives out. As I lean down, my lips near his ear, I whisper in French, knowing it'll drive him insane.

As the song ends, a smirk tugs at my lips as the music fades. Aiden's hand slips from my waist, and I take a slow step back, my fingers instinctively running through my hair to smooth it out. The room around us feels dizzying with the crowd's buzz. Everything else fades when I glance at Alina, whose jaw is practically on the floor, her eyes wide with shock. Aiden's hand shoots out before I can take another step, wrapping around my wrist and halting me in place.

"Come with me," he murmurs, his voice low. His grip slides from my wrist to my hand, intertwining our fingers and without a word, he begins pulling me away from our friends.

I follow, albeit with hesitation, as we weave through the crowd, moving past the haze of flashing lights and pulsing music. His hand in mine feels like a tether, something I can't entirely break free from, not that i'm trying to. I'm both drawn to him and repelled by him in equal measure. We make our way up the stairs, the air thick with tension, until we reach his room. Aiden slams the door behind us, locks it, and then turns to face me, his chest rising and falling with controlled breaths. He steps closer, a glint of fury in his eyes mixed with something darker—something that makes my pulse race. He takes several steps towards me until he is inches away; his presence feels suffocating yet intoxicating.

"What the hell was that?" His voice is tight, barely containing the storm inside of him. I swallow hard, my heart hammering in my chest. I tilt my head slightly, eyes lowering to his lips before flicking back to his gaze.

"I just did my dare," I reply, my voice softer than I want it to be, betraying the nervousness I'm trying to hide. "I don't know what you're talking about." Aiden's expression darkens, his gaze unwavering as he watches me. Without warning, his thumb slid over my bottom lip, pulling it gently from where my teeth had been resting. My breath catches in my throat, and I find myself unable to look away. His eyes are locked on mine, and I can feel the pull between us. The way my body responds to him, betraying every ounce of resistance I'm trying to maintain.

"Don't do that," he says, his voice strained, like he's barely keeping his composure. I could laugh at his attempt to hold back, but the smouldering heat in his eyes is too much to ignore. My breath hitches, and before I can stop myself, I press my lips to his, the kiss raw, urgent, and filled with an energy that feels dangerously un-containable. It's fire. It's chaos. It's everything I've been trying to fight against.

Aiden grabs my waist, pulling me flush against him, and I melt before I can even think to resist. His hands are everywhere—on my back, my hips, tangling in my hair as he kisses me like he's starving for it, like he's been waiting for this just as much as I have. I fist his shirt, pulling him closer, needing more, needing him. For a moment, everything else fades away. The world outside the room, the party downstairs—it's all irrelevant. It's just the two of us, and every second feels like it's stretching into infinity. His touch is firm, possessive, and as he pulls me closer, I lose myself in the kiss.

"I still don't like you," he murmurs against my lips, his words rough, like he's trying to convince himself. I nod in response, my voice equally low.

"Feeling's mutual, Aiden." But the words don't mean anything. They're just a mask, a way to hold onto whatever pretense we've been clinging to.

Aiden's growl vibrates through me as he deepens the kiss, the heat between us escalating in ways I can't ignore.

"It's Knight to you," he says, pulling back briefly, his lips brushing over mine as he speaks. I smirk, biting his bottom lip in retaliation. Aiden's breath catches, and he traces a trail of soft kisses down my jawline, sending shivers down my spine. The tension is unbearable, the way he touches me, the way his presence fills the space between us, and I can't help but moan softly in response.

"It's always going to be Aiden," I whisper back, my fingers grazing the side of his neck, my breath coming faster. His name slips from my lips like a confession, an acknowledgment of something that neither of us is ready to face.

His lips return to mine, urgent, possessive, as he wraps one of my legs around him, grinding his body into mine. The movement is slow and deliberate, the pressure against me is enough to make my body ache with want.

I'm losing control, but I can't stop. Not now, not when he feels so good.

Aiden lifts me effortlessly, his hands strong beneath me, and I wrap my legs around his waist, pulling him closer. He walks us toward his bed, each step pushing the boundaries of what I thought was possible. He throws me onto the bed and hovers above me, his forearms braced on either side of my head, keeping his weight from crushing me. For a moment, everything is still—until he grinds his body against mine, and I can feel his unmistakable hardness. I let out a breathless moan, my hands threading through his hair, pulling him closer.

"Fuck, Aiden," I gasp, the words escaping before I can stop them. Suddenly, a voice cuts through the tension, followed by banging on the door. "Aiden, Roman is fighting. We need you." Aiden freezes. The world shifts, and the intense heat between us dissipates, leaving only the lingering echo of desire in the air. He curses under his breath, pulling away reluctantly.

"Come on, man. It's important," the voice calls again. Aiden groans in frustration, standing up and adjusting himself as if the interruption has pulled him from some haze he was trapped in.

"Don't go anywhere," he says, his voice soft but firm. I nod, still trying to gather my bearings, watching as he walks toward the door. He opens it just enough to slip out, leaving me in his room, the air still heavy with unspoken tension.

Two seconds pass before panic begins creeping up my spine, and before I can stop myself, I run out of his room. My heart races as I rush to my room, locking the door behind me. I can feel my pulse pounding in my ears, the adrenaline of the moment still lingering. I walk to my bathroom, my hands trembling as I change into pyjamas. I text my friends, letting them know I'm heading to bed, though I'm far from ready to sleep. Why the hell would I make out with him? Yeah, he's undeniably hot, but he's a grump and annoying. He's always been nothing but a pain in my side. God save me from this mess, and I promise to behave.

I slip my noise-cancelling headphones in, trying to block out the thoughts that are swirling in my mind. The buzzing in my ears fades into the background, and eventually, my body gives in to exhaustion. Sleep comes slowly, but when it finally takes me, it's with the lingering taste of Aiden's lips and the storm of emotions he's stirred within me.

CHAPTER TWENTY

KATERINA

I should have stayed in bed. I should have feigned sickness, locked my door, thrown my phone into the ocean—anything to avoid this moment. Because I know the second, I step onto the ice, he'll be there. And I don't know what's worse—the fact that I kissed him or the fact that I ran. I ran before he could say anything. Before I could ruin it by letting myself think, by allowing myself want. Because I do.
I do want him. But I can't. He will leave just like everyone else. So, I left. And now, here I am, standing in the middle of the rink, knowing that I have to face him. Knowing that I can't take back what happened. My skates scrape against the ice as I warm up, every movement feeling too sharp, too off-balance, like my body still hasn't caught up to my brain. Like my body still remembers him. I take a deep breath, forcing my

shoulders back, my face blank. It was nothing. I tell myself. You'll see him, and it will be fine. Normal. But then Alexei skates up beside me, grinning.

"How's your ego, Malyshka?" I groan, already regretting everything.

"Shut up."

"What's wrong? Still thinking about your mistake?" He makes air quotes, smirking. Last night, after lying down, I decided to call Alexei into my room and let him know what happened. I called it a mistake, even though I know it's not one.

"You're the worst." I glare at Alexei but he gestures to the rink entrance.

"Not true. He is." I already know. I already feel it. And I make the mistake of looking. Aiden is here, and he's looking right at me. My stomach drops.

He strolls in, hockey bag slung over his shoulder, completely unbothered. His hair is still damp from his shower, his jersey slung lazily over his shoulder, and he moves like someone who knows exactly what he did to me last night. Like someone who's not going to let me forget it.

Our eyes meet. A flicker of amusement, then something more profound—something that makes my breath catch. He smirks at me and I whip back around, my face burning. Nope. Not doing this.

"Angel Face," he calls, voice too casual, too smug. "You gonna be able to focus today?" My grip tightens around my skates' laces. I hate him. I actually hate him. Alexei laughs beside me, skating away before I can shove him into the boards. I take a deep breath, willing myself to ignore him. I can do this. I can skate. I can pretend last night didn't happen. I push off, gliding into my first jump sequence— And fall flat on my ass. Aiden howls with laughter from the sidelines.

I groan, covering my face as Alexei skates back over, grinning. "You're so fucked, Malyshka." Lying on the ice, cheeks burning, I know one thing for sure. This is going to be hell.

I don't even make it to the locker room before I hear him behind me.

"Running away again, Angel Face?" I spin around, ready to murder him, but he's already too close, standing in my space like he owns it. My jaw tightens. "Move." He doesn't. Of course, he doesn't. Instead, he tilts his head, smirk still in place, eyes too sharp, too knowing.

"You left." I force my arms to stay at my sides, fingers twitching.

"So?" I ask in defiance. Aiden hums, his gaze flicking over my face like he's reading every thought I don't want him to see.

"Didn't think you were the type to run."

My spine locks. "I don't run."

"Really? Then what would you call last night?" I cross my arms, forcing myself to meet his gaze, willing my voice to be steady.

"It was a mistake." Something in his expression shifts—just for a second. Then, his smirk is back, but it's slower now, lazier. "Sure it was."

"Don't start." Aiden shrugs, infuriatingly relaxed, clearly amused by our conversation.

"I didn't do anything. You're the one losing your mind."

"I am not—"

He leans in, lowering his voice. "You're the one touching me, Hart." My breath hitches. My traitorous hands are fisted in the fabric of his hoodie, holding on like I forgot how to let go. Shit. I yank them away like he burned me, ignoring the warmth still lingering on my fingertips.

"I can't stand you," I whisper as he invades my space, and I can breathe him in. His eyes flicker, his smirk never fading.

"Try again." Aiden pecks my lips fast with a smug look on his face. I glare, ready to tell him exactly where he can shove his arrogant attitude, but my brain is a mush from the peck— Someone clears their throat. Loudly.

Standing right there, arms crossed, eyebrows raised so high they might fly off her face is Alina. Beside her, Maddie is grinning like a lunatic.

"So… that just happened." I say nervously. Maddie lets out a squeal.

"Oh my God, finally." Alexei just shakes his head, smirking knowingly. "Took longer than I expected." I groan, covering my face with my hands.

"We are not talking about this." Alina snorts.

"Oh, we absolutely are." I drop my hands and glare at Aiden.

"This is your fault." He shrugs, completely unbothered.

"Happy to take the credit, angel face," I swear, I might actually murder him. Before I can launch myself at him, Alexei claps his hands.

"Alright, lovebirds. Let's go. We've got a full day of practice today. We are going to be busy." I jump at the distraction, turning away before Aiden can say something else that makes me lose my mind.

"Yes. Great idea."

Alina cackles. "You hate long practice days." I flip her off, storming towards the other side of the rink. I do not look back at Aiden.

Because if I do—if I let myself see whatever's in his eyes—I might not walk away this time.

CHAPTER TWENTY - ONE

AIDEN

The knock at the door comes earlier than expected. I'm in the kitchen, gripping my second cup of coffee like it's the only thing keeping me sane. Will and the guys are still half-asleep in the living room, draped across the couches, with last night's game footage on the TV. I glance at the clock. Too early. My stomach tightens. Will groans from the couch. "If it's another freshman, I swear to God—" But I already know it's not. I set my mug down and rub the back of my neck before heading to the door. The second I open it a tiny blur launches at me.
"Aidy!"
I catch her effortlessly, lifting her up before she can knock me over. Her laugh is soft but bright, and I feel

something in my chest unwind. "Hey, princess," I murmur. "Miss me?"

"Duh! It's been forever!" I smile.

"It's been two weeks, Soph." Sophia grins, her arms still locked around my neck. She's lighter than she should be. Always too light.

Behind her, Aunt Maria steps into the doorway, shaking her head. "Are you going to bring us inside, or should we just live in the hallway?"

I roll my eyes but step back, letting them in. Kat's standing near the kitchen, watching the scene unfold like she's stepped into an alternate universe. Her gaze lands on Sophia's headscarf, and her expression shifts—like she's piecing something together.

"Oh!" Maria's eyes light up when she spots Kat. "You must be Katerina."

Kat blinks, surprised my aunt knows her name. "Uh. Yeah?"

Maria grins at her, wrapping her into a hug. "Oh, we've heard about you." I feel every muscle in my body tighten.

"Nope," I say quickly. "We're not doing this. "Maria ignores me, stepping towards Kat like she's about to share my entire life story.

"It's so nice to finally meet the girl my nephew can't stop talking about." I groan. "Maria." Sophia gasps dramatically, twisting in my arms to stare at me.

"She doesn't know you talk about her?" Kat crosses her arms, her lips twitching. "Aw, Aidy. You talk about me?" I glare at her. "More like complain."

"Oh, sure you do." Sophia giggles. "I like her Aidy. She looks like a princess!" Maria pats my shoulder, smirking. "You're in trouble, Aidy." I sigh, resigned to my fate.

Will steps out of the living room, and Sophia lights up. "Willy!" She wriggles out of my arms and sprints toward him, jumping into his arms. I watch them, something heavy settling in my chest. I know how much she loves Will, and I understand why. He reminds her of Dad. And Dad's not here. He hasn't been for a while. He treats Sophia like a disease; he only wants someone to take over his business. So Maria stepped in, took over, and made sure Sophia always had a place to call home.

Sophia clings to Kat for the rest of the day. I don't know how it happens, but one second, Kat awkwardly tolerates it first, and the next minute, she's completely taken in by my sister. Sophia bombards her with questions about skating, insists on seeing old videos, and eventually convinces Kat to spin her around the living room floor. Sophia shrieks with laughter as Kat twirls her. "Again!" Kat chuckles. "You're a little demanding, huh?" Maria sips her tea, watching with an amused expression. "She doesn't warm up to people this fast, you know."

Kat glances down at Sophia, who's now sitting in her lap, playing with the sleeve of her hoodie.

"Really?"

Maria nods. "Trust doesn't come easy for her." I stay silent on the couch, arms crossed, just watching. Kat doesn't know the half of it. Later, after dinner, Maria is in the kitchen chatting with Will, and Sophia is curled up in my lap, fighting sleep.

Kat sits across from us, her expression more serious than usual. She hesitates before speaking, her voice quiet.

"She's sick, isn't she?" I tense. The question shouldn't catch me off guard, but it does. I exhale, running a hand over Sophia's back. "Yeah." Kat watches me before speaking again.

"How bad?"

I don't answer right away. I don't want to say it out loud again. But eventually, I force the words out. "She's fighting it for the second time." Kat stills. "Leukemia," I say. "First diagnosed when at four years old. She went into remission, but it came back last year. She's been in and out of treatments ever since."

Kat glances at Sophia, then back at me. She looks like she's searching for the right thing to say, but what can you say to that?

"Will and I…" My throat tightens. "We're both matches for her. But the doctors still aren't sure if the transplant will work. We're just… waiting. Hoping." Kat nods slowly, eyes softening.

"I'm sorry."

"Don't be." I meet her gaze. "Just—don't treat her like she's made of glass, okay? She hates that." Kat tilts her head, considering. Then she nods. "I won't."

I study her for a long moment, searching for any hint of pity, but there's none.

For once, I don't feel like making a snarky remark.

And for once, neither does she.

CHAPTER TWENTY - TWO

KATERINA

The energy in the arena is powerful, the kind that makes the hair on the back of my neck stand up. The next round of qualifiers. Another chance to prove that Alexei and I belong here. I exhale slowly, bouncing on my skates as I watch the pairs before us. Their routines blur together— good, clean lines, solid jumps, but nothing that scares me. Alexei nudges me.

"Relax, Malyshka. You look like you're about to stab someone."
"Maybe I am. If you don't land our throws today, you're first on my list."
He smirks. "Ah, my favourite kind of motivation. Death threats." Before I can snap back, my eyes land on Aiden. His presence is like a shift in gravity, and suddenly, I'm hyper-aware of every breath, every inch of space between us.

"What do you want, Knight?" I say without looking at him, my nerves already getting the best of me.

"Just checking to see if you're about to flake under pressure." I do turn then, meeting his annoyingly smug expression.

"Oh, please. The only thing I flake on is showing up when you expect me to care." I snap. His smirk deepens. "Sure, Angel Face." I roll my eyes.

"Stop calling me that."

"No." I glare at him, then an idea pops in my head. I'm a genius.

"Then I'm calling you Aidy." His jaw twitches. "Oh, what's the matter?" I coo. "Not a fan?"

"Angel Face," he says, voice dropping low, teasing. "You don't want to start something you can't finish."

Before I can retort, Alexei throws an arm around my shoulder. "If you two are going to flirt, can you at least wait until after our program?" I shove him off.

"We are not flirting."

Aiden shrugs. "She wishes." I narrow my eyes at him, while he has a stupid grin on his face.

"Is that right? Aidy." His nostrils flare slightly, and for the first time, I think I might actually win this one. But then he steps closer, invading my space. "I'll remember that." The way he says it—low, full of promise—sends an entirely

different kind of chill down my spine. Done with this conversation, Alexei mutters something in Russian and skates off to stretch.

I square my shoulders. "Are you done?"

"Not yet." Before I can react, he cups my jaw, leans in, and presses a firm, fleeting kiss against my lips. My brain short-circuits. My heart starts pounding against my ribcage. By the time I process what just happened, he's already pulling back, that cocky, insufferable grin back in place.

"Go win, Angel Face." Aiden walks off, leaving me stunned, my heart pounding, and my brain refusing to function. Alexei skates back up to me.
"Did I just see that correctly?" I snap out of it. "Shut up." Alexei grins at me.
"You're bright red." I nudge his arm with a glare on my face. "I will push you on the ice." He laughs, holding up his hands in surrender. "Fine, fine. But at least now I know where your head's at." I inhale sharply, pushing every thought of Aiden out of my head. Focus. Compete now. Kill Aiden later.

We take our positions, the announcer calls our names, and as the first note of our music plays, I let everything else fall away. The fire in my veins is stronger than ever. Game on. The second the music starts, my body moves on instinct. Every step, every glide, every jump—I don't think, I just do. The ice is mine, and nothing exists beyond the routine Alexei and I have perfected.

The tension from Aiden, the way his lips felt on mine before the program—I shove it down. It doesn't belong here. Alexei and I move as one. The opening step sequence flows effortlessly into the side-by-side triple salchows, and our timing is flawless. The energy in the arena shifts, the crowd catching on, realizing that we're not just skating—we're performing. Aiden said to win. So I will.

Alexei throws me into a triple twist, and I land it with perfect precision, the blades of my skates carving clean into the ice. I can feel his grip tighten when he catches me in the final lift, and as we glide into the closing spin, I hear the audience roar before the final note even plays.

When we finish, my chest heaves, the adrenaline still pulsing through my veins. The arena erupts in cheers.

Alexei grins, spinning me in a tight hug before lifting our clasped hands in the air. "We did it," he breathes, his forehead pressing against mine for a second. "That was flawless, Malyshka." The moment we step off the ice, the cameras swarm. The interviews blur together, my responses automatic, but my mind is elsewhere. All I can think about lately is the grumpy hockey player I live with and how his lips felt on mine.

I know he stayed for the performance. I can feel him watching me. His presence burns at the edges of my awareness, even as Alexei's arm stays firmly draped over my shoulder.

My body still buzzes from the performance when we reach the locker room. I leave Alexei to celebrate, but when I turn the corner, I nearly crash into a solid wall of Aiden. He's leaning against the wall, arms crossed, with an unreadable expression.

"What do you want, Aidy?" His jaw tightens, but he doesn't take the bait. Instead, he pushes off the wall, stepping closer until I have to tilt my chin to meet his gaze. "You skated well," he says, voice lower than usual.

I blink. "That almost sounded like a compliment."

"It was. Don't get used to it." I roll my eyes.

"And here I was, thinking you might be capable of saying something nice." Aiden smirks. "I kissed you before your program, didn't I?"

My stomach flips, but I force myself to scoff. "You ambushed me." He shrugs. "You didn't stop me." I hate that he's right. I hate that the warmth of his lips is still lingering on mine, that my heartbeat hasn't quite settled since it happened. "Enjoying yourself?" I ask dryly. Aiden leans in slightly, and I don't step back. "Immensely."

I let out a frustrated breath. "You're impossible." He chuckles, and for a second, something soft flickers in his gaze.
"Yet, here you are, still talking to me." I hate that he's right. I hate that I like it.
I don't know how long I stand there, staring at Aiden like he's some impossible puzzle I can't solve.

His eyes flicker over my face, something unreadable in them, but his usual smirk is nowhere to be found. Instead, he's watching me like he's waiting for me to say something first. I won't because I don't know what to say. The memory of his lips on mine is still fresh, lingering, and I hate that it's all I can think about. The warmth, the pressure, the way he pulled away like he hadn't just completely thrown me off my game.
Aiden's fingers twitch at his side like he's debating something.

"You gonna keep staring, Angel Face, or do you want to get another round of interviews where you pretend you don't love the attention I give you?" And there it is—the arrogance. His smirk creeping back in like he's reclaiming his territory.
"Oh, shut up, Knight. You love it just as much."
"You know, the last time someone told me to shut up, I kissed them." He adds with a grin, as his gaze lands on my lips. My face burns, and he knows it. I see the flicker of amusement in his expression, the way his lips twitch as if he's daring me to react. I take a slow breath and cross my arms. "Do it again, and I'll break your nose."

Aiden tilts his head, stepping closer, and I hate that my body reacts before my brain does. The heat, the anticipation, the way-too-much awareness of him.
"Tempting," he murmurs, eyes dropping to my lips before

flicking back up. "But I'd rather wait until you want it. I open my mouth to fire back some snarky remark, but Alexei's voice cuts through the thick air between us.

"Kat! Come on! The scores are going up!" I tear my gaze away from Aiden, yanking myself back to reality. Right. Scores. Skating. My actual life the thing that should matter more than whatever the hell this is between me and Aiden Knight.

I storm past him, refusing to look back, but I feel his stare on me the entire way.

The crowd gets louder as Alexei and I approach the scoring area. Everyone gathers around the screen as our final score flashes across the monitor.

A hundred and eight points. We won Gold again. I let out a breath, the tension in my chest finally releasing as Alexei pulls me into a tight hug.

"Another win for us, Malyshka!" he laughs, lifting me off my feet before spinning me. I laugh, but my mind is still clouded. We did it. We won. And yet, my thoughts are tangled in him. I glance over my shoulder, my eyes instinctively searching the crowd, and of course, I find him immediately.

Aiden's standing off to the side, arms crossed, watching. He's not smiling, not clapping, just watching. Something about it sends a shiver down my spine.

But before I can process what it means and figure out what the hell is going on between us, I hear Alina's voice calling my name.

"Kat! We're celebrating tonight!" I snap my focus back, forcing myself to push Aiden out of my head. Right. Celebrating. I glance at Alexei, and he grins, already knowing my answer. "Hell yes, we are."

Tonight, I'm not thinking about Aiden Knight. I refuse.

The celebration is in full swing when we arrive at the bar. Music thrums through the air and the neon lights cast a moody glow over the packed crowd. Alina, Alexei, Maddie, and I push through the sea of bodies, heading straight for the VIP section Roman somehow managed to snag for us. It should be a perfect night. We won. We dominated. I should be riding the high of victory, soaking in the attention, basking in the feeling of success. But instead, my eyes keep searching for him.

The moment I spot him, my stomach twists because he's not alone. Some tall blonde girl is draped over him, fingers tracing the tattoos on his forearm like she has every right to. She's laughing at something he says, flipping her hair like girls do when they want to be noticed. And Aiden— Aiden is letting her.

Something bitter curdles in my stomach. It's stupid. So stupid. I have no claim over him. He's an arrogant, cocky, infuriating hockey player who gets under my skin like no one else. I don't like it. I don't like the way she's touching him. I don't like how he leans in slightly like he's enjoying the attention. And I don't like the way my chest tightens and my hands clench into fists at my sides.

"Kat." Alina's voice snaps me out of it. I turn, forcing a smile that probably looks as fake as it feels.

"What?" She follows my gaze, and the second she sees what I'm looking at, her lips curve into a knowing smirk.

"Oh my God," she says, sing-song. "You're jealous."

"I am not." A scoff slips past my lips at the ridiculous idea.

Alina grins. "You so are." I sip my drink, ignoring the heat rising in my cheeks. "Please. He can do whatever he wants. It's his life."

"Mhm."

"I don't care."

"Right," Alina says with a teasing smile.

"I don't!" I insist. Alina raises a brow. "So, if I dared you to go over there right now and introduce yourself to his little friend, you'd do it?" I freeze, my throat tightening. Shit. Alina laughs. "Yeah, that's what I thought." I grit my teeth.

"It's not jealousy." She pats my shoulder, looking way too amused for my liking. "Whatever you say, Ale."

I groan, turning away, determined not to look at him anymore. Instead, I focus on Alexei, who's already on his second drink, gesturing wildly as he tells some dramatic story to Roman and Will. I slide onto the couch next to him. "You're already this drunk?" He smirks, leaning over to clink his glass against mine. "I'm celebrating, Malyshka." I roll my eyes but take a sip anyway, letting the warmth of the alcohol settle in my stomach. It works—for about two minutes. Because then, I hear her giggling again. What the fuck is she laughing at? Aiden isn't even that funny.

I make the mistake of glancing over just in time to see her press a hand against Aiden's chest, leaning in close. Too close. Aiden doesn't push her away.
He doesn't even look at me. Something inside of me snaps. I don't think—I just act. Before I can stop myself, I grab Alexei's hand and pull him onto the dance floor. He stumbles slightly, laughing. "Kat, what—"

"Dance with me." He raises a brow. "Oh? Is this to make someone jealous? I'm gay, it won't work." I glare. "Shut up and dance," Alexei smirks but obliges, spinning me into the rhythm of the music. The bass pounds in my chest, my heart hammering with something far more complicated than adrenaline. I let myself get lost in it—the movement, the heat, the feeling of Alexei's hands at my waist as we move.

I feel eyes on me. With every move I make, my skin burns from the attention. I don't even have to look to know Aiden is watching. It's like a magnet, the way my body instinctively knows where he is. I risk a glance, and sure enough, his eyes are locked on me, dark and unreadable. The girl is still talking to him, but he's not listening. His jaw is tight, and his grip on his drink is stiff. Good, be jealous, Asshole.

I spin closer to Alexei, laughing a little louder than necessary. Glancing at Aiden again, I see him move. One second, he's across the room. The next, he's right behind me, his presence demanding.

Alexei notices first. Before he can say anything, a warm hand wraps around my wrist, tugging me back. I turn—
And I crash into Aiden. My breath catches. His grip is firm, his eyes burning into mine, and suddenly, the air between us is thick.

"What are you doing?" I ask, my voice steady despite the way my heart is pounding. His jaw clenches. "What the hell was that?" I blink. "What was what?" Aiden narrows his eyes at me. "Don't play dumb, Angel Face." I tilt my head, pretending to think.

"Ohhh, do you mean me dancing? Because last I checked, you looked plenty entertained over there." His grip tightens on my hand, as if he doesn't want to let go of me. "That's what this is about? You're jealous?"

"I don't care what you do, Aiden." I snap, glaring into his eyes. His expression darkens. "Bullshit." We're too close. I should pull away. I don't. His hand is still wrapped around my wrist, his thumb absently brushing against my skin.

"Why do you care?" he asks in a murmur, voice lower now. I hate that I don't have an answer. Because I do care. And I don't know why.

"I don't." I lie. Aiden studies me, his gaze flickering to my lips for half a second before he stares into my eyes again. "You sure about that, Angel Face?"
I swallow hard, my heart pounding out of my chest. "Positive." His smirk is slow, knowing.
"What are you so afraid of?" I refuse to answer. Then, just to infuriate me, he leans in—so close that I can feel his breath against my ear. "Let me know when you're ready to be honest." And then he lets go.

Just like that, he walks away, leaving me standing there, breathless and furious.
Alexei slides up next to me, sipping his drink. "Well, that was hot." I groan, pressing my fingers against my temple. "I can't stand him." Alexei grins.
"Oh, Malyshka. I think you might be in trouble." I roll my eyes.
"I'm not in trouble."
Alexei tilts his head. "Then why do you look like you're about
to pass out?" I glare, but my stomach twists because—damn it—he's right.

My hands shake from interacting with Aiden, and my heart is still pounding. I feel like I just stepped off the ice after a perfect routine— electrified, high, completely on edge. Except this isn't the ice. It's him. Aiden Knight.

I glance around, my eyes instinctively searching for him again, but he's nowhere to be seen. The blonde girl is also gone, and I hate how much I care about that detail. Alina suddenly appears beside me, offering me a fresh drink.

"Here. You look like you need this." I take it without question, chugging half of it before finally exhaling. "Thank you." She watches me for a second, then raises a brow. "So, are we going to talk about that?"
"No," Alina smirks. "Oh, we absolutely are." I groan, throwing my head back. "Why does everyone suddenly think I have some kind of thing with Aiden?" Alina snorts.

"Because you do. "I whip my head toward her in disbelief.
"I do not."
"Kat." Alina says my name, as if asking me to be honest right now.
I cross my arms. "Alina." She sighs, like I'm a child she has to be patient with. "Fine. Let's put it this way. If you don't have a thing for him, why did you pull Alexei onto the dance floor the second you saw Aiden with that girl?"
I open my mouth. Close it. Open it again. Damn it. Alina grins.
I groan. "I don't like him, okay?" She takes a sip of her drink while rolling her eyes at me. "Sure you don't."
I glare. "I don't." Alina just pats my arm.

"Oh, honey. You can keep lying to me, but at some point, you're going to have to stop lying to yourself."
"He will leave me, or worse, hurt me," I say, picking the red polish that coats my left thumb. Alina sighs, wrapping her arms to hug me.
"Maybe he won't. Maybe he'll stay and love you right." I scowl, chugging the rest of my drink as she walks away, laughing under her breath.

I avoid Aiden most of the night, but I see him the second I step outside for fresh air. The cool breeze does nothing to soothe the fire in my veins, the remnants of alcohol buzzing beneath my skin as I lean against the wall, closing my eyes. I just need a second. Just one moment to breathe without feeling like I'm suffocating under the weight of him—

"I was wondering when you'd run." I snap my eyes open, my body immediately locking up at the sound of his voice. Aiden is leaning against the railing a few feet away, watching me like he expected me to come out here. Like he knew I wouldn't be able to stay inside any longer. I inhale slowly, steeling myself before meeting his gaze.

"I wasn't running." He shakes his head at me with a glint of amusement on his face. "Sure, Angel." I cross my arms, scowling at his pretty face. "Stop calling me that."

"No." I groan in annoyance, and Aiden chuckles, taking a slow step toward me.

"You didn't answer my question." I narrow my eyes, "What question?" I ask, my voice laced with confusion. "The one I asked before I walked away." My stomach twists at the reminder, but i feign ignorance. "I don't remember." He tilts his head like he sees right through me.

"Liar."

I hate him. I hate how easily he gets under my skin. I shift, feigning nonchalance. "You ask a lot of questions, Knight. Maybe if you weren't so—"

"What are you so afraid of?" I freeze. His voice is low and quiet, but there's something sharp underneath it. Something raw. Something that makes my breath catch. I swallow hard, my throat dry.

"I'm not afraid." Aiden steps closer, the distance between us almost gone. His scent makes my mind hazy. I feel drunk on him.

"Then why do you keep running?" I don't move. I can't. My back is already against the wall, and he's right there, his presence suffocating, intoxicating, too much.

"I'm not," I whisper, but it's weak, even to my own ears. Aiden exhales through his nose, shaking his head slightly like I'm exhausting him.
"You can dance with Alexei all you want. You can pretend you don't care, pretend I don't get to you. But you and I both know the truth, Kat."

I hate how easily he says it. Like it's a fact. Like he's already won. I lift my chin, meeting his stare head-on. "And what truth is that?" A slow smirk tugs at the corner of his lips, but his eyes are dark, full of something I don't want to name.

"That no matter how hard you fight it…" Aiden whispers, leaning in, his breath warm against my ear. "You want me just as much as I want you."

My body betrays me, shivering at the sound of his voice, at the heat of his presence. And unfortunately for me, he notices. His smirk deepens, his fingers twitching at his side like he wants to touch me like he's waiting for me to break first. I swallow hard, forcing myself to find my voice. "You don't know anything, Aiden."
His grin is slow and confident, as he right fingers graze my left arm from top to bottom. Burning my skin with his touch "Keep telling yourself that, baby." And just like before, he turns and leaves, walking away from me for the second time tonight.
Leaving me standing there, breathless, frustrated, and completely undone.

CHAPTER TWENTY - THREE

KATERINA

Pretending nothing happened is more challenging than I thought. But I do it anyway. The following day, I wake up, throw on my usual training gear, and show up at the rink like Aiden Knight hasn't been invading my thoughts since the second he walked away from me last night. I don't think about his voice in my ear, the way his presence suffocated me in the best, most infuriating way. I don't think about how my body reacted to his words, how he knew exactly what he was doing, and how much he was getting to me. I shove it all down, tuck it into the darkest corner of my mind, and focus on the only thing that matters. Winning.

Training starts as usual. Alexei and I run through our warm-up, step sequences, and spins. My body is tired, still recovering from the night before, but I push through it. Everything is fine until Aiden shows up with Roman.

Aiden leans against the boards, arms crossed, watching me like he has every right to be here. His dark eyes scan the rink, his expression unreadable, but I can feel the tension radiating from him. He hasn't said a word yet, but I can already tell he's about to say something stupid. I grit my teeth, skating to a stop near Alexei, ignoring the way my pulse kicks up when Aiden pushes off the wall and takes a few slow steps closer to where I've stopped.

"What are you doing here, Knight?" I ask, voice clipped. He smirks, shoving his hands into his hoodie pockets.

"Watching." I roll my eyes, annoyed at his presence. "Don't you have hockey practice?" I snap, avoiding eye contact.

"Don't you have a routine to land?" My jaw tightens at his comment. Alexei glances between us, amused but smart enough not to say anything. I scowl, turning away and ignoring him.

"Let's go again," I tell Alexei. I push off, moving through our following sequence, doing everything I can to pretend Aiden isn't standing there, burning holes into me with his stare. And for a while, it works until the throw.

Alexei's grip is perfect; his strength is precisely where it needs to be as he launches me into the air. It should be flawless. It should be routine, but something isn't right. Maybe it's the exhaustion. Perhaps it's the tension thrumming beneath my skin. Maybe it's the fact that my mind hasn't been as clear as I thought it was. Either way—I fall.

It happens fast. Too fast. One second, I'm rotating through the air, everything precise and controlled, and the next—
Pain. I slam into the ice, my left shoulder taking the full force of the impact. It's the same shoulder that keeps bugging me. A sickening snap rings in my ears. Sharp. Deep. Wrong. Gasps ripple through the rink, but I barely hear them. All I hear is the roaring in my ears. The way my breath comes too fast, too shallow. My shoulder—
Something is wrong with my shoulder. Alexei kneels beside me, hands hovering near me but not touching.

"Kat," he says, voice tight. "Are you okay?" No. I am not okay. But I force a breath out, gritting my teeth against the pain. "I—" And then, he's there. Aiden. The sight of him standing over me is the final straw. "Stay away," I snap before he can even say anything. Aiden freezes, his eyes narrowing.
"Kat—"
"I said stay away." His jaw clenches, but I don't care. I can't care. Not when my shoulder is screaming in pain. Not when reality sets in— I might have just lost my shot at gold. Tears burn the back of my eyes, but I blink them away, swallowing the lump in my throat. Alexei helps me sit up his face pinched with concern.

"We need to get you checked out." I nod stiffly, refusing to look at Aiden and acknowledge that he's still standing there, still watching me, like he wants to fix something he has no business fixing. This is my battle. My career. My life. And if I lost everything I've been working for, the last thing I need is Aiden Knight acting like he cares.

I don't even remember the drive to the hospital. Alina and Alexei came with me, but their voices blurred into the background the second we arrived. The doctor confirmed what I already knew deep down. Rotator cuff tear. Not a large one. But small enough to need surgery long enough to keep me off the ice for at least three months. The moment they tell me, I refuse to believe it. I don't cry. I don't break down in front of everyone. I just sit there, fists clenched, nails digging into my palm as reality crushes me. I have four months until the next qualifier. And I won't even be able to skate for the next three.

I feel like I can't breathe. Alina tries to talk to me, but I barely hear her. She and Alexei eventually leave to grab food, giving me space, and for the first time, I'm entirely alone. Until I'm not. A shadow shifts outside the doorway. My stomach twists painfully as I look at him.

Aiden.

I should have known he'd show up. He doesn't step inside. Doesn't say a word. He just stands there, watching me, hands shoved in his pockets, expression unreadable. For a moment, neither of us moves. Then Alina's voice rings from down the hall. "What are you doing here?" Aiden doesn't look at her. His eyes stay on me. Alina approaches him and says something I can't hear while he nods. I should tell him to leave. I should tell him he has no reason to be here. But I don't. I don't speak. I feel too weak. I just look outside of the hospital window.

Aiden looks at me again and walks out the door without saying anything. And for the first time since I fell, I felt something other than pain.

Something worse that I don't want to name. Because the truth is, I don't know what hurts more—my shoulder or ignoring Aiden.

CHAPTER TWENTY - FOUR

KATERINA

Pain is the first thing I register when I wake up. A deep, pulsing ache radiates from my shoulder, the kind that even the heavy doses of painkillers can't completely erase. My body feels sluggish, my mind foggy from the anesthesia, and for a few blissful seconds, I forget why I feel like this. Then reality slams into me. I had surgery because I fell. Because I tore my rotator cuff. Because I was reckless and distracted, and now- Now, I might have just lost everything.

A choked sob lodges itself in my throat, but I swallow it down, blinking hard at the ceiling. I can't cry. I won't cry. Not in this sterile hospital room where everything smells like antiseptic and pity. The door creaks open, and I brace myself, expecting another nurse, another doctor, coming in with more reminders of what I already know.

Instead, it's Alina and Alexei—my best friends. Alina rushes to my side immediately; her expression twisted in worry.

"Oh, Malyshka," she whispers, carefully avoiding my shoulder as she perches on the edge of the bed. "How are you feeling?" I force a weak smile. "Like I got hit by a Zamboni." Alexei snorts, standing behind her with his arms crossed.

"Well, at least your sense of humor is intact." I roll my eyes but wince when the movement tugs at my shoulder. Alina glares at Alexei.

"Don't make her laugh, idiot." He raises his hands in surrender.

"She started it." I shake my head, exhaustion settling deep in my bones.

"You guys don't have to stay." Alina glares at me.

" We absolutely do. And we will. So shut up." I sigh, knowing it's pointless to argue.

Alexei gives me a knowing smirk before his expression softens slightly.

"Your dad was here to check on you, but you were still under the anesthesia. I called your mom and filled her in. She is currently looking for flights." I nodded at the information. My estranged father stopped by to see me. The realization that my father cared enough to check on me made me feel lighter.

"Coach says she'll come by later. She's waiting on the official recovery timeline."

My stomach knots.

"Right." Neither says anything, but the unspoken words are loud enough—the Olympics. I try not to think about it, to let the possibility of missing everything consume me. But it does—it already does. So I do the only thing I can do. I shut down.

It's been two weeks since my surgery, and I feel like a shell of the old me. I can't skate, I can't practice, I can't do anything. I have barely spoken to the boys, mostly spending my days in class or in bed. At class, I take the farthest seat from them to be alone with my thoughts. The only people who still have access to me are Alina and Alexei. Who are now trying to get me to eat something so I don't starve myself.

"Come on, Kat, you have to eat something. Please." Alina's voice is tired, full of worry. I sit at the kitchen table, poking at my food, dragging my fork back and forth across the plate, but never actually lifting it to my mouth. I should just eat, but I can't– because every bite reminds me of how I've lost control of everything. One more week, I can start physical therapy. But I still have two more months before I can skate again. There's no way I'll be ready for our next qualifiers on time. My dream is over. It's over. Alina sighs, pushing her plate away.

"You can't keep starving yourself. I understand you're going through it, but we cannot help you if you don't let us." I don't respond. I walk out of the kitchen and head upstairs to my room. When I shut the door, my tears came fast, hot, and heavy. I lay down, curling into myself, silent sobs wracking my body. I don't know how to do this. I don't know who I am without skating. The door creaks open, but I don't turn to look.

"Roomie, can i come in?" I nod at Will, who moves closer, sitting beside me on the bed. I wait for him to say something, but he doesn't. He just wraps his arms around me, carefully, gently, like I might break, giving me a big hug. "Please bring back our sassy roommate. I'd take her over Depressed Kat any day." A sob escapes before I can stop it. And I just cry. Will lets me. He doesn't say a word. Just rubs my back, letting me fall apart.

"I'm sorry, Will," I choke out. "I don't know what the hell is wrong with me. I can't stop crying." He presses a hand to my back.

"We'd be more worried if you didn't cry." I try to laugh, but it comes out strangled. Will places a kiss on top of my head and leaves the room without another word.

I try to sleep. But the pain in my shoulder is unbearable. I sit up on my bed in the darkness of my room, my arm throbbing even through the pain meds, and the weight of it all—the surgery, the recovery, the lost time—crushes me.

Tears slip down my cheeks before I can stop them, silent and heavy, and I bite my lip to keep the sob inside, but it's no use. My heart starts pounding out of my chest as I sob. The door creaks open. At first, I think it's Alina. But I see him.

Aiden steps inside quietly and carefully, as if he knows he's walking

straight into a war zone. I stiffen, scrubbing at my face quickly, forcing myself to sit up even though my body protests the movement.

"Get out," I yell, but he doesn't. He just closes the door behind him, his gaze locked onto mine, dark and unreadable.

"No." Anger flares in my chest.

"I don't want you here." He slowly steps towards me, stopping at the edge of my bed.

"I don't care." I glare, but he doesn't move, doesn't flinch.

"Go away, Aiden." He exhales through his nose, like he's barely holding onto his patience.

"You've been shutting everyone out," he states, anger dripping from his voice.

"So what?" I snap. "It's my life, my career—"

"And you're just going to give up?" I freeze.

"I didn't say that."

"You didn't have to," he mutters. "I see it all over your face." Something cracks inside me.

"What do you want from me, Aiden?" My voice breaks on his name, and I hate it. I hate how weak I sound, how raw I feel. Aiden doesn't answer right away. He just looks at me, his expression unreadable, but there's something in his eyes— something that makes my throat tighten.

"I want you to let me be here for you." I let out a shaky breath, staring at him like I don't know who he is.

"Why?" I whisper. His gaze flickers, something unreadable passing over his face before he says, low and rough—

"Because I can't stand seeing you like this." My lip trembles, and I shake my head. "I—" Before I can say anything else, he's closing the space between us, carefully sitting on the edge of my bed. He doesn't touch me, doesn't push—just waits. And I hate that it works. I hate that my walls are already cracking. So I do the only thing I can do. I let go. I fall. Aiden catches me the second I do. I don't know who moves first, but suddenly, I'm in his arms, my face buried in his chest, and I'm crying. Not silent tears. Not quiet grief. Broken.

I sob, leaning into him, my body trembling, and Aiden just holds me, his grip tight, solid, real. He runs his right hand through my hair to comfort me, pressing his lips against my temple, and he doesn't say a word—just lets me fall apart in his arms. I shouldn't be doing this. I shouldn't be letting this happen. But right now, I don't care. Because the pain—the aching, burning, all-consuming pain that has settled deep in my chest—won't stop, and I need something to drown it out. I need him to drown it out. So, when Aiden dark eyes flicker to my lips, I don't hesitate.

"Aiden. Make me forget. Please?" A single tear slips down my cheek.

His entire body goes still. I place my left hand on his jaw, my thumb rubbing his jaw. "Please, make me feel something other than pain."

Whatever restraint he had left shatters. Aiden crushes his lips against mine, his hands immediately claiming me, one gripping the back of my neck, the other wrapping around my throat firmly. I melt into him, letting the kiss consume me, devour me. My tongue glides over his bottom lip, and when he groans, I smile against his mouth. He pulls me onto his lap, his strong hands guiding me as I straddle him. Aiden grabs my ass and pulls me down against him, forcing a gasp out of me.

"Aiden," I moan, my lips brushing against his ear. His entire body tenses beneath me, his grip tightens, and his mouth latches onto my neck, sucking, biting, owning. I arch against him, my fingers tangling in his hair, tugging when he finds the sensitive spot beneath my jaw. God. I can barely breathe.

I rock against him, feeling every hard, heated inch of his pressed against me, and my mind goes blank. Aiden groans, flipping me onto my back, careful not to jostle my injured shoulder. He hovers above me, his hands trailing up my sides, slipping beneath my shirt, his touch burning against my skin. Then, his eyes darken.

"Careful, my angel. I don't want you to hurt yourself." His voice is hoarse, thick with restraint. I bite my bottom lip, my chest rising and falling rapidly as I stare down at him, drunk on the way he looks at me like I'm something holy. He slides his hands higher, fingers grazing the bottom of my breasts, and my breath catches. I need more.

I don't even hesitate. I pull my shirt over my head, baring myself to him. Aiden sucks in a sharp breath, his eyes dropping. He licks his lips, his throat bobbing as he takes me in. "Fuck Goldie." He whispers, taking me in. Heat pools low in my stomach, my core tightening. Aiden's hands roam over my ribs, and his touch is both soft and desperate. He leans down, pressing open-mouthed kisses along my stomach, then up—higher, higher—until his lips brush the top of my chest. Then he sucks hard, leaving his mark, claiming me. I whimper, my fingers digging into his shoulders, my body writhing beneath him.

"You're so fucking beautiful," he murmurs against my skin, his voice raw like he's trying to memorize me. I reach for him, letting my hands explore every inch of his body—the solid lines of his abs, the dip of his waist, the way his muscles flex under my touch.

"It's not fair." I lean forward, brushing my lips over his stomach. "You're built like a fucking sculpture." Aiden lets out a deep chuckle, but it dies quickly when I kiss each ridge of his abs, my tongue flicking against his skin. His entire body shudders.

"You're one to talk. You look like a fucking Godess Kat." His voice is wrecked, his eyes hungry as they rake over me.

I smirk, pulling his bottom lip between my teeth before sucking on it. Aiden groans, gripping my waist tightly, his fingers digging into my skin.

"You feel so good," I whisper against his ear before sucking on his earlobe.

His dick twitches beneath me, his jaw clenching as he grits his teeth.

I feel drunk on him, on the way his body reacts to mine, the way he holds himself back like he's on the edge of losing control. "I don't want this ever to end." I grip his face, slamming my lips against his.

He groans into my mouth, his hands guiding my hips, urging me to grind against him, and I do. It's everything. The friction. The heat. The way his body tenses beneath me. I can feel him everywhere, and I can't stop, don't want to stop. Aiden curses, his fingers digging into my skin, and suddenly—the coil inside me snaps. A shudder rips through me as I reach my peak, my mouth falling open, my fingers clutching onto Aiden for dear life. I gas, burying my face against his shoulder as I whisper his name, my entire body trembling. His arms wrap around me, holding me through it, his breathing just as ragged. Holy shit. I collapse against him, my cheek resting on his chest, my heart still racing. Aiden's hand slides through my hair, his fingers tangling in the strands, and when I look up at him, he's grinning.

"Hi," I smirk, breathless. Aiden chuckles.

"Hi." He kisses me again, deep and slow, like he never wants to stop, and I never want him to. Aiden pulls away, his hands settling on my waist, lifting me off him. "I need to use the bathroom," he mutters, standing quickly. My eyes drop to his crotch, and I bite my lip to keep from grinning. Aiden shoots me a glare, shaking his head. I point toward the bathroom, barely holding in my laughter. He mutters under his breath, stalking toward the door and shutting it behind him. I hear the faucet turn on, but it's not loud enough to swallow Aidens words. "Old lady, naked grandma, think, Aiden, think." I burst out laughing, burying my face in the pillow. A few minutes later, the bathroom door opens, and Aiden steps out, looking much calmer.

"Are you going to stay?" I ask, my voice smaller than I intended. His eyes meet mine, and he nods. I smile as he slides into bed beside me, pulling the covers over us. I turn onto my side, keeping a safe distance between us. But Aiden frowns, wrapping an arm around my waist and pulling me flush against him, his chest pressed to my back. I can feel his heartbeat against my spine, fast and heavy, just like mine.

He breathes against my neck, his voice low, deep, raw—
"No more space, Angel Face." I exhale slowly, closing my eyes as exhaustion overtakes me, my body sinking into his warmth, my fingers curled into his hoodie like I'm afraid he'll disappear if I let go. But he doesn't.

He stays, and for the first time since surgery, the weight on my chest lifts just enough for me to breathe. I wake up hours later, still tangled against him. I shift slightly, expecting him to move or pull away, but his arms tighten around me, his voice barely above a whisper as he speaks. "Go back to sleep, Angel Face." And for once— I do.

CHAPTER TWENTY - FIVE

KATERINA

Aiden has been avoiding me. I admit, i deserve it. I did it to him, and this is karma. My heart has been palpitating all day, and it seems like it won't calm down.

'I told you he didn't want you'.

No, no, no, no, not now please.

'Why would he? You don't have a heart, and you treat others like shit. The only person who ever loved you was me, princess.'

"Stop! You're not real." My voice is barely a whisper as I run my hands through my hair, tugging at the strands at the nape of my neck.

'I'm real, Katerina. You should've never turned your back on me.'
'Look at you now.'
'A fucking loser. No more career. A nobody. A nothing. A waste of space.'

I try to inhale, but my lungs refuse to cooperate. The more I breathe in, the more it feels like I'm suffocating. My ears ring. My heart is beating so fast it hurts. My vision blurs, and panic digs its claws into my chest.
"Kat, look at me." Aiden's voice slices through the fear, distant at first, but the more he repeats my name, the more the fog lifts. "Angel Face. Take a deep breath for me, please. Tell me five things you can see." I try, but my throat feels too tight. It's like I'm choking on nothing.
"Your black eyes," I whisper, my voice trembling. "My backpack. My Hello Kitty shorts. Your red shirt. My books." Aiden nods, his big palms cradling my cheeks. His touch is grounding. Real.
"Good, good. Four things you can touch." I lean into his hands, forcing air into my lungs.
"Your hands. My hair. Your shirt. My bed sheets."
"You got this, baby. Tell me three things you can hear." I gulp, my vision blurry. Why is he here helping me? I thought he was ignoring me.
"Your voice. My breathing. The boys downstairs." He strokes my cheek, his thumbs moving in slow, steady circles.

"Okay, almost done. Two things you can smell." I inhale deeply, drowning in the familiar scent of his cologne.

"Your cologne… and my smelly self," I say with a broken smile. Aiden laughs, the sound easing my chest's last bit of tension.

"You don't smell. What are you talking about?" His grin fades as his fingers tighten slightly on my face. "Last one. One thing you can taste."

"My tears," I whisper, sniffling.

Aiden pulls back slightly, but his hands stay on me, steady and warm, as my heart calms down and my mind stops racing. "Uhm… thank you for helping me out right now. I appreciate it." His black eyes search mine, and for the first time tonight, I notice just how devastatingly handsome he is. He could be doing nothing, and I'd pay just to watch him exist. His shaggy black hair falls over his eyes, and without thinking, I reach out and push it back.

"Why have you been avoiding me?" I ask, barely above a whisper. Aiden hesitates, his gaze flickering toward the window before landing back on me.

"I didn't want you to tell me you regretted it. You didn't say it the first time we kissed, but you avoided me, so I just didn't want the same thing to happen."

"So you avoided me instead?" He nods. I nod back, understanding. "Well, I'm sorry I did that. It fucking sucks being ignored." Aiden chuckles as he sinks onto the bed next to me. "It does. But I'm sorry, too. I should've just talked to you." I place my hand over his, giving it a slight squeeze.

"Come, I'll help you run a bath." I wince, hiding my face in my hand. "It's embarrassing, but I can't. Alina was supposed to help me, but I ruined it by walking away from her." Aiden frowns, confusion written all over his face.

"Why can't you?" I groan, too mortified to say it out loud. "Tell me." His voice is gentle, but his eyes pin me in place. I swallow, then mumble,

"Removing my clothes is impossible by myself, and I can't scrub properly with one arm. So... I can't." Aiden processes my words and then nods. Without hesitation, he pushes himself up from the floor.

"Let's go."

"Where? I ask, confused.

"I'm going to run a bath for you." I freeze. My heart jumps into my throat. "Is that okay with you? I should've asked—sorry." I nod, forcing myself to stay calm.

"It's okay. Yeah. Totally fine." No, it's not fine. He's going to see me naked. Oh my god.

I don't move as Aiden leads me into the bathroom, closes the door, and turns on the water. He adds Epsom salt, and his movements are so casual like this isn't completely uncharted territory. He looks over his shoulder, his expression unreadable.

"Angel Face, it's ready." His hands reach for my sling, and I nod. He undoes it carefully, then moves to my shirt. I hesitate, but eventually, I let him help me slip out of it, leaving me in just

my white lace bra. Aiden gulps as his dark eyes flicker down to my chest before he quickly kneels, his fingers resting on the waistband of my sweats. "Still good?" I nod, barely breathing. Aiden bends down on his knees and pulls them down as he looks at me. I release a shaky breath, not breaking eye contact. I run my left hand through his hair, pulling at it as he looks at me with so much desire as if he would do anything for me. Having him on his knees in front of me makes my core tingle and a whole ass butterfly zoo in my stomach. Don't picture him in between your legs, Kat. No! I step out of my sweats, and my bra grazes his chest as he stands up. I can't think when he is so close to me. "I'll undo your bra, and then you can take it off while I turn around." I nod as Aiden steps closer, wrapping both arms around me. He undoes my bra with me in between his arms as I rest my head on his chest, surrounding myself with his scent. I close my eyes as I take a deep breath. His presence engulfs me, and just like that, Aiden invades my thoughts. I feel my bra loosen up, and my left arm lifts immediately to hold the front of the bra in place. "I'll turn around so you can get in the tub," Aiden says, his voice hoarse.

When he tries to turn around, I wrap my left arm around his right wrist and turn him towards me. His eyes clash with mine, confused at why I stopped him. But I just remove my bra, letting it drop in front of Aidens feet. Aiden looks up at me and gulps as his gaze drops to my chest. I hook my left index finger through my panties and pull them down, letting them fall on the floor. I step out of them and closer to Aiden. Heat floods my body, my pulse hammering in my ears. Aiden's eyes never leave mine, but the hunger in them is undeniable.

"You're trying to kill me, aren't you?" A slow smile tugs at my lips.

"You know you're the first guy that's seen me naked in two years?" His jaw clenches as his gaze caresses my body. "You bet your ass I'll be the last, Goldie."

The air crackles. I barely register him lifting me into the tub, his strong arms holding me like I weigh nothing. The hot water soothes my sore muscles, but nothing compares to the fire in my veins when Aiden crouches beside the tub and starts washing my hair.

His fingers move slowly, massaging my scalp, and I let myself sink into the sensation. His touch is too gentle and careful, making my heart ache.
"You've done this before," I murmur. He exhales through his nose.
"Sophia. When she was too weak from chemo." My heart twists. Neither of us speaks as Aiden rinses the shampoo from my hair, his fingertips trailing through the strands in a way that feels too intimate. After rinsing my hair, he wraps a towel around it and sits on the floor next to the tub, facing me. No one has ever taken care of me like this. I feel so nervous around him, and while he looks at me, I feel like I can do no wrong.

The air shifts, and my pulse races as Aiden's eyes flick to my lips. I don't move. Neither does he. His hand slides along my jaw, tilting my chin just enough before his lips crash into mine. I grab his shirt with my good hand, yanking him closer. His grip tightens in my hair as he deepens the kiss. It's messy and desperate. Aiden groans against my mouth, his fingers skimming my bare skin everywhere but where I need him most. I pull back, panting. "Aiden—" His forehead rests against mine, his breath uneven. "Yeah?" He answers, his eyes full of want.
"This is—"
"Everything," he finishes, his voice rough. And God help me, I agree.

CHAPTER TWENTY - SIX

AIDEN

When Kat finally fell asleep, curled up next to me, I felt something inside my chest shift—something significant, something I couldn't easily dismiss. For weeks, I'd been denying how I felt, telling myself she was nothing more than a distraction, a challenge I had to overcome. But now, looking down at her peaceful face pressed against my chest, it was impossible to pretend anymore. I like her. I really like her.
It wasn't just attraction; I'd felt that many times before. This was deeper, quieter, yet infinitely louder in my heart. Kat was fierce, passionate, and stubborn—but seeing her vulnerable and broken, trusting me enough to let me in when she was at her weakest, had stirred something inside me that I hadn't expected.

She hadn't avoided me after the panic attack. That alone felt huge. Instead, she'd quietly leaned into me, letting me hold her, letting me help her—even accepting my presence when she'd taken a bath to wash away the remnants of her anxiety. The memory of gently washing her skin, carefully and respectfully, was imprinted on my mind, making my heart pound in an almost overwhelming way.

I felt protective, responsible even, like she'd entrusted me with something fragile. For the first time, it didn't feel suffocating—it felt right.

Kat stirred slightly in her sleep, mumbling something unintelligible, and pressed closer. I tightened my arms around her, inhaling the faint scent of her shampoo. Right then, I knew without a doubt—I was utterly screwed. I wasn't just falling for her; I'd already fallen.

The following day came too quickly. Sunlight streaming into her room made her eyelashes flutter open slowly. Her sleepy yet clear gaze met mine, and for a brief moment, neither of us moved or spoke.

"Hey," I whispered, breaking the silence gently.

"Hey," she replied softly, voice hoarse but tender.

"How are you feeling?" I asked cautiously, brushing her hair back from her face.

She hesitated, then smiled faintly. "Better. Thanks to you."

My chest swelled at her admission. "I'm glad you let me stay."

She nods almost shyly. "Me too."

"I have to go see Sophia today. I promised her an ice cream date." Kat grins up at me, rubbing her thumb over my jaw.

"You have such a good heart, Aiden." Smiling, I wrap my arms around her, placing kisses all over her face as I tighten my hold on her.

"Okay. That cute moment is over. I need my coffee." I chuckle, letting her go. Kat gets up and checks that her oversized shirt is okay before leaving the room.

I sigh, gripping my hair and tugging it. Okay, Aiden, don't fuck this up. I stand and put on my sweatpants, which are lying next to the bed, and make my way out of the room to join Kat in the kitchen.

I smile when I see her leaning by the counter, waiting for her coffee, by the espresso machine. I lean in and place a gentle kiss on her right shoulder. Kat turns around and gives me one of her famous smirks.

"Missed me already?" She asks teasingly.

"My heart can't stand being away from you. It's attached." Kat laughs, slapping my chest. The espresso machine beeps, and Kat prepares her coffee while I watch her silently.

The front door slams, and a voice yells, "Breakfast is here." Grayson walks into the kitchen, holding three bags of takeout food.

Kat claps her hands and walks towards Graysen to check what's in the bags, but I stay back and take a couple of sips from her Caramel Iced Latte.

"Aiden. Again? I could make you one; you don't have to drink mine." I shrug, grinning at Kat.

"My dear, dear Angel, haven't you learned? I don't want one. I want to drink yours." She huffs, annoyed, grabs her coffee from my hands, and stalks upstairs back to her room.

After breakfast, Kat assured me she'd be okay alone for a few hours, so I decided to visit Sophia. My sister had been in the hospital too long, and after last night, I needed to see her smiling face.

On the way, I stopped to pick up her favourite—mint chocolate chip ice cream. I used to tease her mercilessly about it being the worst flavour, but secretly, I'd grown to love it too. When I walked into her hospital room, she perked up instantly, her bright eyes sparkling despite the dark circles beneath them.

"Aiden!" she called excitedly, sitting up straighter.

"Hey, kiddo." I smiled widely, holding up the small carton of ice cream. "Brought you something special."

She squealed in delight. "Mint chocolate chip! Yes! Admit it—you're glad I converted you."

I chuckled, handing her the spoon. "Fine, Soph, you win. Best ice cream ever."

She grinned triumphantly. "Knew you'd come around."

Sitting beside her bed, I watched her savour the treat, a rare moment of joy in a place that often felt too heavy. My heart twisted every time I looked at her thin frame, her delicate fingers gripping the spoon as if it weighed more than it should.

"I talked to your doctor earlier," I told her quietly, trying to keep my voice steady.

Sophia paused mid-bite, eyes wide. "And?"

I smiled broadly, unable to contain my excitement. "They found a match for your stem cells."

Her breath caught. "Really?"

I nod, my throat suddenly tight with emotion. "Yeah, Soph. It's me. I'm a 99.9% match."

She stared at me, eyes filling with tears, her lip trembling before she lunged forward, wrapping her arms around my neck tightly.

"Are you going to be my super-hero, Aidy?" she whispered into my shoulder.

"I'd do anything for you," I promised softly, holding her close. "The doctors said your odds are excellent now. We're gonna beat this, okay?"

She sniffled, pulling back to look at me with determination. "We will."

When I finally returned home, my heart felt lighter. Kat was sitting on the couch, her knees drawn to her chest. As I walked in, she looked up, her expression softening. "How's Sophia?" she asked, concern etched into her beautiful face.

I sat down beside her, reaching for her hand without thinking. She let me take it, intertwining her fingers with mine.

"She's good. She asked me to bring you with me next time I visit," I said gently, squeezing her hand reassuringly. "Kat, they had some news for me today—I'm a 99.9% match for Sophia's stem cell transplant."

Her mouth falls open, eyes widening in shock before relief floods her features. Tears welled in her eyes, spilling down her cheeks. "Are you serious?"

"Completely." I smile gently, cupping her cheek and brushing away her tears with my thumb. "She has a real chance now, Kat."

A sob escapes her lips as she throws herself into my arms, clinging tightly. "Oh my god, Aiden. This is huge." I nod as she tightens her arms around me.

"W-when is the transplant going to happen?"

"Wait, do you need surgery?" She asks, her eyes wide.

I hold her tightly, heart pounding fiercely in my chest. "I don't know yet, but you'll be the first one I'll tell." Kat nods, leaning on my chest to comfort me, and as she settled against me, I knew, without any doubt, that I am utterly screwed when it comes to this girl.

CHAPTER TWENTY - SEVEN

KATERINA

I was in enemy territory. Stealing Aiden Knight's clothes should not be this easy. But, to be fair, it's his fault for leaving his closet open and unattended. Aiden Knight's walk-in closet was bigger than my room, lined with neatly arranged suits, jackets, and an excessive number of hoodies for someone who probably never gets cold. I run my fingers over the fabric, stopping at a soft, oversized hoodie that looks too inviting to ignore. I've been staying home for a couple of days now, letting myself
heal, and after the other night—after Aiden had his hands in my hair, his mouth on mine, after everything—I should be keeping my distance.
Instead, I'm standing in the middle of his closet, rummaging through his hoodies like I own the place.
I know I have my own clothes, but the second I saw Aiden's oversized sweatshirts, the temptation became

too much. I deserve this. After everything I've been through, after the pain, the panic, the mess—stealing one of his hoodies is the least he can offer me.

With a smirk, I pull it off the hanger and tug it over my head, inhaling the faint scent of pine and something undeniably Aiden. It's way too big, the sleeves hanging past my hands, the hem skimming my thighs. Perfect.

The problem? I took too long. I feel it.

A prickle at the back of my neck. That unmistakable heat of being watched.

Because the second I turn around, Aiden is right there, leaning against the doorframe, arms crossed, gaze dark, smirk lazy and unmistakably focused on me, more specifically, on my legs, which were utterly bare beneath his stolen shirt. His jaw flexed like he was forcing himself to stay put instead of stalking toward me. I freeze. A slow smile curved my lips as my heart pounded out of my chest. Fuck, I just got caught red-handed. I have to play it cool.

"Like what you see, Captain?" Really? I ask myself, that's what you consider cool? Aidens eyes drag over me, slow and deliberate, his smirk deepening.

"Well, well, well…Didn't realize my closet doubled as your wardrobe."

I clear my throat, tugging the hem of the hoodie down like that'll make this situation less humiliating.

"I—"

"You breaking into my closet, Angel Face?" I cross my arms, pretending I don't feel my face heating. "It's not breaking in if the door was open."

Aiden chuckles, stepping inside and closing the space between us in two slow strides.

"That's what you're going with?" I lift my chin.

"You have too many hoodies. I'm doing you a favour."

Then, tilting my head, I add, "You've been staring an

awfully long. Should I pose, or do you want to take a picture?" His lips twitch, and instantly, he pushes off the doorframe, closing the space between us. My breath hitches, but I refuse to back down, even as he stops a mere inch away.

Aiden reaches up, brushing his fingers along my jaw before tucking a stray strand of hair behind my ear.

"I don't need a picture," he murmurs, voice low, teasing. "I've already memorized every detail." Damn.

Heat curls in my stomach, but I keep my expression playful, raising a brow.

"That so? Sounds like an obsession, Knight. Should I be concerned?" His gaze drops briefly to my lips before meeting my eyes again.

"Maybe," he says, the smirk in his voice evident. "But you don't look too worried."

I roll my eyes, stepping past him—deliberately brushing against his chest as I do.

"Well, if you're done gawking, I'll be keeping this shirt. Consider it a tax for all the times you've annoyed me."

His gaze flickers to my bare legs beneath the hem of the hoodie, and something tightens in the air between us. His tongue swipes along his lower lip like he's thinking about something, and my entire body burns.

I hate him. I hate how easily he can make me feel like this— like I'm seconds away from completely falling apart. Before I can break first, he exhales through his nose and shakes his head.

"Fine. Keep it. But I am collecting payment." I narrow my eyes. "Payment?"

Aiden's smirk returns, slow and dangerous. "You owe me a skate."

It's stupid. I know it's silly. But the second I step onto the rink my body remembers precisely why this is home. I exhale, letting my blades carve into the ice, feeling the familiar resistance beneath me. It's been weeks since I last skated, and even though my shoulder is still healing, the rest of me misses this—the glide, the rhythm, the freedom. Aiden skates up beside me, his movements easy, and effortless. Show-off.

I give him a look.

"I can do this myself you know." Aiden ignores me and continues lacing my skates, much to my dismay.

"I know," he says as I stand up, his hands settling on my waist, steadying me, his touch just enough to remind me that he's there.

"But humor me." I huff but let him guide me, his grip firm but careful, making sure not to strain my shoulder. We move together easily and in sync, and the worst part? It feels good. The best part? I know it's killing him just as much as it's killing me. His fingers flex against my waist, his breathing shallow as I lean into him, letting him support my balance as I push into a slow glide. The rink is empty, the air cold, but everything between us is too hot.

I smirk, tilting my head up at him. "You sure you can handle this, Aidy? His jaw tightens.

"Call me that again, Angel Face," he murmurs, his voice deep, "And see what happens."

I arch a brow. "Aidy." His grip tightens, and he moves. Before I can react, he spins me, his hands keeping me steady, and suddenly, I'm pressed against the boards, my back hitting the cool surface, my breath catching as he cages me in. The tension snaps. His mouth is on mine before I can even think.

It's desperate. Rough. His hands gripping my waist, pulling me flush against him, his body solid and warm. I melt, fisting the front of his hoodie—deepening the kiss like I need this just as badly as he does.

Aiden groans against my lips, his fingers pressing into my sides, everywhere but where I want them, and it's infuriating, it's exhilarating, it's—

"Fucking finally!"

We jerk apart at the sound of our friends' voices. I whip around just in time to see Will, Roman, and Alina standing at the rink's entrance, grinning like idiots.

Oh my God. Aiden growls, running a hand down his face. "You guys have the worst timing." Fuck can't a girl get some in peace around here.

Alina crosses her arms, smirking. "Or the best."

I groan, covering my face with my hands. "I hate all of you."

Will snorts. "No, you don't."

Roman winks at the both of us with a grin on his face as he says. "So, when's the wedding?"

Aiden flips him off while I groan louder. And somewhere beneath the embarrassment, beneath the sheer mortification of being caught, there's something else. Something warm.

CHAPTER TWENTY - EIGHT

KATERINA

I knew this morning was going to go to shit when I woke up and found out Grayson drank my coffee. I was late for practice because I couldn't find my damn leg warmers, and the first thing I saw at the rink was Alina yelling. She is fuming. Roman stands across from her, arms crossed, jaw clenched, while Alina paces before him like she's seconds away from losing it.

"I don't get you," she snaps, throwing her hands in the air. "One second, you're fine, and the next, you shut down like I'm some stranger."

Roman exhales through his nose, visibly restraining himself.

"Alina—"

"No," she cuts him off, her voice shaking. "I don't understand why you can't just talk to me." His expression hardens, but beneath it, I see it—hesitation.

Fear. My best friend likes Roman. She's scared to lose him. The look in her eyes, I've seen it before on her.
"This is getting ugly," Aiden mutters, wrapping his arms around my waist.

I nudge him on the ribs to get him to be quiet. "Stop talking. I can't hear."

Roman shakes his head, exhaling harshly. "Because it's not that simple, Alina." She scoffs at Roman, rolling her eyes.

"No, Roman. It is. You just don't want it to be." A heavy silence stretches between them. Roman's fingers flex at his sides like he wants to reach for her but doesn't dare. Alina's eyes shine with frustration, lips pressed tight like she's holding back something deeper than anger.

She steps back. Not much. But enough for Roman to notice. His jaw ticks, his entire body stiffening, but he doesn't say anything. Alina nods once like she's just made a decision.

"I can't keep doing this, Roman." She walks away before he can respond, her shoulders tense, her hands balled into fists. I don't realize I'm holding my breath until she's gone.

Aiden blows out a low whistle, shaking his head. "Damn." I elbow him.

"Not the time." I spat at Aiden through gritted teeth. Roman stands there momentarily, staring at the spot where Alina disappeared, his fingers tightening into fists before he turns and storms off in the opposite direction. I sigh, rubbing my temple.

"That's gonna be a mess." Aiden nudges my side, wiggling his brows, while he rubs his hands together in anticipation.

"Wanna make a bet?" I glare at him, annoyed at his reaction.

"You're insufferable."

He smirks. "And yet, you love spending time with me."

I roll my eyes but don't argue. Because he's right. Ever since my shoulder injury, my thoughts have shifted. Don't get me wrong—I still want to be a gold medalist in the upcoming Olympics. Scratch that. I will be.

But this past week, focusing on my studies and having Aiden help me skate just enough to stay prepared for my return has made me realize something. I wasn't living. I mean, sure, technically, I was, but not really. I was so consumed by figure skating, so obsessed with winning that stupid gold medal, that I lost sight of why I even started. I used to skate because I loved it, it made me feel alive. Not for a medal. My new goal? Reignite my passion for figure skating.

I shake my thoughts off and skate around the rink, gaining speed with each glide.

"Bend those knees, angel face," Aiden commands, his voice firm but laced with something that makes my stomach flip. I bend my right knee slightly, casting him a grin.

"Just like that. You're doing so good." A rush of heat spreads through me at his praise. My core tingles and I have to fight the sudden urge to press my thighs together. What the hell is wrong with me? One compliment, and I'm in shambles.

"You're such a—"

"Aiden, stop it." I come to a sharp halt, skidding on the ice, and turn to face the devil himself. Aiden stops and smirks at me, knowing exactly what he's doing. My heart slams against my ribs. I hate this. I hate how he makes me lose control.

"Stop what?" I glare at his stupidly attractive grin and shove him with my left arm, but my balance wavers.

Before I can fall, two strong arms wrap around my waist, steadying me.

Suddenly, being held by Aiden is far worse than the teasing. His scent—clean, woodsy, intoxicating—wraps around me, making my head spin.

"Stop what?" he asks again, his tone lower this time. I press my lips into a thin line, looking everywhere except his eyes.

"You know what. Stop with the compliments." Aiden's smirk widens, a knowing glint sparking in his gaze.

"I didn't know you had a praise kink, angel." My jaw drops. The audacity—

I slap his chest with my left arm, attempting to wiggle out of his hold, but he only tightens his grip, keeping me close.

"I don't," I say, my voice firm despite the warmth creeping up my neck. "I think we're done for today. I want to go home and take a bath." Aiden quirks a brow, licking his bottom lip. "Ugh, yes, you can join. Let's go." He gives me a full-blown smile—the kind that could make me collapse if he wasn't holding me up. Aiden doesn't smile often. Most of the time, he walks around with a resting bitch face or an annoying smirk, but when he does smile, I want to take a picture, print it out, and lock it away in a safe where only I have the key. So I can look at it whenever I want to.

"Are you and the girls coming to the game tonight?" Aiden asks as he effortlessly intertwines our hands and skates by my side toward the bench.

"Yeah. Roman is still being an ass to Alina, and I don't like it, but I'm pretty sure she will still go to support him." I sit on the bench as Aiden kneels in front of me and starts undoing my laces.

"I promise you, he cares about her," Aiden says.

"Roman's been through a lot. It's just… hard for him to

express himself. Meanwhile, your best friend? She's very expressive." I chuckle, nodding in agreement. Aiden finishes with his skates first, swaps them for slides, and then kneels again— this time to put mine on.
"Aiden, it's just slides. You don't have to do that." He ignores me, grabs our bags, slings them over his shoulder, and reaches for my hand.
This man will be the death of me. I stand and let him take my hand, a soft smile tugging at my lips.
"Let's go take that bath."
I roll my eyes, chuckling. "You're such a guy."

Twenty minutes later, we step into the house, and my jaw drops when I see Will and Maddie cuddled up on the couch. Aiden freezes beside me, equally stunned.
"When she's gone, he's dead," Roman announces from the staircase. I grin at how stressed he looks. The vein in his forehead is ready to pop, and if it does… I want front-row seats.
"This fucker came up to me and said, I like your sister. You can do whatever you want to me, but I won't stop wanting her. I punched his dumb-ass, and he just grinned at me like a damn psychopath."
I bite my lip, fighting back a laugh, and glance at Aiden, who looks just as amused.
"We're right here, Roman. I can hear you—"
"I don't give a fuck, Will."
Roman spits the words out, and this time, I laugh. Roman glares at me, so I shut up, pressing my lips together to stop laughing. I love how protective he is of Maddie. I often wish I had a sibling, someone to share

all my joy and sadness with, someone who could be there for me when I feel lonely.

"Sorry, Rome. Maybe you should call my best friend and have her come over," I say, placing my right hand on his shoulder for comfort. His glare fades into something softer and sadder, and my chest tightens.

"She won't answer my calls," he mutters. "I think I fucked everything up." I sigh, stepping forward to wrap my arms around his waist.

"It doesn't hurt to try. The Alina I know would come here in a heartbeat if you needed her to." Aiden claps a hand on Roman's back.

"Go get her, tiger. Stop acting like a little bitch and get your girl." Roman shoots him a glare before turning to me.

"Please tell him to shut the fuck up. He just ruined a great bonding moment."

I glare at Aiden, who raises his hands in mock innocence, taking a step back. I swear Aiden has no filter whatsoever.

"We're here if you need to talk. Bye!" Aiden snaps, grabbing my hand and dragging me upstairs to my room. He shuts the door behind us and locks it, slamming me against the door. I gasp as his hands trap me on both sides.

"God, he talks too much," Aiden mutters, his lips brushing against mine.

"All I wanted was to have you all to myself." His mouth trails down my collarbone, his lips grazing the sensitive skin. I tilt my head, giving him more access, and he takes it.

"Aiden…" I whisper, my breathing erratic. A deep sound rumbles from his chest, and I feel it everywhere. My left-hand sneaks into his hair, fingers curling as I pull. I force his head back and meet his gaze with a teasing smile.

"Are you going to fuck me?" I ask my voice barely a whisper. Aiden's pupils dilate. His eyes flick to my lips, dark and dangerous, as if I've just awoken something untamed inside him.

"Do you want me to?" Aiden asks, as his eyes analyze my face for any sign of hesitation. A whimper escapes me when he pulls me to his front, our bodies meshed together.

"Y-Yes." I manage to get out as his hand slides up, cupping my breast, squeezing just enough to make me arch into him. Then he grips my thighs, lifting me against him. I wrap my legs around his waist, crashing my lips against his, swallowing the groan he lets out. His tongue sweeps into my mouth, claiming, devouring—

"Guys, I need to talk to you." That was no Aiden. Fuck. I groan, hitting my head against the door at the sound of Roman's voice.

"No," Aiden whispers. "Pretend you're sleeping." I laugh softly, shaking my head. "Aiden, he's your best friend," I whisper, pulling his bottom lips between my thumb.

"I don't care. I want you. Right now."

"Please." Roman pleads, his voice cracking at the end. Aiden lifts his fist to his mouth and bites it in irritation, his entire body stiff with frustration. His eyes are dark, still clouded with desire, and I don't miss the way his jaw clenches, his patience running razor-thin. I chuckle, amused despite the heat still coursing through my veins. My heart is racing from what almost happened— what would have happened if we hadn't been interrupted.

With a sigh, I turn and open the door. Roman practically barrels into my room, not even waiting for an invitation.

"Oh, thank God," he mutters, running a hand through his hair before dropping onto my bed, shoulders slumping forward. His whole body screams exhaustion like he's been carrying the weight of something heavy for far too long.

"I need help," he admits, his voice rough and strained. I exchange a glance with Aiden, who still looks like he's debating whether or not to kick Roman out. Roman exhales sharply and leans forward, elbows on his knees.

"I can't lose Ali... She's the best thing that's ever happened to me, and I'm—" His voice cracks, and he shakes his head in frustration.

"I'm self-sabotaging and don't even know how to stop. I don't know how to love her, right. I've never known how to love someone right, Kat." My chest tightens—my poor friends. You can see how much they care about each other. Maybe this is a right person, wrong time situation. Roman doesn't do vulnerable. He doesn't let people see him break. But right now? He's breaking. I step closer, sitting on the bed beside him.

"Roman," I say softly, "Just talk to her. You know what Alina has been through. She needs communication. She needs honesty. You can't keep shutting her out." Roman lets out a hollow laugh, rubbing his hands over his face.

"And how do I even do that? Open up about what?" He looks up at me, eyes guarded yet desperate for an answer. I hold his gaze.

"Your past. Your fears. Why you act the way that you do. She doesn't need perfection, Roman—she just needs the truth." His Adam's apple bobs as he swallows.

"I don't want to hurt her. What if I say the wrong thing? What if I get angry? What if—"

"You won't," I interrupt.

"Not if you go into this remembering that she's on your side. She just wants to know you." Roman stands, pacing the room, dragging a hand through his hair.

"I don't want to blow up on her. Especially when she asks questions I don't want to answer. I want to be able to talk without—" His hands tighten into fists.

"Without shutting down." I stand, too, trying to place myself before him so he stays grounded in the conversation.

"Then start small. Tell her that it's hard for you, but you're trying. She'll understand." Roman stares at me for a long moment before nodding.

"Yeah… okay." Then, without warning, he wraps his arms around me in a tight hug. Before I can even return it, Aiden clears his throat—loudly.

"Uhm, yeah, take your hands off her now," he says, his voice laced with warning. I glare at Aiden, but Roman just smirks, unfazed. He squeezes me one last time before pulling back.

"Jealous much?" Aiden doesn't deny it. Instead, he grabs a pillow from my bed and launches it at Roman's head, which Roman quickly catches, laughing.

"Seriously, man?"

"Seriously," Aiden deadpans. I roll my eyes. They act like they are ten years old sometimes.

"Roman, just try, okay? Talk to Alina after the game. Take her out to eat, spend time together, and then bring her back to talk." Roman nods, determination flickering in his eyes. I hope he understood what I said and really tries to open up to Ali.

"Yeah. Yeah, I can do that." He exhales, shoving his hands into his pockets before giving me one last hug—purely to piss off Aiden, I'm sure. Aiden retaliates by hurling another pillow at him, this time nailing him right in the face.

"Fuck you, you jealous prick," Roman mutters, dodging the next pillow. "She's like my sister." I smile, shaking my head as he heads for the door.

"Thanks, KitKat. I appreciate it." He yells through the hallway.

"You got this," I ye. He throws one last glare at Aiden before disappearing down the hallway. The moment the door clicks shut, I spin on my heel, arms crossed.

"Why would you do that?" Aiden shrugs, unapologetic. "Because he ruined our fun time." I sigh. Of course. Aiden flops onto my bed, stretching his arms above his head, his shirt lifting just enough to reveal a sliver of skin. My eyes betray me, flickering downward before snapping back up. He notices, and a smirk tugs at his lips. "But let's go get that bath," he says, voice smug. I grab a pillow and smack him in the chest. "You're impossible." Aiden laughs, but before I can move away, he grabs me by the wrist, pulling me down onto the bed with him. His hands frame my face, his touch warm, steady—

possessive.

And then his lips are on mine. It's slow at first, teasing like he's savoring how I melt against him. But then something shifts, and suddenly, we're not just kissing—we're drowning in each other. His hand slips to my waist, fingers digging in, pulling me closer. My hands tangle in his hair, nails scratching lightly against his scalp, making him groan into my mouth. The sound sends a shiver down my spine.

I need him. But just as his hands start to roam, a familiar fear creeps in. I want to keep him, and I want this. But what happens when he learns about my past? What happens when he sees the parts of me I've kept buried? Will he still look at me the same way? Will he still want me? The thoughts are suffocating as Aiden pulls back slightly, brushing his lips over my jaw.
"You okay?" he murmurs, his voice low, gentle. I force a smile, pushing the doubts away—for now.
"Yeah," I whisper, pressing my lips to his again.
Maybe I can hold onto this a little longer before it all comes crashing down.

CHAPTER TWENTY - NINE

KATERINA

The following day, I wake up next to him. Aiden's arm is draped over my waist, his body curled around mine like it's the most natural thing in the world. His warmth seeps into me, his slow, steady breathing the only sound in the quiet room, and I hate how much I like it. How much I don't want to
move. How much I want to stay in this stolen moment, pretend that this is normal—that we are normal.
But reality crashes in too fast, too sharp because this isn't normal. We aren't normal. Whatever this is—whatever we keep doing—it isn't safe.
So, I move. I shift carefully, trying to slip out from under him without waking him up. But the second I do, Aiden grumbles in his sleep, his arm tightening around me, his nose brushing against my neck. My breath catches.

"You're not sneaky, Angel Face," he murmurs, voice rough with sleep.

I freeze. His grip tightens just enough to pull me back against his chest.

"Where do you think you're going?" I swallow, forcing myself to sound unbothered.

"To get coffee."

Aiden makes a low noise in his throat as if he doesn't believe me, but after a moment, he sighs and loosens his hold.

"Fine. But I'm stealing some." I roll my eyes as I finally escape, tugging the hem of his hoodie over my thighs before making my way to the kitchen.

The second I step into the main room, Alina is already there, sipping coffee, arms crossed, waiting.

I pause.

She tilts her head. "So, you're wearing his hoodie again." I

scowl.

"Good morning to you, too."

Alina smirks. "Didn't answer the question."

I groan, grabbing a mug and pouring my coffee like I can ignore her.

"It's comfortable."

"Mhm," she hums. "And not because you two are screwing."

I choke on my coffee. "Alina!" She laughs, propping her chin on her hand.

"Relax, Malyshka. Your secret is safe with me. For now." I

glare.

"There's no secret. Nothing is going on." Alina gives me a look.

"Kat."

"Alina." She sighs, rolling her eyes.

"Fine. Pretend all you want. But just so you know, you're the worst liar I've ever met."
I groan. "You're the worst." Alina grins before answering.
"I know."
Before I can come up with a comeback, the source of my problems walks in the kitchen—shirtless, messy hair from sleeping in and looking like he owns the place. Which, technically, he does. But still. Aiden steps behind me, his chest brushing my back as he reaches over my head to grab a mug. I tense. He leans down, his breath warm against my ear.
"Told you I was stealing some." I glare at him over my shoulder.
"You're insufferable," Aiden smirks, taking a slow sip.
"And yet, you keep ending up in my bed." My face burns while Alina chokes on her coffee, cackling. I can't believe he said that in front of Alina.

By the time I get to class, my morning irritation has doubled.
Mostly because Aiden insisted on driving me to school as if I was some fragile thing that couldn't handle the walk. We argued about it, but somehow, I still ended up in his car, listening to his annoying music, trying to ignore how my stomach flipped whenever he smirked at me. I grab his phone and lift it towards his face to unlock it. Aiden glares at me, but I ignore him. Clicking his music app, I search for Cigarettes After Sex and shuffle their playlist.
"What's with the sad music?" Aiden asks, glancing at me and then back at the road.

"It's not sad. It's just calm, soft music." Surprisingly, Aiden doesn't say anything back and lets me be until we get to campus.

And now? Now, I'm stuck next to him in class because our professor switched seating arrangements for a stupid "collaborative learning experience."

"Try to look less miserable," Aiden murmurs, leaning over as he lazily spins a pen between his fingers. I glare at him.

"I wouldn't be miserable if I didn't have to sit next to you." Aiden grins, leaning in just enough that I can smell his cologne.

"Liar. You love sitting next to me." I scoff, turning back to

my notebook. "I tolerate sitting next to you." He chuckles.

"Tolerate? Is that what you call it when you cuddle me in your sleep?" My hand tightens around my pen.

"I do not cuddle you."

"You do," he says with a grin, like he's enjoying this too much. "It's adorable, really. You even nuzzle—" I whip my head around, whispering harshly,

"If you finish that sentence, I will stab you with my pen." Aiden laughs, completely unfazed.

"Kinky." I slam my pen down and pinch the bridge of my nose, inhaling deeply. "I hate you."

"No, you don't." I open my mouth to fire back, but our professor clears her throat, cutting me off. I don't miss the victorious look Aiden shoots me. Smug bastard. Somehow, despite my best efforts, I end up back in his room. One second, we're watching a movie on his couch, and the next— His fingers are tangled in my hair, his lips on mine, his body pressing me down into the mattress, his weight everywhere on me.

"Aiden," I gasp, as his mouth trails down my jaw, his hands sliding under the hem of my hoodie— His hoodie. Aiden groans, dragging his lips back to mine, kissing me so intensely my head spins. I should stop this. But I don't. Because his hands feel too good, his body feels too right, and when he pulls away just enough to whisper,

"You drive me insane, Angel Face," my heart nearly shatters. Because I believe him.

His room is too small. Or maybe it just feels that way because he's here. Aiden stretches out on his bed, propped up against the headboard, his long legs sprawled out comfortably. I'm curled up at the other end of the bed, pretending to be invested in the movie playing on his TV. I'm not. Because all I can think about is him. The way his forearms flex when he runs a hand through his hair. The way his jaw tightens when a scene annoys him. The way his fingers drum absently against his stomach, make my gaze drop lower than it should.

I shift, tucking my legs under me. I should have left an hour ago, I have a test to study for. But I don't move. And now, in the quiet hum of his room, it feels like it's going to snap. Aiden exhales slowly. I glance up at him just as he turns his head, his dark eyes locking onto mine.

Something shifts in the air. Heavy. Charged.

I swallow hard, gripping the edge of his blanket like it might ground me.

"You're not even watching," he says, his voice rough, low,

something deeper laced beneath it. I lick my lips.

"Neither are you."

Aiden tilts his head slightly, eyes dropping to my mouth for

half a second before flicking back up. "You keep looking at me," he murmurs.
My heart slams against my ribs. "You keep looking at me
first."
His lips twitch, but there's no amusement in his expression. Only heat.
The kind that steals the air from my lungs, makes my skin
burn beneath his gaze.
I should say something sharp, something to break this tension, to remind him that I still haven't forgiven him. That I'm still mad at him for walking away, for pulling back when I wanted him to stay. But the words get stuck.
Because he's watching me like that again, like he's trying to decide if he should touch me.
Like he wants to, but knows it'll ruin everything. I turn away, pretending to adjust the blanket over my lap. "You want me to leave?"
"No," Aiden says finally, voice rough. "I don't." That admission is dangerous, because I don't want to leave either. I shift again, stretching my legs out so that my foot accidentally brushes his thigh. He stills, and so do I.
I should move away. But I don't and neither does Aiden. His breathing is deeper now, heavier, as if he's fighting something.
I bite my lip. "Aiden—"
"Come here," he says suddenly. My stomach free-falls. His voice is different now—not a demand, not a plea, but something in between. I should hesitate. I should question it.
But I don't, because I want this. More than anything.

I shift, slowly crawling toward him, my pulse wild as I settle next to him, my thigh brushing his.
Close.
Too close.
Aiden doesn't move for a long moment.
Then, slowly, he lifts his arm, giving me room to lean into him. I shouldn't but I do. His warmth is immediate, overwhelming, wrapping around me like a second skin. I rest my head against his shoulder, pretending this is normal, that my entire body isn't on fire. His fingers brush against my arm, featherlight. I suck in a sharp breath and Aiden tenses, like he wasn't expecting that reaction, but he doesn't stop. His fingers trace my skin, slow, testing and it's suddenly too much.
I pull back, turning toward him, our faces inches apart.
Big mistake.
Because now I can see everything. The way his chest rises and falls, his jaw tight with restraint. The way his eyes—black, endless, stormy with something unreadable—flicker down to my lips. Aiden exhales sharply, like he's reached his breaking point.
And before I can say a single word, he kisses me. The moment his lips crash into mine, I forget how to breathe. It's not soft, needy, raw, filled with everything we've been holding back. I gasp against him, my hands gripping his hoodie, pulling him closer even as he presses me deeper into the bed. He growls against my mouth, one hand cupping my jaw, the other gripping my waist like he's afraid I'll disappear. Like he's afraid this is all some fever dream. I tug at his hoodie, needing more, needing to feel him. Aiden pulls away just enough to yank it over his head, his breath ragged, his pupils blown wide with heat. I barely have time to take him

in before he's kissing me again, deeper, slower this time. Like he wants to memorize me.
Like he's afraid this will end too soon.
I slide my hands over his bare skin, feeling the sharp ridges of his muscles, the way his breath catches when I drag my nails down his back. He groans, pressing his forehead against mine.
What is he doing to me?

CHAPTER THIRTY

KATERINA

It started playfully. We were watching a movie and somehow, we ended up tangled with each other. I should push him away, create distance, remind myself that this is reckless, dangerous, a road we can't come back from.
But I don't.
Because Aiden Knight is everywhere—his hands on my waist, his breath against my skin, his lips trailing slow, agonizing kisses down my neck. Every touch sends a spark skittering across my nerves, my body burning too hot, my mind losing the ability to think about anything except him.
I grip my hoodie—
his hoodie that I'm still wearing—as he presses me into the mattress, his weight solid and grounding, his knee

nudging between my thighs, parting them like it's the most natural thing in the world.

His name leaves my lips in a breathy whisper, and he growls in response, his grip tightening, his fingers teasing against the bare skin of my hip beneath the oversized fabric.

"You love driving me insane, don't you?" I smirk, even though my breathing is uneven, my pulse pounding.

"Maybe."

Aiden's eyes darken. "Angel." The way he says it—low, almost possessive—sends a full- body shiver through me. I arch against him, seeking friction, something, but he just grins, dragging this moment out like he wants me to beg.

So, I do the only thing I can—I kiss him hard.

He groans, his hands sliding beneath the hoodie, fingers tracing up my ribs, slow and reverent.

"You're going to be the death of me." I bite my lip, tugging at the hem of his shirt. "Then die already."

Aiden laughs, but the sound is strained, his pupils blown wide, his gaze flicking over my face like he's committing this—me—to

memory.

Then, with a deliberate slowness, he pulls my stolen hoodie over my head, leaving me bare beneath him. He stops breathing as he looks at me, and for the first time, he's speechless.

I smirk, even though my body is burning, even though I feel like I might shatter under his gaze. "What?"

Aiden swallows, his Adam's apple bobbing. "You're fucking perfect." Warmth floods my chest, my confidence faltering for just a second before he leans down, his lips tracing a slow, torturous path down my collarbone, across my chest, and my stomach.

I let out a shaky breath. "Aiden—" I wrap one arm around his neck, and with the other hand, I pull his chain bringing his mouth into mine. My breasts press into his bare chest, and the contact sends a soft whimper past my lips. Aiden stiffens, his grip tightening on my waist.

"Kat, I won't be able to stop," he rasps, his voice thick with restraint. "My patience is wearing thin." A slow smirk tugs at my lips as I run my fingers through his hair.

"I don't want you to stop," I whisper. "I want all of you." Aiden lets out a low groan, his fingers tangling in my hair as he yanks me closer, slamming our lips together in a searing kiss. My right hand grips the nape of his neck, while my other trails down his hard, sculpted chest. My nails scratch lightly along his skin, savouring the way his muscles twitch under my touch.

"God, I've wanted to have you like this for so long," he murmurs against my lips. His hands grip the back of my thighs, wrapping them around his waist.

For a moment, he just stares at me, his eyes devouring every inch of my body, like he's trying to memorize me—trying to get his fill before he ruins me. Then, he moves.

His hips thrust forward, hitting my core and i whimper at the contact. His broad frame covering mine as he hovers over me, his forearms caging me in on either side.

A sharp moan escapes me as his mouth attacks my neck, sucking at the sensitive skin. I don't think I've told him before, but neck kisses? They're my weakness. And Aiden? He's ruthless about exploiting it.

He grinds against me, his arousal pressing hard into my core. A shudder rolls through me as I lock my legs around his waist, trying to get more friction, needing more.

"God, baby, you look unreal," he groans, his lips dragging along my collarbone.

I gasp as he sucks on the same spot again, making me see stars.

Aiden moves lower, trailing kisses down my chest, leaving love bites along the tops of my breasts. Marking me. Claiming me. His lips travel lower, stopping at my navel.

"Open your legs for me, Angel Face," he murmurs. "I want to

see all of you." A deep flush crawls up my neck, but I do as he says,

spreading myself wide for him. His eyes darken, his gaze fixed on my core like it's his next meal.

"You better take a deep breath, baby, because I'm about to leave you breathless." Before I can process his words, he pulls me to the edge of the bed and licks me from top to bottom. A sharp gasp tears from my throat.

"Aiden—"

"So fucking wet for me, Kat," he groans. "You taste so damn good."

My hips jerk off the bed as his tongue flicks over my clit, teasing, tormenting. I tangle my fingers into his hair, holding him there, needing more. Aiden slides one finger inside me, moving in sync with his tongue.

A choked moan escapes me as he curls his finger, pressing against that spot. My hips try to lift again, but his strong grip holds me still.

"I can't wait to see those pouty lips wrapped around my cock," he murmurs against me. I whimper, pleasure tightening deep in my belly.

"Aiden… I—I'm gonna come if you keep—" He slides in a second finger, filling me. The combination of his fingers and tongue sends me over the edge so fast I can't even warn him. I shatter, my entire body trembling as my orgasm crashes through me.

"Aiden-Ah" I moan his name as I shake from the mind-blowing pleasure. Aiden pulls his fingers out, and I whimper at the loss of contact.

Then, I watch as he licks them clean, eyes locked onto mine.

"Are you going to be a good girl and suck my cock, Kat?" His voice is hoarse, full of raw desire. "I'm dying to feel your mouth around me." I nod, biting my bottom lip. Aiden stands, stripping off his boxers and shorts in one go. And I freeze. My eyes widen as I stare at him. How the hell is that supposed to fit? Anywhere? Aiden notices my expression and smiles smugly.

"Don't worry, Goldie" he rasps. "We'll make it fit." I swallow hard, shifting onto my knees and moving closer. He stands above me, his cock level with my face.

"Damn, baby," he groans. "You look like a fucking wet dream right now." I wrap my fingers around him, stroking slowly, watching as his breath hitches.

I swirl my tongue around the tip, feeling his body tense. "Fuck," Aiden groans. "That feels so good, baby." I take more of him, bobbing my head up and down, letting the tip hit the back of my throat. His fingers tangle in my hair, guiding my pace.

"God, you are unreal," he mutters. I spit on the tip, stroking him faster, sucking harder, determined to ruin him. Aiden pulls back suddenly, lifting me and laying me flat on the bed. He crashes his lips onto mine, kissing me hungrily, his right hand palming my breast, fingers pinching my nipple. I moan when I feel the tip of his cock at my entrance.

"Fuck. I don't have a condom. I didn't know-" I shake my head, pulling him closer.

"I'm on birth control," I whisper against his lips, arching my back to get more friction, "And I'm clean. I swear."

"Me too. I promise." Aiden says, restraint wearing thin. I nod as he kisses me

deeply, his hand running along my inner thigh.

Then, he pushes in. I gasp, my nails digging into his back as his cock stretches me open. Aiden stills, breathing heavily.

"Fuck, Angel," he groans. "If you keep clenching my cock like that, this is gonna be over really quick." I giggle, capturing his lips in a soft kiss.

Aiden pulls out and thrusts back in, hard. I cry out, pleasure crashing through me as Aiden starts thrusting in and out, his pace steady, deep, relentless.

"Fuck, Angel. I love how your cunt swallows me whole. Made just for me."

His hand wraps around my throat, and I realize the pressure makes everything more intense.

"Harder, Aiden. I need more." Aiden adjusts himself, placing a pillow under my hips, lifting my legs, slamming into me deeper. He grips my thigh, his eyes wild as he takes all of me.

"Tell me you're mine, Angel Face," he rasps. "Tell me this pussy belongs to me." My lips part, his words only heightening the pleasure I'm feeling.

"All yours, Aiden. Only yours." And when I come again, screaming his name, I know it's true. I belong to him.

And God help me, because I think I always have.

CHAPTER THIRTY - ONE

KATERINA

The morning after is different. Not in a bad way—not in the way that makes me regret everything and push Aiden away like I probably should. But in a way that makes my heart feel too full, like it's carrying something too big for my body to hold.
I wake up still tangled in his sheets, his arm draped over my waist, his body warm and solid against mine. I shift slightly, my muscles sore in the best way, and before I can slip out of bed, Aiden tightens his hold, pulling me back against his chest with a low, sleepy groan.
"Where do you think you're going, Angel Face?" His voice is hoarse from sleep, rough and deep, making my stomach tighten.
I roll my eyes, though my lips twitch. "To get coffee."
Aiden buries his face in my neck, pressing a slow, lazy kiss against my skin. "No."
I shiver. "No?"

He smirks against my shoulder. "No. You're staying right here."

I huff a breath, twisting in his grip just enough to glare at him. "Are you kidnapping me, Knight?"

He tilts his head, pretending to think about it. "Mmm... that depends."

"On?"

His fingers trace slow, teasing circles along my bare hip. "How much you fight me on it."

I bite my lip, hating the way my body immediately responds to him, heat creeping up my neck. "You're insufferable."

Aiden smirks. "And yet baby, you still ended up in my bed."

I gasp, shoving at his chest, but he just laughs, catching my wrist and rolling us over so that he's hovering above me, his weight pressing me into the mattress. His smirk fades as he studies me, his gaze dark and unreadable.

"You okay?"

The question knocks the air from my lungs.

Because he means it. It's not just an empty phrase—he's really asking. Really checking in. And for a moment, the weight of it—of him—is almost too much.

I swallow hard, nodding. "Yeah."

Aiden watches me for a second longer, then nods, pressing a soft kiss to my forehead before finally rolling off me, giving me space.

And that—more than anything—makes my chest ache.

Eventually, I do escape his room, slipping into the kitchen to find Alina already there, sipping coffee and scrolling through her phone.

The second she looks up, her eyes narrow. "Oh my God," breathes. "You finally did it." I freeze.

"What—" She gasps, smacking the counter. "You did! You and Aiden—" I lunge for her, clapping a hand over her mouth.

"Shut up!"

Alina's eyes are gleaming as she pulls my hand away, grinning like she just won the lottery. "Was it good?"

I groan. "I hate you."

"You love me."

"I regret telling you anything."

She wiggles her eyebrows. "Oh, but you didn't tell me everything." I groan again, grabbing my coffee and stomping toward the living room. "I'm leaving."

Alina cackles behind me. "I love this day!"

I should tease her back, say something about Roman, but this thing between them is very confusing. She has been sleeping over almost everyday and i know she loves Roman, but i hate when they argue and fight. The walls in this house are too thin.

Later that day, Aiden and I end up at the rink again. Because as much as my body still aches from last night, I need this. I need the ice, the movement, the reminder that I'm still me—still capable of fighting for what I want, for what I deserve.

Aiden skates beside me, hands in his pockets, watching as I test my limits, stretching, moving carefully.

"You're pushing too hard," he says eventually.

I exhale, rolling my shoulders, testing the ache.

"I have to." Aiden sighs, stopping in front of me, his brows furrowed.

"Kat—"

"I need this, Aiden."

His jaw tightens. "I know."

I swallow, shifting my weight on my blades. "Then let me." For a second, he doesn't say anything. Then—

He nods. "Okay." I blink. "Okay?"

Aiden nods again, a small smile tugging on his lips.
"You think I'm gonna stop you?" I raise an eyebrow.
"Yes?" Aiden shakes his head, stepping closer, gripping my waist, as he pulls me closer to him. My heart starts picking up at the proximity, flashbacks of last night replaying in my head.
"I'm not here to stop you, Angel Face." I inhale sharply as he
Looks at me, his stare steady, grounding. "Then what are you here for?" He smirks, leaning in, his lips grazing my ear. Goosebumps erupt all over my body, at such a simple gesture.
"To make sure you don't fall." I nod, as I lose the battle against my own heart. He lets me skate as he watches, giving me pointers or helping me here and then. Around eight pm, Aiden drives us home. We end up tangled on the couch, a movie playing in the background that neither of us is paying attention to. I'm still wearing his hoodie, curled up against his side, his fingers lazily tracing patterns on my thigh.
And for the first time in forever—
I don't feel like I'm running from anything. I feel safe. I feel home.
Aiden presses a slow kiss to my temple, his voice quiet.
"I'm going to ruin you for any other man out there." I tilt my head up, smirking. "Not if I ruin you first."
His gaze darkens, his fingers tightening on my thigh.
"Angel Face."
I grin. "Knight." He smiles and lowers his head down to kiss me. Slow and deep and devastating.
And I let him.

CHAPTER THIRTY - TWO

AIDEN

I've spent weeks thinking about how to make this night perfect. Not just good. Not decent. Perfect. Because Kat deserves perfect.

It starts with a hoodie she wears once—oversized, washed-out black, with "Cigarettes After Sex" written across the front in white letters. I remember her tucked into my side one rainy evening, humming along to a song with no beat, no drop, no chorus—just soft melancholy and floating lyrics that stick with you long after the sound fades.

That's when I know. That's when the idea starts forming.

And tonight? Tonight, is the night.

She has no clue.

I pace in front of her dorm like an idiot, the ticket QR codes already sitting in my Apple Wallet. I've even splurged on merch ahead of time—the hoodie she's been eyeing is folded up in the backseat of my car. I can't remember the last time I tried this hard.

Hell, I don't think I ever have.

The door creaks open and there she is—Kat, with her usual soft expression and that half-smile she only gives me when I catch her off guard. She's wearing light-washed jeans, a black crop top, and a zip-up jacket. Simple. Beautiful. So her.

"You look like you're about to pass out," she teases, closing the door behind her.

"I was starting to think you were standing me up."

She rolls her eyes but slips her hand into mine like it belongs there. "Where are we going?"

"You'll see."

"You and your damn surprises." She leans into me as we walk. "If this ends with you handing me a slice of pizza, I'm not complaining."

I grin but stay quiet. Let her guess.

We get into my car, and I adjust the aux cord so it's queued. The moment I turn the ignition, "Sweet" by Cigarettes After Sex comes on.

She stills.

"You didn't—" I keep driving. Still don't say a word.

"Oh my god," she whispers, her voice cracking with emotion. "Aiden."

I glance over—just long enough to see her eyes go wide, like her heart leaps into her throat. "You didn't."

"I did."

She covers her face with both hands, then pulls them away just as fast. "Wait—seriously? You got tickets?"

"Yep."

"Cigarettes After Sex?"

"Yes, Kat."

"Tonight?"

I laugh, can't stop smiling. "We're gonna be late if you don't buckle in."

She lets out a squeal that bounces around the car, pure joy vibrating from her. "You didn't even like them when I first played them for you!"

"I never said I didn't like them. I said they were slow."

"They are slow."

"They're sad, too."

"Yeah, but it's the kind of sad that makes you feel good."

I nod. "I get it now."

She doesn't speak for the next ten minutes—just sits there with her hand in mine, a dazed look on her face like she can't believe this is real. Every so often, she squeezes my fingers or glances over and smiles like she's taking mental pictures of every second.

That alone makes every dollar worth it.

The venue is packed.

Lights buzz overhead as people shuffle in from every direction. It smells like popcorn, perfume, and rain—the kind of summer night you don't forget.

Kat's practically bouncing. "We're really here."

I reach into my jacket and hand her the hoodie I stashed.

She blinks, then gasps, pulling it from the bag. "This is the one I said I wanted last month."

"I remember."

She holds it to her chest, grinning so wide it makes her nose scrunch. "I don't know how to explain this, but this… this means so much."

I lean in, brushing my lips against her temple. "I'm glad."

She slips it on immediately—even though it's still warm—and pulls the hood over her head with a smug little smile like the luckiest girl in the world. She looks cozy. And a little like trouble.

God help me.

We get to our seats and I realize just how close we are to the stage. I hadn't noticed when I bought the tickets.

Kat turns in a slow circle, taking it all in. "This is insane. We're so close. You must've spent—"

"Don't worry about it."

"Aiden."

I look at her, dead serious. "You're worth it."

She blinks like she doesn't know what to say, then stands on her tiptoes and kisses me. Not just a peck—a soft, slow kiss that says she feels everything I feel. That her heart's racing too.

The lights dim. People start screaming.

Kat included.

She grabs my hand, and the first note rings out across the venue—low, echoing, hypnotic.

The band walks out, and the entire crowd dissolves into silence. Then applause. Then silence again.

It's the most peaceful chaos I've ever seen.

She knows every word.

I don't know all the songs, but I don't care. I spend more time watching her than the stage.

She sings, sways, whispers lyrics under her breath. Her thumb brushes the back of my hand again and again, like she can't stop touching me, like she doesn't want to let go. And when they start "Apocalypse," she turns to me, her lips already moving before she leans in.

"This one's my favorite," she whispers against my ear. "It reminds me of you."

I swallow hard, then smile. "Yeah?"

She nods, her nose brushing mine. "Every time I hear it. It's like... how I feel when I'm around you."

My heart slams against my ribs. "I don't think anyone's ever said anything like that to me before."

She smiles. "Good. I like being your first."

Then she kisses me—slow, deep, deliberate. I feel her heartbeat in her lips, in her fingers, in the way she presses into me like the rest of the world has fallen away.

I wrap my arms around her and pull her closer.

She doesn't let go for a long time.

After the encore, we stay in our seats even as the crowd starts to thin out. Kat tugs the hoodie sleeves down over her hands and leans her head on my shoulder.

"I'm never forgetting tonight," she says quietly.

"Good," I say. "Neither am I."

She turns to look at me. "Why'd you do all this?"

I think about it. I could joke. Deflect. Say something easy.

But I don't want to.

I look her in the eyes and say, "Because I've never wanted to try this hard with anyone. Ever. And you... you make me want to be better. You make me want more."

She stares at me, her bottom lip quivering slightly.

"I didn't know I was lonely until you came along," I say.

"But I was. For a long time."

Kat blinks fast, then leans in again, her hands on either side of my face. She kisses me like she's giving me something sacred.

"I feel the same," she whispers.

I pull her into my chest, and we sit there while the crew sweeps up confetti and the amps buzz into silence. The afterglow of the concert still hums through the air, but all I can focus on is the girl wrapped in my arms.

Kat.

Mine.

Getting out of a concert arena is not joke, especially when twenty thousand other people are there with you. Outside, the air has cooled. Kat kicks off her heels and walks barefoot next to me, holding them in one hand while her other stays looped through mine.

I wave down a cab and open the door for her, helping her in. As the cab pulls away from the curb, she leans into me and lays her head against my chest.

Her voice is soft when she asks, "Are you staying with me tonight?"

My heart does that stutter-thing it always does when she catches me off guard.

"Do you want me to?"

She nods without lifting her head. "More than anything."

I swallow. "Okay." We get back to the hotel and don't say much on the ride up the elevator. There's a weight in the air—not heavy, not tense. Just charged.

Like we both know something has shifted between us. When we reach her room, she unlocks the door, steps inside, then turns to look at me. "You coming in?"

I follow her.

The moment the door clicks shut, she wraps her arms around me again, her face in my chest.

"Thank you," she whispers. "This was the best night of my life."
I run my fingers through her hair, kiss the top of her head. "It's the best night of mine, too."
We stay like that for a while—her in my hoodie, barefoot and beautiful, with her heart pressed against mine.
And for once, everything feels right.
Simple. Real. Ours

I don't know how long I've been staring at the ceiling. Kat sleeps beside me, her leg slung over mine, her breathing soft and steady. The hoodie I gave her is half-slid off one shoulder, exposing bare skin in the dim hotel room light. Her fingers are curled into the fabric of my shirt like she's afraid I'll vanish.
And part of me feels like I might.
Tomorrow is the surgery.
The thought alone makes me sore—not in my body, but deep in my chest. The kind of ache that doesn't come from anything physical. It's the weight of everything ahead, pressing down, trying to squeeze the breath out of me. I've done all the tests. I know the risks. The logistics. The science.
But none of that helps right now.
Sophia needs this.
She barely said anything when we talked on the phone two nights ago. She doesn't anymore. Not about this. Not about how it feels. She's tired. I can hear it in every pause, every breath.
All she said was, "There's time to back out." Like I could.

She's my little sister—the only person who's known every version of me and never stopped seeing someone worth believing in. She believed in me before I had any idea who I was. I'm giving her my stem cells. But if I could give her everything—my strength, my future, my lungs, my heart—I would.

I close my eyes for a second and try to breathe through the anxiety. It hums beneath my ribs like an engine idling, waiting to roar. My hand finds Kat's back on instinct, fingers brushing across warm skin.

She shifts slightly. "Are you okay?" Her voice is low and raspy, thick with sleep.

I nod. "Didn't mean to wake you."

"You didn't." She props herself up on one elbow and looks at me. Her eyes are barely open, but they see straight through me. "Your chest is tight again. I can feel it."

Of course she can. She always does.

I let out a long breath. "Just thinking."

Kat moves closer, resting her head on my shoulder. Her hand finds my chest, like she's trying to quiet whatever lives there.

"About tomorrow?"

"Yeah."

She doesn't fill the silence. She never does. She just lays there with me, grounding me with her body, her breath, her presence. That's her way. She doesn't push. She anchors.

"I'm not scared of the surgery," I say finally. My voice feels small. "I'm scared it won't be enough."

"It will be," she whispers.

I glance down at her. "You don't know that."

"No," she says, meeting my gaze. "But I believe it. And so does Sophia."

That belief—it feels heavier than doubt, somehow. I swallow hard.

"She wouldn't say it out loud, but I know she thinks... I'm all she has."

"You are."

The room goes still again. Not quiet, exactly—just thick. Like there's meaning in every unspoken word between us. Kat runs her fingers across my ribs, slow and careful.

I speak without thinking. "Did I ever tell you what my dad said the day we found out she relapsed?"

Kat's body tenses just slightly. "No."

"He didn't even look up from his laptop," I say. "Just muttered something like, 'It's always something with that girl.'" My jaw clenches. "Like she was a burden."

Kat sits up, cross-legged beside me now. There's steel in her eyes even though her hair's a mess and she's still half-asleep.

"I'm going to say something, and I need you to hear me."

I meet her eyes.

"You are not your father. And Sophia is not a burden."

I nod, throat tight. The words hit harder than I expect.

"She's lucky to have you," Kat says, softer now. "You don't talk about it, but you've practically raised her."

"Maria helped."

"Yeah, but Maria's not the one missing sleep every night. Or carrying guilt like it's stitched into her spine."

I stare at her. At the way she's looking at me like she sees something I can't. I don't know how I thought I could do any of this without her.

She leans in and presses a kiss to my cheek, letting it linger.

"I'll be there after. When you wake up. I'm not going anywhere."

That almost undoes me.
I pull her into my chest and bury my face in her hair.
"Thank you," I murmur. "Just… thank you."

The hospital is cold.
Not the usual cold. Not just air-conditioned. This kind of cold lives in the tiles, in the lighting, in the walls. It gets into your skin.
Even though I've been here before—for tests, blood draws, briefings—today is different.
This is game day.
Aunt Maria meets me at the check-in waiting room. Her hair's pulled back in a rushed, messy bun. Her eyes look tired, but when she sees me, she smiles like she's trying to transfer all the strength she has into me.
"There's my brave boy." I hug her and let myself sink into it. For a second, I don't have to be strong. She holds my hand as the nurse walks me through the final steps. There's an IV. Paperwork. Monitors. She kisses my forehead before they start to wheel me away.
Kat hasn't come yet.
And part of me thinks—maybe that's for the best. She doesn't need to see me like this. Pale. Hooked up. Half-dressed in a gown that doesn't even close right in the back. But then the curtain slides open, and she steps in. She's in sweats and my hoodie, no makeup, hair in a braid she clearly slept in. Her eyes land on mine and everything in me just… stills.
"You shouldn't be back here," I whisper. She walks straight to me like I didn't say anything and grabs my hand.
"I told you I'd be here."

I stare at her. "They're going to give me anesthesia in a few minutes. I might say some weird shit."
She smiles. "Can't wait."
I want to say more, but I'm suddenly tired. More tired than I've ever felt. "Kat—"
"Shh." She brushes my hair off my forehead. "You've already done the hard part. Just rest now."
The nurse steps in. "Ready?"
I look at Kat. Then back to the nurse. "Yeah. Ready."
The meds hit fast.
Everything slows.
My last thought before the dark swallows me is Sophia's laugh.
And Kat's hand still in mine.
I wake up groggy. And sore as hell.
It feels like someone took a hammer to my lower back and then backed a car over my hips for good measure. My body is lead. My brain fog. But I'm awake.
The nurse leans over to adjust my blankets. "You're doing great, Aiden. Everything went as expected." I nod slowly, my head swimming.
"Your aunt's outside. And your... girlfriend?"
"Let her in," I mumble.
A few seconds later, Kat walks in. She's holding a coffee and a giant water bottle, but the second she sees me, her whole face softens.
"You look like hell," she says, voice gentle but teasing.
"Feel worse."
She sets everything down and moves beside me. Her fingers brush my hair back from my forehead, careful, familiar. "I brought you a hoodie. It's cold in here."
"Don't move me," I croak. "I might scream."
She laughs under her breath and sits down, taking my hand. "Okay. No movement. I got you."

Aunt Maria steps in next, her eyes red but smiling.
"You did good, baby."
"Is Sophia okay?" I ask, even though my voice barely works.
"She's doing great," Maria says. "Resting. The doctors are optimistic."
Relief floods my system like a second dose of anesthesia. Heavy. Warm. Kat doesn't leave my side. She holds my hand the whole time. Whispers things I'll barely remember later. But I remember he head on my thigh, resting when the painkillers finally kick in.
Her soft humming under her breath—one of the songs from last night.
And her voice, just before I drift off again:
"You're her hero, you know that?"
No. But hearing it in Kat's voice makes me believe it. Just a little. And for the first time in weeks, I let myself rest.
Because the girl I love is here. And my sister has a real shot now. That's everything, I could ever ask for.

CHAPTER THIRTY - THREE

KATERINA

The hospital room is too quiet. Too sterile. Too still. Too much like every worst-case scenario that has ever haunted me.

Aiden is lying in the hospital bed, pale against the stark white sheets, an IV hooked up to his arm, his normally sharp eyes dulled with exhaustion.

He looks small like this, vulnerable in a way I've never seen before. And I don't like it. But I hate the alternative more.

Because this? This means Sophia has a chance. And now, I'm here—watching over him, waiting for him to wake up, wishing I could somehow absorb his pain, do something to make this easier.

The door opens softly, and I glance up to see Will standing
there, his face drawn with worry. "He's still out?" he asks quietly.

I nod, looking back at Aiden's face. "Yeah."
Will exhales, rubbing a hand down his face as he walks further into the room. "You know, he acts like nothing gets to him, but this? This took a lot out of him."
I swallow the lump in my throat, my fingers curling around Aiden's hand. "I know."
Will watches me for a moment before sitting down across from me. "Thanks for being here." I glance at him, surprised. "Of course I'm here. Where else would I be?"
Will smirks slightly. "If you'd asked me a few months ago, I'd have guessed anywhere but here."
I let out a dry laugh. "Yeah, well. A lot has changed."
Will's smirk fades into something softer. "Yeah. It has."
Silence stretches between us, comfortable but heavy. Finally, Will sighs, pushing himself up. "I'm going to check on Sophia. Maria's with her now, but she'll want an update."
I nod. "Tell her I'll come by soon."
Will hesitates for a second, then nods and slips out of the room, leaving me alone with Aiden again.
I exhale, shifting in my chair, adjusting the blanket I threw over him earlier.
His fingers twitch and my heart leaps into my throat. "Aiden?"
His eyelids flutter, his brow pinching slightly before his eyes slowly open, unfocused and hazy.
"Angel Face?" His voice is hoarse, barely above a whisper.
I bite my lip, relief crashing over me. "Yeah. I'm here."
Aiden blinks up at me, confusion flickering across his features as he takes in his surroundings. "Hospital?"

I nod, squeezing his hand. "You just had surgery, remember?" His eyes close for a second before he groans, shifting slightly.

"Feels like I got hit by a truck."

I roll my eyes, biting back a smile. "That's because you decided to donate part of your actual body, of course you'll feel like shit."

He smirks weakly. "Flattering, Goldie."

I huff, but my chest is tight, my heart still hammering in my ribs. "You scared me, you know."

Aiden's smirk falters. He studies me for a long moment, his expression unreadable, before his fingers squeeze mine lightly. "I'm okay."

I shake my head, my throat burning. "I was terrified of something happening to you."

His eyes soften. "It's Sophia." I sigh, pressing my forehead against our joined hands.

"You're impossible." I mutter, caressing his jaw, as I gaze at his eyes.

Aiden chuckles weakly. "And yet, you love me." My breath catches.

I freeze.

Aiden's smirk is still in place, but there's something real behind his words, something raw and unguarded. Something that terrifies me. I don't say anything. I can't.

Because I don't know what to say, but Aiden just watches me, his fingers tracing slow, lazy circles against my skin, like he's waiting for me to catch up. Like he already knows.

I swallow hard, glancing toward the door. "Will went to check on Sophia. I should—"

Aiden's grip tightens. "Stay."

I inhale sharply, looking back at him.

His gaze is steady, unwavering, even as exhaustion weighs down his features.
"Stay with me."
My heart stumbles over itself. How can I say no?

Aiden is the worst patient. I should've expected it. The guy doesn't know how to sit still for more than five minutes, and now, being forced to recover after donating his stem cells, he's practically climbing the walls.
"Kat, I swear to God, if you try to make me drink another smoothie, I'm going to lose my mind." I narrow my eyes at him from across the kitchen.
"You just had surgery, Aiden. Your body needs proper nutrition." He groans, slumping further into the couch like a petulant child.
"I need real food." I cross my arms.
"You need to stop being a stubborn idiot and listen to me." Aiden lifts a brow, smirking. "You like bossing me around, don't you?" I grab a pillow from the armchair and chuck it at him.
"Shut up and drink your smoothie, Aidy." He catches it easily, grinning.
"You're lucky I'm too weak to fight back." I roll my eyes but bite back a smile.
The truth is, I don't mind taking care of him. If anything, it's nice—making sure he's resting, keeping him from overexerting himself, having an excuse to be close to him without overthinking it. It feels normal in a way I wasn't expecting.

And it's easier to focus on him than on the what-ifs that still linger in the back of my mind. But today, for the first time in weeks, we finally get some good
News. Sophia's numbers are up.
Her body is responding to the transplant, and when Will calls to tell us, I watch Aiden's entire body sag with relief.
"That's—" He exhales, shaking his head like he can't believe it. "That's good. That's really fucking good."
I nod, squeezing his hand. "It's working."
Aiden blinks rapidly, looking away like he's trying to keep it together. "Yeah."
I don't say anything else. I just slide my fingers between his,
letting him hold on as tightly as he needs.
Later that night, I wake up to the sound of his voice. It takes me a second to register what's happening. I'm half-asleep, curled up under a blanket on the couch, when I hear him in the other room. His voice is low, tight with frustration.
"No, Dad, you don't get to pretend you care now." I freeze.
Dad.
Aiden's dad. The one who barely exists in his life, the one who has never been there for Sophia, the one who walked away and stayed away.
I sit up, my stomach twisting as Aiden's voice grows sharper. "She's not a fucking disease," he snaps, his voice getting louder
. "She's your daughter, and she's fighting for her life, and you can't even be bothered to—"
A pause. A long one.
I hear Aiden exhale, the kind of breath that sounds like he's trying not to break something.

"Right," he finally says, voice quieter now. "That's what I thought."

Another silence, then a harsh laugh, bitter and cold. "Yeah, well. Don't worry. I've been taking care of things without you for a long time. We don't need you now."

And then— Aiden hangs up. I don't know how long I sit there, my heart pounding, waiting for him to come back into the living room. When he finally does, his jaw is tight, his hands clenched into fists at his sides.

He stops when he sees me awake, his expression flickering with something unreadable. "You heard that?" I nod slowly. "Yeah."

Aiden rubs a hand over his face, letting out a rough sigh. "It's fine."

I raise an eyebrow. "That didn't sound fine."

He exhales through his nose, shaking his head. "It's nothing I didn't already know."

I hesitate, watching the way his muscles are tensed, like he's holding everything inside, refusing to let himself feel it.

So, I stand up, crossing the room before I can talk myself out of it, and wrap my arms around his waist. Aiden stiffens. For a second, he doesn't react at all, but then his arms wrap around me, his body sinking into mine as he exhales slowly, his breath warm against my hair. We don't speak. We don't need to. He just holds onto me, and I let him.

And for once, Aiden Knight doesn't have to be strong alone.

CHAPTER THIRTY - FOUR

KATERINA

It's been a week since the surgery and Aiden is feeling better. He was cleared by his doctor yesterday, so he is good to get back on ice. We're currently at our house right now, having dinner with Roman and Graysen. I'm mad at him. Roman. He keeps hurting my best friend, but he is also my best friend. I know he is not doing it intentionally, but it doesn't make it hurt less.

Truth is, I had missed sitting down with all the boys. With everything that's been happening, we haven't had a proper meal in a a good minute.

"How's Sophia doing?" Roman asks as he stabs his steak. I grimace at the sight of his almost raw meat. I don't know how he eats that.

"Something wrong, Kat?" Roman smirks, cutting his steak and chewing a piece.

"I think I'm going to throw up. That is raw. I can see it moving." I gag a little, covering my mouth with my hand as I look away from him.

Aiden, who's sitting next to me, laughs, wrapping his large hand around my left thigh.

"Breathe, Angel Face."

I shake my head and look away from Roman, straight into Aiden's beautiful eyes. God, I'm obsessed with this man. He is so selfless and kind.

Aiden looks away from me and returns his attention to Roman.

"To answer your question, she is doing great. Her numbers are improving, and it seems like her body is accepting my cells." I bring my left hand over Aiden's and give it a squeeze.

"Will is with her right now. That's why he isn't here," Aiden adds, taking a bite of his steak. I see Roman roll his eyes, and I giggle.

"Is that where he is? I thought he was with my sister, eating each other's faces." I laugh at his dig against Will. I know Roman loves Will, but I also know he hates seeing them both, kiss around him.

"Why are you so mad, Roman?" I ask, raising an eyebrow. "Are you mad because you blew it with Ali? I keep telling you to give it time, but you won't listen to me." Roman stabs his food, clearly angry at my comment, but I don't care. Aiden and I tried to help him see reason, but with Roman, that word doesn't exist in his vocabulary. So, what does he do? Hurt my best friend over and over again with his stupid decisions.

"Stay out of it, Kat. That's between Alina and I."

I press my lips into a thin line and nod. "Whatever." Aiden squeezes my thigh again to reassure me, and I take a deep breath.

"Are you guys coming to Alexei's birthday bash tomorrow night?" I ask, taking a bite of my salad.
Graysen chuckles, shaking his head.
"If I don't kill him beforehand, yes, I'll be there." I let out a chuckle as Graysen's phone goes off.
"Speak of the devil. Why is your friend such a diva?" I laugh, and Aiden joins in.
Alexei is definitely a diva. He is the loudest person in the room but the one person who will never make you feel alone. If he sees you by yourself, he will make sure to introduce you to everyone and stick by your side. A great friend.
"He keeps asking my opinions about how clothes look on him. They are clothes. They all look good on him," Graysen grumbles.
Roman starts laughing, shaking his head.
"He wants your opinion, dude. He knows he looks good. He just wants you to say it. YOU."
I turn my head toward Aiden, tilting it in Roman's direction.
This guy gives great advice, but I wish he would take it himself.
I think Roman is a great person. A little childish, of course, but I know he loves my best friend. He just doesn't know how to love her right. Unfortunately for him and Maddie, their family life wasn't the best. Giving out their love to someone is something foreign for them.
"God, I'm so stupid. That's why he keeps pouting."
Roman pats Graysen's back, pressing his lips together.
After dinner, I follow Aiden upstairs into his room.
I jump onto his bed and lay down with a smile. Aiden joins me, resting his head on my tummy.
"I know you're mad at Roman about Alina, but please talk to him about it."

I huff as Aiden lifts his head and turns to look at me. "Roman's dad used to beat his mom in front of him and then move on to Roman." A gasp leaves my mouth at the information.

"Roman would sleep in front of Maddie's door, just in case his dad ever decided to hurt her. That's the kind of person he is. It's hard for him to open up and let people in. He doesn't trust easy and has been through a lot. I understand Alina's frustration, but he has a lot of trauma."

I nod, pressing my lips together as memories flood my mind. "Max used to drop me on purpose whenever he was mad at

me and then apologize, saying it was an accident." Aiden wraps his arms around my hips, pulling me closer to him.

"You don't have to tell me."

I shake my head. "I want to. I really want to."

Aiden nods, placing small kisses on the top of my thighs. "Whenever guys would talk to me at school or the academy,

he would get jealous. He hated that I was a better skater than him, so he would always pick at my insecurities." A tear drops down my cheek as I continue talking.

"You're going to think I'm crazy, but I still hear him in my head. Even now. Whenever something important is happening, or my anxiety kicks in, I hear his voice telling me I'm not good enough."

"He did a number on me for sure. Fucked with my head so bad. But it wasn't that what ruined us. Before our last qualifier for the Olympics, he saw me talking to one another skater and he started arguing with me, yelling me and telling me i was a cheating bitch." I let out a scoff at the memory.

"For talking with a fucking guy who, by the way, was on our team."

"We started our routine and he dropped me on my head. I ended up in a coma for almost 3 weeks because of that fall. I guess I hit the ice so bad, that I fractured my skull." Aiden uses his thumb to rub shapes on my thigh over and over, the gesture calming me down.

"When I woke up at the hospital, he was the first person I saw. He told me that he wished I had died. That was the day he tried to rape me, while I was in a fucking hospital bed." I gulp, still hearing the screams I let out until a nurse heard.

I feel Aidens thumbs rub away tears, I didn't know had escaped.

"Did the bastard hurt you?" I shake my head staring at his pretty brown eyes.

"No. Thankfully one of the nurses heard me scream and he stopped. After that whole mess, I told my coach I quit. She ended up yelling at me, and told me, I was ruining everything and that Max didn't do anything, I just overreacted and tried to ruin his life, cause he didn't want to be with me."

"I opened up to her and she stepped all over my feelings, not caring. I fucking hate her so much." Two arms circle around me as Aiden pulls me towards his chest. Aiden rubs circles into my skin, grounding me.

"At first, it was just scratches or bruises, nothing bad. He made me feel awful about my hips and weight, saying I needed to be under a certain number."

Aiden tightens his grip around me. "You are enough, Kat. You are perfect."

I take a deep breath, letting his words sink in, giving him a small smile.

"When we filed the lawsuit, the news spread everywhere. Everyone called me names, saying I just wanted a big payout."
Aiden's eyes burn with anger, but he stays quiet, letting me speak.
"That's when my dad found me, and the rest, well… you know the rest. Here I am."
Aiden gives me a smile before bringing his lips to mine. His kiss is slow, reassuring, and filled with something I've been searching for my entire life.
Love.
"He deserves all the punches I gave him. Next time, I won't stop until it's him in a coma." I shake my head, wrapping my arms around him.
"If you do that, you'll end up in jail. I hate him but he is not worth your future." Aiden nods placing a kiss on the top off my head. I take a deep breath feeling relieved. I have been holding this in for so long. My friends are the only people that know. It feels so good to tell Aiden.
"You are so strong, Angel Face. Don't let an ugly, cowardly bastard bring you down." I laugh, throwing my head back cause Aiden is right. Max is a fucking coward.
"I wish instead of hearing him, you could hear me or your friends telling you how proud we are of you." I stare into Aiden's eyes, brushing his hair from his forehead. "Thank you for telling me." He whispers, pressing his lips to mine again, and this time, I let myself get completely lost in him.
"Thank you for listening to me." I say pulling away.
"Always Angel Face. Let's get some sleep." I nod laying down next to him and drift into a deep sleep feeling safe in Aidens arms.

I wake up to Aiden's alarm blaring, the sound cutting through the early morning stillness. His face is nestled in the crook of my neck, his arms wrapped securely around me, his steady breaths warming my skin.

A slow smile tugs at my lips as I run my hand up and down his back, savouring the feel of him so close.

"Baby, if you keep doing that, I'm going to be late for practice," he murmurs, his deep, sleep-laced voice sending shivers down my spine.

So hot. Yep, I'm never sleeping in my own bed again if it means waking up to this.

"I wish you didn't have practice. I just want to stay in bed with you all day." I tighten my arms around him, pressing my face against his chest.

"Me too," he sighs, pressing a kiss to my hair. "But unfortunately, we both have to be responsible adults."

I groan, but when he pats my back playfully, I roll away, reluctantly slipping out of bed.

After a quick shower, I braid my hair, leaving a few loose strands to frame my face, and apply some mascara, blush, and a soft pink lipstick. I pull on my Lululemon leggings, a fitted long sleeve top, and my thick jacket before grabbing my backpack and gym bag. I double-check that I have everything I need, before heading downstairs.

Roman is leaning against the kitchen island, chatting with Aiden when I walk in. The moment he sees me, he grabs a coffee from the cupholder and holds it out to me like a peace offering.

"Truce? Don't hate me, please. You're my best friend."

I can't help but smile as I take the cup from him.
"You're lucky I love coffee."
"Hey, what about me?" Aiden protests, raising his hands in mock outrage.
I glance at him with a smirk.
"You already know I love you." Roman says to Aiden with chuckles, shaking his head before his expression turns serious.
"I'm sorry for how I acted yesterday, Kat. I know relationships are hard, especially when you're not used to understanding the love you're getting."
His words soften my irritation, and I reach out, squeezing his arm.
"I don't hate you, Roman. I just want you to stop running from something that could be good for you."
He nods before wrapping me in a quick hug. Aiden clears his throat loudly.
"You have two seconds, Roman. Yep, time's up. Hands off."
Roman groans, stepping away. "I really don't like you sometimes. You won't even let me hug her."
Aiden shrugs unapologetically. "Hug the wall, not my girl."
I laugh, sipping my coffee as Aiden strides toward me. He bends down and presses a lingering kiss to the top of my head before wrapping his arms around me.
"My girl, Roman. Only I can give her hugs." My heart stutters.
My girl.
We haven't talked about labels, but something about the way he says it makes warmth bloom in my chest. Aiden's lips move, but I realize I'm too distracted to process his words.
"What did you say, babe?" I ask, squeezing his arm.
"Let's go before we're late."

I nod, waving goodbye to Roman as Aiden and I head out to his car. We make it to the arena just in time. Aiden and I go our separate ways, but not before he pulls me in for a quick kiss.

As soon as I step into the locker room, I'm immediately tackled into a group hug.

"Morning, pookie! Are you excited for my party tonight?" Alexei grins, practically bouncing.

I chuckle and nod. "Of course. Wouldn't miss it."

Alexei launches into a dramatic rant about his outfit choices, and Maddie joins in. I turn toward Alina, noticing the way she forces a smile, nodding at the conversation but not really engaging. It's fake. I've seen that look before.

As Alexei and Maddie head toward the ice, I linger behind with her. "Are you okay?" I ask, squeezing her arm.

She hesitates before shaking her head. "I'm not. I fucking am not. I keep thinking about him, Kat. I care about him so much, and I'm scared to lose him."

I sigh, pulling her into a hug as she buries her face in my shoulder. "You won't lose him, Ali. He cares about you, too. He just needs help figuring it out. Give it time, please. That guy is wrapped around your finger, I promise you."

She wipes her tears away. "I don't know how to give it time. I'm scared. The way he shuts down and runs from questions scares me."

I nod, rubbing her arm. "I get it. Sometimes men don't know how to be vulnerable. But that doesn't mean he doesn't care about you. He had a really hard life, Ali. He's never had someone try to be there for him. Give it time."

She exhales shakily, tightening her ponytail. "Okay. I'll try. I just... miss you. I need you to move into the figure skating house already so I can crawl into your bed when I'm sad."

I smile, linking my arm through hers. "I miss you, too."

We head onto the ice, where Alina delivers a flawless routine. I catch Roman sneaking glances at her every five seconds. Every time their eyes meet, they both look away.

These two, I swear.

My own gaze searches the ice until it lands on Aiden. The moment he looks up, our eyes lock. My heart stumbles, my breath catching in my throat. He grins and winks at me. My knees nearly buckle, and I clutch Alina's arm for support. I grin back and blow him a kiss, which he pretends to catch.

"You guys are so cute, it makes me sick," Alina teases.

I laugh, turning toward her. "You deserve this too, Ali."

She squeezes me tight, and I hug her back.

Hours later, I find Aiden on the phone. The second he says my name, a squeal erupts from the speaker. "Kit-Kat, can you come see me?"

I grab the phone, my face lighting up when I see Sophia's tiny, excited expression. "Hi, pretty girl! How are you feeling?"

Aiden wraps his arms around my waist, resting his chin on my shoulder as I talk to his sister.

"I'm doing so much better. My superhero healed me," she says, pointing to Aiden. My cheeks ache from smiling.

"Do you want us to bring you anything?" She shakes her head. "Just my favorite person."

Aiden feigns offense. "Me, right?" Sophia giggles. "I was talking about Kat, but you're okay too, I guess."

Aiden gasps in mock betrayal.

"I've been replaced?"

Sophia grins. "Can you blame me?" Aiden glances at me, his gaze softening.

"No, I can't blame you at all. She's my favorite person, too." My breath catches.

"We'll head out there now and see you in a little, okay?" Sophia nods eagerly before saying goodbye and hanging up.

As soon as the call ends, I turn to Aiden with pleading eyes, and he smirks like he already knew this was coming.

"Fine, Angel Face," he murmurs, pressing a quick kiss to my forehead before grabbing his keys. We gather our things, tossing them into the backseat of his car before heading out. The drive is easy, familiar, filled with quiet conversations and Aiden's hand resting on my thigh. Halfway there, he makes a quick stop at the store to grab Sophia's favorite ice cream, and I can't help but smile at how effortlessly thoughtful he is.

Twenty minutes later, we arrive at the hospital. The second Sophia sees me, she throws herself off her bed and into my arms.

"Oh my gosh, I missed you so much!" she squeals, wrapping her tiny arms around my neck.

I laugh, holding her close, careful not to squeeze too tight. "I missed you too, pretty girl. Are you ready to get your hair braided?"

Sophia gasps, nodding rapidly, excitement buzzing off her in waves.

"I see how it is—you don't care about your brother at all," I tease.

She giggles mischievously before turning and rushing over to Aiden. He effortlessly scoops her up, spinning her in the air as she squeals.

"Where's Auntie Maria?" Aiden asks, glancing around the room as he sets her down gently.

"She went to grab some food," Sophia answers, still grinning.

Aiden nods before pulling out the small ice cream tub and placing it inside her small mini fridge. "Alright, I take it back—you're my favorite person, Aiden."

I burst out laughing as Aiden gapes at her in mock betrayal. "Ice cream bribery works so fast with you," I say, shaking my head. Sophia shrugs, completely unbothered.

The three of us play uno, while chatting about the skating class Aiden and I teach. Sophia's eyes light up as she declares that she's going to join once she's cleared, and the excitement in her voice makes me smile so hard my cheeks ache.

Once we finish, I settle in beside her on the bed, carefully braiding her hair as we watch a movie. Her tiny fingers relax against the blanket, and before long, she drifts off to sleep. The steady rhythm of her breathing fills the room, and I take a moment to watch her, feeling a warmth settle deep in my chest. Just as I tuck the last strand of hair into place, the door opens, and Maria steps inside, her face lighting up when she sees us. "It's so good to see you both," she says, her eyes filled with gratitude.

"You too," I reply, standing to greet her. We chat for a while, catching up as she glances between Sophia's peaceful form and Aiden, who looks completely at ease beside me.

Eventually, we say our goodbyes and head back to the house to get ready for Alexei's party.

Spending time with Sophia always fills me with so much energy. She's a burst of light in my life, and being with her and Aiden feels so right.

CHAPTER THIRTY - FIVE

AIDEN

 I am definitely beating up people tonight. No, not because of me. Not at all. Alexei's birthday party is tonight and my girl looks like a fucking goddess. I know I will have to check motherfuckers all night and I'm not looking forward to that.

The moment Kat walked into my room to ask me if she looked good, I just wanted to grab her, throw her in my bed and lock us in my room forever. So no one could take her away.

Kat has on a pair of light pink low waist cargo pants, that hug her curves too well. For a top, she has on a small black bralette shirt, that makes her look so good. Her hair is wavy and reaches her hips. Her tiny waist and toned stomach are on display and she looks beautiful. She applies her lipstick in front of my mirror and I can't take my eyes off of her. I let out a groan and rub my face with my left hand as my right rests on my hips. "What is it?" Kat asks turning towards me, her eyebrows dipping in confusion. I walk towards her wrapping my arms around her waist bringing her closer to me.

"You are so fucking beautiful it drives me crazy." My angels face breaks into a full blown grin. I lean down and give her a chaste kiss.

"Aiden! I just put lipstick on." Kat whines getting out of my hold and turning around to face the mirror. She makes sure her lipstick is good and runs her fingers through her hair to make sure it isn't tangled. I decided to put on a pair of black denim jeans with a black short sleeve, simple as always.

I put on my white sneakers as Kat puts on hers and then we walk out of my room hand in hand.

"God I'm excited to see Maddie and Alina tonight. Also baby, we need to Uber back cause I really want to drink tonight." I smile at Kat's rambling but nod my head at every word she says. "Aiden, please dance with me tonight. I really want too." I chuckle as she squeezes my hand. She's so cute. We get inside my car and I start driving towards the figure skating house. Kat will be moving out in two months and this will be her future home. For some reason it hurts to think that she won't be living with us anymore. That I won't be able to walk across the hall and give her a kiss or just see her after a long day of practice.

I wrap my right hand around her thigh and Kat's lips part in surprise.

Oh… someone's s in the mood tonight. I smirk rubbing her thigh up and down as Kat parts her legs open and turns her head to look at me.

"What is it angel face?" I ask my eyes dropping to her lips as they part open more.

"Aiden?" I tilt my head as my eyes go from the road to my beautiful girl.

"Yes baby?" I reply my eyes roaming her face, that is full of lust as she looks at me with the same hazy look on her face.

"Touch me please." Kat whispers. I grip the steering wheel with my left hand, hard enough that my knuckles turn white. My right hand moves from her thigh and into her core. I rub her through her pants, and Kat lets out a moan as she bites her lower lip.

"Fuck Kat, I won't be able to drive us there in one piece if you moan like that again." Kat grinds her hips into my hand as she tries to hold in her moans. Undoing her cargo pants belt, I slide my hand inside her pants and into her heat. When my bare skin makes contact with her wet folds, my girl moans again.

"Fuck Aiden, that feels so good." I groan, taking a sharp turn, which makes Kat squeal and park next to a tree.

"I'm so hard angel, I fucking need you. I can't go to this party like this." Kat grins, getting out of her cargo pants, while I pull my jeans down. My cock sprung free and Kat giggles, as she straddles my lap naked. I let out a breath of air, feeling the pool between her legs hug my cock. "So hard, so fucking ready for my pussy." Kat whispers in my ear, making my skin break out in gooseflesh. Kat rubs her pussy over my cock and I groan at the wet feel of her heat.

"I need you Aiden. I need you to fuck me." I smile wrapping my hand around her neck and bringing her face down on me.

"Fuck." Kat whispers as she looks at her pussy sliding up and down my length. I lift her up by her hips as she guides the head of my cock on her wet pussy. I lower her down slowly, as she adjusts around me.

I hiss when I feel her tightness clench around me. Kat leans into my neck and nibbles the spot right under my ear, sucking my neck and leaving sweet kisses.

"Fuck Kat, your needy pussy takes my cock in so well angel. All fucking mine." I thrust up as she lowers into me and Kat moans wrapping her arms around my neck. I grip her neck with my hand bringing her down to slam my lips against her. "Just like that baby, ride my cock like the good girl you are."

Kat's moans are all I hear as she bounces on my dick. Up and down, faster and faster. Wrapping her hair around my hand I pull her head back and lean into her, sucking on her sweet neck. I love her log her. I can't wait to double fist it, as i pound on her from behind.

I graze her skin my teeth numerous times, making sure to mark what's mine. When we go to the party, everyone will know she belongs to me and no one else. My fucking girl.

"Fuck Aiden, this feels so good, don't stop." I bring my hands up to her bralette and slide them under, cupping her breasts.

So fucking hot. "You look so beautiful riding my cock Angel. Like a fucking Goddess." I grab her hips and thrust into her mercifully fast. Kat shrieks and moans of pleasure are all I hear, telling me to go faster.

"If-i'm Only-y your goddess, then what are you-u?" Kat asks tugging the back of my hair. I hiss, wrapping my left hand around her neck, to bring her lips into mine.

"I'm your God." I say as I thrust into her. "Only mine?" She asks between moans, sliding up and down on my cock.

"Only yours angel." I whisper. Kat digs her nails into my chest as she explodes around my dick. She clenches and un-clenches my cock as she rides her orgasm out. I thrust a couple more times and my vision blacks out as I reach my own orgasm. I grunt placing a kiss on my baby's neck and digging my fingers on her hips.

"Fuck that was mind blowing." I say smashing my lips on hers for a last taste. Kat depends the kiss and before I know it, my cock is hard again and still inside of her. Kat groans slapping my chest.

"Aiden. It hasn't even been 30 seconds and you're hard again." I let out a laugh raising my shoulders and hands up in defense.

"Don't blame me. Have you looked at yourself? You are a walking dream baby." I lift my hips and Kat moans.

I lift her off me and move her to the back seat. I join her and just like that I'm balls deep into her again for round two.

Twenty Five minutes later we make it to the party. Kat had to redo her lipstick and fix her hair before we got out of the car. She asked me for my spare shirt to clean herself up, but I told her no.

I want her to walk around with my cum dripping down her legs, reminding her who she fucking belongs to.

Just me.

We walk up the stairs to the entrance of the house and I smile as my eyes roam Kat's body. She doesn't look like she was freshly fucked, but she can't hide the huge hickey on her neck, which she yelled at me at least twenty times on our way here.

We make our way inside hand in hand. People stop to say hi and I don't miss how my "teammates" eyes roam Kat's body like it's a desert. I wrap an arm around her waist, as we walk towards her friends. Kat squeals when she spots her friends, running up the them and getting into a group hug.

"Aiden." I look to my left and see Roman with Will. I make my way towards them and bro hug both of them, as Will offers me a beer. I take a sip, glancing towards my angel as she continues talking with her friends.

"Hard launch tonight huh?" I chuckle at Romans words, shaking my head.

"I've been hard launching for a long time, she is it for me man. That girl has me wrapped around her fucking fingers." Will lets out a laugh patting my back.

"We can tell. You guys both have matching hickeys." My hand moves up to my neck and I touch the spot she was sucking on earlier, wincing.

Sneaky vixen, left me a hickey. "Someone is territorial huh?" Roman asks smirking. I grin. You should see the one in her neck. I don't say it out loud though. What Kat and I do, it's our business. The girls make their way towards us and I notice the way Roman stiffens when Alina looks at him.

These two needs someone to lock them in a room together, so they can make up.

Kat wraps her arms around my waist and looks up at me with a grin. She wraps her right hand on the back of my neck and brings it down to her level.

"I can feel your cum dripping down my legs and it's making me so fucking horny." Kat whispers, her breathy words, giving me goosebumps. I grin wrapping my right arm around her tiny waist bringing her closer to me.

"Mine Angel. I love knowing you're walking around with my cum all over you. All fucking mine." I whisper kissing the side of her head.

"Okay love birds, we get it. But as the kind of the party, y'all should be paying attention to me." Kat unwraps her arms around me and squeals hugging Alexei.
"Happy birthday you diva." Kat says twirling him around. "Happy Birthday man." I say giving him a hug. Alexei grins as he nods at me and Kat.
"You look so fucking good Kat." Kat blushes looking down, shy from the attention she is getting. She fucking deserves it. She is so beautiful.
"Let's go dance." Maddie yells and my friends nod. They all go in the middle of the make shift dance floor and start dancing to some Latin hits. My angel moves her hips to the beat and I'm mesmerized.
"Aiden, oh my god. I haven't seen you in so long." My view has been ruined when a blonde chick stops right in front of me. "Hi Molly. Good to see you too." I say deciding to be nice, instead of telling her to fuck off, so I can look at my girl in peace.
Molly hand grips my right bicep, stepping closer to me. "We have missed you around here. You're always busy lately."
I take a step back, shaking her hand off of my arm.
"Yeah, I've been busy." She opens her mouth to say something, but my short pretty Goldie, places herself between us.
"Aiden, I want to dance." I smirk nodding as she grabs my hand and leads us towards the dance floor.
A remix of Baby by me from 50 cent starts playing and Kat moves her hips to the beat grinding against me. I wrap my hands around her hips bringing her closer to me I dip my head into her neck, the tip of my nose grazing her neck. Kats lips part and she turns around to face me, looking at me all mad.

"I leave you alone for 5 minutes and girls are all over you." I smirk wrapping my right hand on her back of her head, lifting her head up.

"Are you jealous angel face?" Kat scoffs as she looks away from me. "I'm only yours." Her eyes soften at my words, her body melting into mine. "I promise." I whisper slamming my lips into hers. Kat responds to the kiss wrapping her arms around my neck, bringing our bodies closer together. A couple minutes later we pull apart, to breath.

We dance for a couple more songs and then join our friends playing some card games and talking for hours. When the party ends Kat is drunk out of her ass, but we make it back home in one piece.

"I'm happy with you." My angel whispers as I lay her down in my bed.

"You bring out a side of me that I thought was gone. It's easy to fall in love with you." I gulp standing up, as my heart starts racing.

I pull my blanket over her shoulders and walk into my closet to grab a pair of pyjamas. After getting them on, I take of my shirt and join my angel in my bed.

The moment I lay down, Kat immediately turns around and wraps herself with me. Her legs over mine and her arms around my waist.

This girl will be the death of me.

CHAPTER THIRTY - SIX

KATERINA

Aiden is slacking and I see it before anyone else does. The way his footwork is just a fraction slower than usual, the way his shots aren't hitting as cleanly, the way he keeps glancing toward me during practice like he's not fully focused. It's subtle—subtle enough that most people wouldn't catch it—but I know Aiden. I know the way he moves, the precision he carries, the intensity that usually burns behind every shift he takes on the ice.

And right now? It's off.

I shift uncomfortably from my place on the other side of the
rink, watching as Aiden skates down the ice, taking another shot that barely misses the net. He curses under his breath, frustration evident in the way he tightens his grip on his stick.

Coach Matthews notices it, too.

"Knight! Get your head in the game!" he barks, his voice cutting through the cold air of the rink. Aiden clenches his jaw but nods, skating back into line with the rest of his teammates.

I exhale, trying to ignore the uneasy feeling settling in my chest. Half an hour later, the inevitable happens. Practice stops cold as Coach blows his whistle, the sharp sound echoing through the arena. Everyone turns as he stalks toward Aiden, his expression stormy.

"Knight, what the hell is going on with you?"

Aiden exhales sharply, running a hand through his damp hair. "I'm fine."

Coach's glare darkens. "Bullshit. You've been missing practices, showing up late, and when you do show up, your head isn't in it. What the fuck is wrong with you?"

I shift uncomfortably from where I'm standing, fully aware of the reason Aiden has been slacking.

Me.

He's been helping me practice every night, making sure I get my strength back after surgery. He's been there for me, making sure I don't push too hard, that I don't fall apart under the pressure of recovery. And now, it's costing him.

Aiden's jaw ticks, but he doesn't say anything.

Coach scoffs, shaking his head. "You're distracted, Knight. And I can see exactly what's doing it."

My stomach drops as Coach's gaze flickers toward me. Aiden tenses beside him.

"I'm not distracted," Aiden grits out.

Coach laughs coldly. "Really? Because from where I'm standing, it looks like you're too caught up with her to remember what the hell you're playing for."

My face burns. Aiden snaps.

"That is not what's happening." His voice is sharp, dangerous, filled with barely contained anger. "Kat has nothing to do with this."

Coach crosses his arms. "You sure about that? Because it seems to me like your head is too far up her ass to focus on the team."

Aiden steps forward.

I react before he can do something stupid, skating towards him and grabbing his arm before he can get too close to Coach.

"Aiden," I say quietly. "It's fine."

He whips his head toward me, his eyes burning. "No, it's not."

I squeeze his wrist, trying to ground him, trying to remind him that this isn't a battle he needs to fight.

But Aiden isn't the type to back down.

"Stay out of my personal life," he tells Coach, his voice low and deadly. "What I do off the ice is none of your business."

Coach's gaze narrows. "It is my business when it affects your performance."

Aiden's nostrils flare, but before he can say anything else,

Coach takes a step back, shaking his head in disappointment. "Figure out your priorities, Knight. Because if you keep playing like this, you won't have a place on this team."

Aiden's entire body locks up, his hands curling into fists at his sides.

Coach doesn't wait for a response. He just turns and walks

off the ice, leaving Aiden standing there, seething. The silence that follows is suffocating.

I swallow hard, my fingers still wrapped around Aiden's wrist. "Aiden—"

He yanks away, his eyes stormy when they meet mine. "Don't." I flinch, but nod.
Because there's nothing else to say. Because I know exactly what he's feeling. Because he's right—this isn't my fight.
Even if it feels like I'm the reason he's losing it.
The tension lingers long after practice ends.
Aiden storms off the ice without a word, his jaw tight, his hands clenched. I watch as he disappears into the locker room, my stomach twisting uncomfortably.
He's pissed—at Coach, at himself, at me. And I don't know how to fix it.
I linger by the rink, running my fingers over the smooth edge of the boards, trying to work through the tangled mess of emotions in my head. Guilt, frustration, something heavier that I don't want to name.
"Give him space."
I turn to find Will standing a few feet away, arms crossed. His expression is unreadable, but there's something knowing in his gaze.
I exhale. "He's ruining his own game because of me."
Will shakes his head. "No, he's ruining his game because he cares about you. And Aiden doesn't do anything halfway." My chest tightens. "I never wanted him to put me first."
Will shrugs. "That's not how he works. You should know that by now." I do. That's what makes this worse. I nod, biting my lip. "Thanks, Will."
He just offers a small smirk before walking off, leaving me alone with my thoughts.
 When I finally make it back to the house, Aiden is already there, sitting on the couch, watching an old hockey game on the TV. He doesn't look up when I walk in.

I close the door softly, hesitating for a second before stepping forward. "Aiden."

I sigh, moving closer. "Can you at least look at me?"

He exhales harshly, dragging a hand down his face before finally turning his head. His eyes are unreadable, but there's something tired in them. Something frustrated.

I sit on the coffee table in front of him, crossing my arms.

"Are you mad at me?"

His jaw tightens. "I'm mad at myself." I frown. "Why?"

He scoffs, shaking his head. "Because I let myself get distracted. Because I let this"—he gestures between us—"affect my game."

I flinch. "So, I am a distraction."

Aiden's eyes snap to mine, sharp and furious. "No. That's not—" He groans, leaning forward, resting his elbows on his knees. "That's not what I meant."

"Then what did you mean?" I demand, my heart pounding. He exhales, running a hand through his hair. "I mean that I can't stop thinking about you. I mean that every time I'm supposed to be focused, you're right there in my head. I mean that I would drop everything for you, and I don't know if that makes me the dumbest guy alive or just someone who's finally figured out what actually matters."

I stare, my breath catching. Because I wasn't expecting that. Aiden shakes his head, letting out a bitter laugh. "Coach is right. I've been slipping. And it's because I care about you more than I should."

The words hit me like a gut punch. Because I care about him too. More than I should. I swallow hard, shifting closer. "Aiden, I—"

"Don't." He looks up at me, his expression raw. "Not if you don't mean it."

The words die in my throat. Because I don't know what to say. I do the only thing I can. I lean in. Aiden inhales sharply, his hands tightening on his knees, like he's holding himself back. Like he's waiting.

I kiss him.

Soft, slow, but undeniable.

Aiden doesn't hesitate. The second our lips touch, his hands are on me, pulling me into his lap, his fingers digging into my waist. He kisses me like he's making a point, like he's trying to prove something, and maybe he is.

Maybe we both are.

When we finally break apart, I rest my forehead against his, my breathing unsteady.

"We'll figure this out," I whisper.

Aiden lets out a slow breath, his hands still gripping me like he's afraid I'll disappear. "Yeah."

And for now, that's enough.

CHAPTER THIRTY - SEVEN

KATERINA

The atmosphere in the arena is out of this world. The crowd roars, the boards rattle, and the energy is so thick it feels like it could crack the ice. The boys are seconds away from qualifying for the Frozen Four, and if the last three periods have proven anything—it's that Aiden Knight is unstoppable.

He's everywhere on the ice, driving plays, cutting through the defense like they're nothing. His skates carve deep, his shots are lethal, and the way he commands the game is almost terrifying. He plays with the kind of fire that makes it impossible to look away.

And me?

I'm gripping the edge of my seat, heart pounding, watching as Aiden dangles past a defense man, fakes out the goalie, and buries the puck top shelf.

The crowd erupts.

I shoot to my feet as the boys pile on top of him, screaming in victory. The final buzzer sounds, and just like that—

They've won. They're going to the Frozen Four. Alina and Maddie are screaming next to me, jumping up and down, and even Alexei is cheering like he's the one who just scored. I feel my heart swell as I watch Aiden skate to the boards, tilting his helmet up to scan the crowd. The second his eyes find me, my stomach flips. He smirks, tapping his stick against the glass before skating away.
Cocky asshole.

The post-game celebration is chaos. The entire hockey house is packed, music blaring, drinks flowing, and people celebrating like the boys already won the championship. But the real celebration? That's outside. The bonfire is already roaring, casting flickering shadows across the backyard as players, friends, and fans gather around. I'm standing near the fire, bundled in Aiden's hoodie—because, let's be honest, at this point, half my wardrobe is his—when he finally emerges from the house, fresh from a shower, looking infuriatingly good.
His hair is still damp, curling slightly at the ends, and his sweatshirt hangs loosely off his frame. His sharp gaze locks onto me immediately. "You're stealing my clothes again." I smirk, tugging the sleeves over my hands.
"I have no idea what you're talking about." Aiden stops in front of me, arms crossing. "That's my hoodie, Angel Face." I blink innocently.
"Oh? Weird. Must've gotten lost in my drawer." Aiden huffs, but there's a ghost of a smile tugging at his lips. He reaches out, tugging at the hem of the sweatshirt,

pulling me slightly closer. "One of these days, I'm going to start stealing your clothes." I raise an eyebrow. "I'd pay to see you in one of my crop tops." I say with a giggle.

He smirks at me, bitting his bottom lip. "Careful, Hart. I never back down from a challenge."

Before I can respond, Roman's voice booms across the yard. "ALL RIGHT, WHO WANTS TO DO STUPID SHIT?"

The crowd cheers. Aiden sighs, rubbing his temple. "I already regret this." I grin. "Come on, Captain, live a little."

His eyes flick to mine, something undeniable burning there. "Oh, I am, Angel Face. Trust me."

The bonfire burns high, casting flickering shadows across the backyard as the celebration reaches full swing. Laughter echoes, beer bottles clink together, and the smell of smoke lingers in the crisp night air. The boys are still hyped from their win, the energy so contagious that even I can't stop smiling. But Aiden? Aiden is watching me.

I can feel his gaze like a physical touch, searing across my skin, making my heart race. He's leaning against the porch railing, arms crossed, eyes dark and unreadable. He's been watching me all night, ever since I stole his hoodie and refused to give it back.

And I love it.

"So," Roman claps his hands together, stumbling slightly as he steps forward. "Let's play a game." A chorus of cheers erupts around us, and I can't help but laugh. Roman is three drinks in, which means whatever idea he's about to propose is either genius or insane.

Alina smirks, arms crossed. "Is this the kind of game that gets
people arrested?"

Roman gasps, hand to his chest. "Baby, I am offended. I would never—"

"Last time we played one of your games, Will had to bribe campus security to let us go," Aiden drawls, finally pushing off the railing and making his way over.

Roman waves him off. "That was a misunderstanding."

Will sighs. "You tried to convince them we were part of an undercover mission."

"I almost had them fooled," Roman argues.

I shake my head, grinning. "Okay, so what's the game?" Roman's face lights up. "Truth or Dare."

Aiden groans. "Absolutely not. We have played this game too many times, these last couple of months."

But it's too late. The group is already cheering in agreement, and before I know it, everyone is settling into a makeshift circle near the fire.

Alina nudges me as we sit down. "This is going to be a disaster." I smirk. "I know."

The game starts off mild. A few easy truths, a dare that forces
one of the guys to shotgun two beers back-to-back, another that makes Maddie run a lap around the yard in nothing but Roman's jersey. But then—

Roman turns to me.

"Hart," he drawls, smirking. "Truth or dare?" I roll my eyes. "Dare."

The group oohs, and Roman grins. "I love that answer. I dare you to kiss someone in this circle."

I pause, my pulse spiking.

My gaze flickers—without thinking—to Aiden. And he knows.

His smirk fades, his jaw tightening, his entire body going still as he watches me. Daring me to do it.

The tension is thick.

I stand and make my way to Aiden. I lean when i reach him and smile. "Hi baby." I whisper. Aiden grins and smashes his lips with mine, giving me a consuming kiss. My brain shuts down, as i bring my arms around his neck. Aiden pulls me into his lap, as his tongue dances with mine.

Someone clears their throat and I pull away, my cheeks redder than a tomato. Roman smirks at us, so I do the only reasonable thing, I can think of. I flip him off.

Soon it's Aidens turn, and he doesn't even hesitate. He chooses dare. Roman grins, looking way too pleased with himself. "I dare you to pick someone in this circle and carry them into the lake."

The group erupts, cheering and laughing, and before I can even move—

Aiden grabs me.

I let out a yelp as he hauls me over his shoulder, his grip tight

around my legs as he stalks toward the dock. "Aiden, don't you dare—"

"Oh, I definitely dare."

The cold wind bites at my skin as we reach the edge of the dock, the dark water stretching out below.

"Aiden, I swear to God—" He jumps.

The water hits like a shock to my system, stealing my breath as we go under. The chill wraps around me, and for a split second, all I can feel is him—his arms around me, the press of his body against mine as we sink before breaking the surface.

I gasp, shoving my wet hair out of my face. "You asshole!" Aiden is laughing, the deep, rich sound rolling through the night as he shakes the water from his hair.

I glare at him, shoving at his chest. "You are the worst." He smirks. "You're still wearing my hoodie."

I growl, yanking it over my head and throwing it at him. "Not anymore."

Aiden catches it easily, his eyes dark with something else now, something dangerous. He steps forward, water rippling around us, his voice lower when he murmurs—

"You love stealing my clothes."

My breath catches, my body burning despite the cold. "Shut up, Knight."

His smirk deepens. "Make me, Hart." I giggle, swimming away from him. I'm freezing but the icy cold water feels good, numbing me.

I'm still freezing. Even after Aiden and I dragged ourselves out of the lake, even after I wrung out my hair and wrapped myself in a towel someone shoved at me, even after I stole another one of Aiden's hoodies to replace the one, I tossed at him—I cannot shake the chill that has settled into my bones.

Which is why I'm currently curled up on the couch, cocooned in the thickest blanket I could find, glaring at Aiden while he sits beside me, completely unbothered.

"You did that on purpose," I grumble, tucking my freezing feet beneath me.

Aiden, who has the audacity to look pleased with himself, smirks. "I have no idea what you're talking about."

I narrow my eyes. "You're such an asshole."

He stretches his arms over the back of the couch, his long legs sprawled out in front of him. "And yet, here you are, stealing my hoodie again."

I cross my arms over my chest. "You owe me this hoodie."

Aiden chuckles, his eyes flicking over me like he's committing this moment to memory. "Fair enough, Angel Face."

Before I can fire back, Alina plops down beside me, shaking her head dramatically. "That was the best thing I've ever witnessed. The tension? The dramatics? The shameless flirting?"

I groan. "We were not flirting."

Alina and Maddie both burst out laughing.

"Oh my God, you are so in denial," Maddie cackles, nudging me. "I give it two weeks before you cave."

I scoff, tightening the blanket around me. "I am not caving."

Roman flops onto the armrest, sipping his beer with a lazy grin. "That's what they all say, Hart."

Aiden smirks, clearly enjoying this way too much. "She's stubborn."

I scowl at him. "And you're infuriating."

He leans in slightly, voice dropping just enough for only me to hear. "You love it."

My breath catches in my throat because he's not wrong. I do love it—the push and pull, the tension that's always simmering between us, the way he challenges me, the way he sees me.

Instead of responding, I steal his beer right out of his hand

and take a long, slow sip as Aiden watches me, his lips curving into something dangerous.

CHAPTER THIRTY - EIGHT

KATERINA

Practice today was different. Coach has been ruthless. "Straighten up your leg, Katerina. Push up." I sigh at the coach's words and lift my foot higher, ensuring my leg is perfectly straight.

"Just like that. Keep it going." Alexei lowers me down and skates beside me, perfectly in sync, as Lover by Taylor Swift plays in the background.

I'm proud of how effortlessly we move together, each step
and movement flowing like second nature. I also know we're doing well because our coach has stopped yelling at us... well, mostly.

I reach for Alexei's hand, and he grips mine firmly, pulling me toward him before lifting me into the air. His strong hands hold me securely at my lower back as

I extend gracefully, reaching for the blade of my skate while he spins us around.

As he lowers me down, I wrap my calves around his neck, letting him spin us four times before he gently sets me back on the ice.

"Alright, take a break. Good job." I high-five Alexei before wrapping my arms around his neck, and he playfully lifts me up in response.

My gaze drifts to the edge of the ice rink, where my handsome hockey player stands. His eyes are already locked onto mine. My lips curl into a soft smile, and he grins, pushing off and skating toward me.

My heart starts thudding against my chest—so hard I swear it might break free.

Come on, heart. I thought we got over this. He's already mine. I know that. But it doesn't change the way he still makes me feel. It's infuriating.

"Angel face, that was freaking phenomenal," Aiden says as he reaches me. I beam at his praise, wrapping my arms around his waist.

"Low-key, I got anxious that you'd slice Alexei's face with your skate, but thank God you didn't." I giggle at his comment, and he takes my hand in his, rubbing slow circles against my palm.

"That would've been a bloody scene," I joke, watching as Aiden chuckles and nods.

He tilts his head slightly, his expression softening. His grip
tightens around me, as he presses a gentle kiss to the side of my head.

"How did I get so damn lucky to score you?" he murmurs, tapping my nose playfully.

I grin, my cheeks heating up as I look away. Before I can say

anything, a sharp voice catches my attention. Aiden and I both turn our heads toward the rink, where we see Alina and Roman arguing. My heart clenches. Oh no. Not again. Alina's hands fly up in
frustration.
"It's your fucking fault, Roman! I try and try and try, while all you do is shut down and push me away!" Roman's jaw tightens.
"Then leave." His voice is raw, broken. "That's all I know how to do, Lina. So just leave. Save yourself from me. You don't need me." Alina takes a shaky step back, defeated. Her voice trembles.
"All I want is you, Roman. I do need you." She shakes her head, and before he can say anything, she turns and skates toward the exit.
I immediately follow. "Alina, wait!"
Hopping off the ice, I quickly slip on my skate guards and chase after her.
She barely makes it a few steps before turning around and throwing herself into my arms, breaking down into sobs.
I hold her tighter. "Shh, Ali. I'm here." Her body trembles against mine.
"Why does he treat me like that?" she chokes out. "I want him, Kat. I only want him, and he doesn't want me at all." I rub slow, soothing circles on her back.
"It's okay, Ali. Things will work out for the best. Right now, I
think you both need space."
She shakes her head violently, her sobs intensifying. "I don't want to lose him. You don't understand, Kat. He's the only one who sees me—sees everything." I tighten my hold on her. "I know, babe. I know."
She takes a deep, shuddering breath before pulling away,

wiping at her tears.
"I need to go. I'll be fine. Don't worry about me." And that is exactly when I do worry.
Alina never asks people not to worry about her unless she's drowning. For the rest of the day, I can't stop thinking about her. I text her. Call her. Leave voicemails. No response. Alexei says she's locked herself in her room, drowning in sad music. I feel helpless. My phone pings, and my heart leaps. Ali? When I unlock it, I see it's from Aiden.
Aidy

> Live with me tonight?

Huh?

Angel Face

> ?

My phone vibrates again almost instantly.
Aidy

> *Be ready in 5. Dress warm and cozy.*

I bite my lower lip, a soft smile creeping onto my face. Without hesitation, I pull one of Aiden's oversized hoodies from my closet, slipping it on over my black leggings. I tuck part of it in at the front to make it cuter, then add a beanie, leg warmers, and my boots.
By the time I reach the kitchen, Aiden is already there, waiting for me. The moment I see him, my stomach flutters.
"Ready to go, angel face?" he asks, his voice warm. I nod quickly, and he takes my hand in his.
Before we leave, he tilts his head down, capturing my lips in a soft kiss.

"You look so pretty," he murmurs. I shake my head, blushing. "I put zero effort into this."

Aiden laughs, bringing my hand up to his lips and pressing a

soft kiss against my palm.

"Still beautiful." We step outside, and I slide into the passenger seat of his car.

He drives for almost an hour before pulling over in the middle of nowhere. It's dark—no city lights, just the moon above us.

I squint at the surroundings. "Are you killing me and dumping my body here?"

Aiden laughs—full, deep, and beautiful—before popping open the trunk.

When he pulls out our skating bags, my eyes widen in excitement.

"We're going ice skating at my favorite frozen pond." My entire face lights up.

I clap my hands together, giddy. "Best. Night. Ever."

Aiden tells me it's a short hike to the pond, but I shrug and start walking ahead. He quickly catches up, falling in step beside me as we move in comfortable silence.

"Is Alina okay?" he asks after a moment. I shrug again, my lips pressing into a tight line. "I don't know. She won't answer my calls or texts." I pause before asking, "Roman?"

This time, Aiden is the one who shrugs. "I bet he's self-destructing somewhere. Will said he was going to keep an eye on him tonight." I nod, reaching for his hand and squeezing it gently.

When we finally reach the pond, I gasp at the sight before me. The ice stretches out, vast and untouched, shimmering under the soft glow of the moonlight.

"Oh my god," I breathe. "This is a pond?"

Aiden chuckles. "Told you it was big." I sit onto a nearby rock, grabbing my bag from him and pulling out my skates. Aiden kneels in front of me, motioning for me to stay put before he gently starts lacing up my skates for me. My heart stumbles in my chest. This boy has no idea how much power he holds over me. He could ruin me—completely—because I'm already in too deep. Whatever this is between us, it's not casual. Not light.

I am falling for him. Every day, more and more. And my heart can't handle it.

Aiden looks down just as I grin up at him, reaching up to

press a soft kiss to his lips.

"You got to stop doing cute things like this for me," I murmur, placing a hand over my heart. He smirks. "Why? Your heart giving up or something?"

I chuckle, nodding. "Or something." He shakes his head, finishing with my skates before lacing up his own. Then, he takes my hand, guiding me onto the ice. "Just be careful," he warns. "The ice here isn't smoothed out." I nod before pushing off, skating around in slow circles.

Aiden follows behind, keeping his distance, watching me with that soft, unreadable look he always gets when he thinks I'm not paying attention. I spin around once, coming to a stop just as two strong hands find my waist. "This is the best night ever," I whisper, pressing my lips to his. We skate together, fingers intertwined, and I fall more times than I care to admit. Aiden tries to catch me each time, but we usually end up tripping together, landing on our asses like a couple of idiots. The last time he falls, I die laughing, struggling to catch my breath.

"Oh, you think that was funny, huh?" he teases, pushing him- self up and skating toward me. I squeal, quickly maneuvering away.

"Aiden, no—"

Too late. He chases me around the pond, but I keep dodging him, giggling as he tries to corner me. Then, a sharp voice slices through the night.

"Hey, kids! This is private property—you can't be here!" I gasp

as Aiden mutters a low, "Shit."

The man pulls out his phone. "Stay right there. I'm calling the cops."

Fuck.

I slap Aiden's arm. "Move!" We skate fast toward our belongings, yanking off our skates and shoving our feet into our shoes. Grabbing our bags, we sprint toward the trail we came from, slipping on the frozen ground as we go.

We don't stop running for a full ten minutes, until we make it back to Aiden's car.

I double over, laughing as I clutch my stomach. "Oh my god—" Aiden bends over next to me, catching his breath before pulling me into him.

"That was fucking hilarious," he says, pressing his forehead against my shoulder.

I nod, still breathless. "Let's go before the cops actually show

up and find us here."

He grins, pulling away. "Agreed." We hop into the car and drive back into the city, still laughing. Aiden takes us straight home, and we move quietly as we slip inside—it's already past 1 AM. The second we step into his room, Aiden pulls me toward his bed, laying me down before crawling in next to me.

"Stay with me tonight," he murmurs, brushing his fingers
through my hair. "Let's watch a movie. Drink hot chocolate or something." I nod, smiling as I run a hand through his hair.

Kicking off my leggings and sweater, I accept one of his oversized t-shirts and slip it on before settling into bed. Aiden slides in beside me, propping himself up on one elbow.

"Ten questions?"

I raise an eyebrow. "I thought it was twenty questions?"

He shrugs. "Too long. Ten's better."

I chuckle. "Fine."

His lips curve into a lazy smirk. "Favourite ice cream flavour?" I pretend to think about it. "Cookies and cream. Yours?" His lips press into a thin line.

I gasp. "No. Not mint chocolate chip—" Aiden nods. I groan dramatically, rolling out of bed. "That's it. We're done." His hand grabs my wrist, yanking me back. Before I can react, he turns me around and pulls me against his chest.

"We will never be done," he murmurs, his voice low and firm. "You keep forgetting—you're mine, angel. Only mine."

My breath catches in my throat.

"I used to like cookies and cream, but I got converted."

I know who, the moment the words leave his mouth. "Sophia." I whisper. Aiden nods with a smile on his face.

"It's her comfort food. During chemo treatments, she couldn't each much, so ice-cream was a favourite. She refused to eat cookies and cream, and would try to stuff my mouth with the mint flavour."

"I finally gave in and stopped buying cookies and cream. I like cookies and cream ice cream but I love

Sophia more. Anything to make her happy." My eyes tear up as I look at him. Aiden Knight is the most selfless man I know, and I am so lucky to have him in my life.

Before I can respond, his lips crash into mine, deep and consuming. I melt instantly, my arms wrapping around his neck. I pull back only to push him onto the bed, straddling his lap, my knees framing his hips.

"Why didn't you want to share the ice with me when we first

met?" I ask, dragging my fingers slowly down his chest.

I feel his muscles flex beneath my touch. His voice comes out rough, barely above a whisper. "I couldn't breathe." I blink.

"What?"

"The first time I saw you," he says, swallowing hard. "I couldn't breathe." His hands settle on my waist.

"You're the most beautiful girl I've ever met, and I honestly thought that if we shared the ice, I wouldn't be able to concentrate—because all I'd do was look at you."

My heart stutters. I smile, wrapping my arms around his neck, lowering my head to press a lingering kiss to his lips. Then, a knock interrupts us.

We break apart as the door creaks open. Will pokes his head

inside.

"I don't want to break up your love-making session," he deadpans,

"But, Kat? Alina's in your room." I jump out of Aiden's bed and stand up. I look at Aiden who nods at me. "Go," Aiden murmurs standing up and pressing a soft kiss to my forehead.

"I'll see you in the morning."

He pats my butt, and I roll my eyes before rushing across the hall.

I push open the door to my room and find Alina curled up in my bed, knees to her chest, her shoulders shaking. My heart aches.

I slip under the covers, wrapping my arms around her. Alina turns into me immediately, burying her face against my chest, sobbing quietly. No matter what—no matter where—she is my best friend. A moment later, the door opens again, and Maddie and Alexei step inside. I motion for them to join us, and without hesitation, they do.

We lay there together, wrapping Alina up in our warmth,

whispering soft reassurances into her ear until she finally drifts off to sleep. I sigh, pressing a kiss to her forehead.

Thank god I have a California king bed—because soon after, we all fall asleep too.

And honestly?

I wouldn't have it any other way.

CHAPTER THIRTY - NINE

KATERINA

After talking to Alina and Aiden, I decided to meet with my father and talk. My nerves are killing me as I wait for him.
The coffee in my hands is lukewarm now, untouched since the moment the barista set it down in front of me. My fingers wrap around the cup, desperate for warmth, but my whole body feels cold. I shouldn't be this nervous. It's just a conversation. Just words.
Just… my father.
I take a slow breath, staring at the rain tapping against the café window, trying to ignore the way my heart is pounding. I hadn't planned to answer his call last night. I hadn't planned to hear his voice at all. But when I did—when I finally picked up—I heard something I wasn't expecting.
Regret.

It cracked through the line like thunder. And now, here I am, sitting in a quiet café, waiting for a man I barely know to walk through the door.
He is doing so much for me that i thought a talk couldn't hurt. A talk with a man I once convinced myself never wanted me. The door chimes, and my pulse stutters.
I don't need to turn around to know it's him.
I just know it. The way the air shifts. The way the weight in my chest grows heavier.
I finally force myself to look.
He's standing just a few feet away, scanning the room, his movements hesitant, unsure. The same dark hair as mine, streaked with a bit of gray, lines on his face and the same eyes as mine.
His gaze lands on me, and for a second, he just… stares, then gives me a weak smile.
Slowly, he walks toward me. "Kat," he says, almost breathless, like he's been waiting forever to say my name.
I nod, swallowing thickly. "Jake." He flinches. Just barely. But I catch it.
I don't call him Dad. I'm not ready for that. Not yet.
He clears his throat and hesitates before pulling out the chair
across from me. "May I?"
I nod again, and he sits, his hands clasped together tightly, like he's trying to keep himself steady.
For a few moments, neither of us speaks. Until he does. "Ever since i went to Russia to see you, you have ignored me.
Making it clear you want no relationship with me, but i need you to know the truth."
Then, finally, he exhales shakily and says the words that have haunted me for years.

"I never left you."

A bitter laugh escapes before I can stop it. "You're sitting here saying that like it's the truth."

"It is the truth," he insists, voice quiet but firm. "I didn't know, Kat. I swear to you—I didn't know." I shake my head, looking away.

"I don't understand. How could you not know? You were with my mom. You left her."

His face twists, like my words physically hurt him. "I left

because I thought she wanted me to."

"She didn't," I say sharply. "She never did." He looks down at his hands, exhaling deeply.

"I know that now." My throat tightens. Jake—my father—drags a hand through his hair, his frustration evident.

"She never told me, Kat. I swear to you, if I had known, I never would have left. I would have been there. I would have been your father." His voice cracks, and something in my chest clenches painfully. I want to believe him.

But how do you undo a lifetime of hurt with just words?

"Then why—" I hesitate, my voice barely a whisper. "Why didn't she tell you?"

He looks away, jaw clenching before he finally mutters, "She did."

The room spins. I blink, my heart hammering. "What?"

His hands tighten into fists. "She did, Kat. She sent me a letter."

A thick, suffocating silence falls between us.

A letter.

My mother told him. And he still left?

I knew this was a mistake. I knew meeting him would only— "Kat," he says urgently, pulling me from my spiral. "I never got
it." I stare at him, barely breathing.

"What?" He swallows hard. "I never got the letter. I only found out about you a few months ago. Precisely two weeks before your lawsuit, was in every news outlet out there. And the reason I didn't get it…" He hesitates. "It was burned."

I shake my head. "I don't understand—"

"My wife at the time," he says, voice laced with anger and something close to shame. "Your stepmother." My blood runs cold.

"She found the letter," he continues. "She was drunk. Con-
fused. I don't know what the hell was going through her head, but she burned it, Kat. She destroyed it before I ever even knew it existed." I can't breathe.

"She didn't even remember doing it until recently. And the moment I knew—the moment I knew you existed— I dropped everything and went to Russia to find you."

Tears blur my vision.

No.

No, no, no.

I spent years hating him. Thinking he chose to leave. Thinking I wasn't enough to make him stay. But he never even knew.

I choke out a sharp breath, covering my face with my hands.

"Oh, Kat," he whispers. "I'm so sorry."

I should still be angry. I should still push him away. But suddenly, all I can think about is how much time we've lost.

Years.

Years of him not knowing. Years of me thinking I didn't matter. When all this time, I did.

I did. When I lift my head again, his eyes are wet.

"I missed your entire life," he murmurs, his voice trembling. "I missed everything."

A sob breaks from my throat. "I don't—I don't know how to—"

"You don't have to," he says quickly, shaking his head. "I don't expect anything from you, Kat. But if you're willing… I'd like to try. To be in your life. In any way you'll let me."

I close my eyes, my heart aching from everything we've lost. Then, slowly, I nod.

And for the first time in my life, I let myself believe that

maybe… just maybe… I don't have to carry this hurt alone anymore.

The second I step inside the house Aiden is waiting sprawled out in our living room couch.

I don't even get two steps in before his arms are around me, pulling me against his chest.

"How'd it go?" he murmurs into my hair. I take a deep breath, melting into him.

I don't even realize I'm crying until I feel his hand in my hair, soothing, grounding.

"It wasn't what I expected," I whisper. "I thought I'd hate him. I wanted to hate him."

Aiden's hold on me tightens, silent, patient.

"But he didn't leave me, Aiden," I whisper, voice cracking. "He didn't even know about me. He never knew."

Aiden's lips press against my temple. "Oh, baby."
I let out a shaky breath. "We're going to try. I don't know how, or where we even start, but… I think I want to give him a chance."
Aiden pulls back just enough to cup my face. "You don't have to figure it all out right now, Kat."
I nod, my throat tight, and he kisses my forehead. "Come on," he murmurs, tugging me toward the couch. "Let's just lay down for a while."
I don't argue. I let him pull me onto the couch, wrapping myself around him as he blankets me in warmth, his fingers tracing slow circles against my back.
And for the first time in a long, long time… I don't feel so alone.

CHAPTER FORTY

KATERINA

Tonight is Christmas Eve, and we're celebrating it at our place.
Both my mom and dad showed up together, which confused the absolute shit out of me, but I refuse to overthink it.
Not tonight. It's Christmas, and I just want to enjoy it.
Aiden's auntie Maria, came with Sophia, and their presence makes me nervous as hell. It's the first time our families are meeting, and I can't shake the anxiety that something might go wrong.
I try to stay calm, but on the inside, I'm freaking out. My mind is racing, my heart hammering in my chest, and I'm so distracted that I've asked Aiden's mom to repeat her questions three times already.
It's bad.

Needing air, I quietly slip away from the kitchen and head toward the backyard. As I push the sliding door open, a wave of cold air hits me, making me shudder. Wrapping my arms around myself, I take a deep breath, hoping it'll help settle the restlessness inside me.
But it doesn't.
"This isn't working," I mutter, rubbing my arms up and down in a desperate attempt to warm up.
The back door slides open behind me, and I turn to see who's followed me outside.
The moment my eyes land on him, my lips twitch into a small smile.
Aiden.
He steps outside, his expression soft as he studies me.
"Angel face, why are you out here in the cold all by yourself?"
I shrug, glancing away.
He doesn't hesitate. He closes the space between us and wraps his arms around my waist, resting his chin on my shoulder.
The moment he touches me, my entire body relaxes. I let out a shaky breath, finally feeling like I can breathe again.
"What's going on, baby?" he whispers.
I shake my head, taking another deep breath. "I-I don't know." My voice wavers, but I push forward.
"Sometimes, it feels like I have this whole anxiety and panic attack thing figured out. There are days when I feel so happy, like I'll never have another attack again... but then there are days like today."
I pull back slightly, staring at the stars as I continue. "My heart
has been hammering out of my chest all day. I keep shaking, and the worst part is... I don't even know why. I had a great day—shopping with the girls, spending

time with my mom— but my body still feels alert."
Aiden listens carefully, his grip tightening around me.
"It used to only happen when something triggered me,"
I admit, "But lately, it just happens. And it scares me."
Aiden sighs softly before pressing a lingering kiss
against my neck. "Thank you for telling me," he
murmurs. "I know it must
be weighing on you a lot."
I nod, tilting my head back to blink away the tears
threatening to spill. You are not ruining your bad bitch
makeup, Katerina.
I swear, if Aiden ever heard the way I talk to myself in
my
head, he'd probably run for the hills.
"How can I help?" he asks, his voice full of genuine
concern. "What can I do to make it go away?" I smile
faintly, turning in his arms to face him. Wrapping my
arms around his waist, I whisper, "You already are.
Distracting me from my thoughts helps a lot."
Aiden presses his lips together in a thin line before
nodding. "Okay, distraction… Anything else?" I shrug,
but before I can say anything else, he suddenly pulls
away.
Then—the betrayal.
Aiden bends down, grabs a handful of snow, and
chucks it at me. A squeal leaves my lips as I bolt off the
deck and into the backyard.
"Aiden, don't you dare!" I yell, already knowing what's
coming next. I barely make it a few steps before a cold
thud hits me square in the back. I spin around, glaring
daggers at my traitorous boyfriend.
"You asshole," I seethe. "Now you'll get it." Bending
down, I grab a handful of snow and pack it into a tight
ball.

Aiden smirks. "Thanks for the view, angel. God damn."
I grin, turning just in time to launch the snowball at his chest. The impact stuns him. His smirk drops.
"Baby," he says, eyes widening. "I don't have a coat on.
Remember that." I scoff.
"Not my problem." Before I can react, Aiden lunges. I scream, trying to escape, but his strong arms wrap around my waist, lifting me effortlessly off the ground.
"Aiden, no!" I wiggle, trying to free myself, but it's too late. Aiden smashes a snowball against the side of my face, making me gasp.
"I, am going to kill you." He laughs, sliding a hand to the back of my head and pulling me in for a kiss.
"No, you won't," he murmurs against my lips. And, of course, he's right.
I melt into his embrace, my arms wrapping around his neck
as his lips move against mine. His tongue slides into my mouth, deepening the kiss, and when his hand slips down to squeeze my ass, a quiet moan escapes me.
"How's that for a distraction?" he smirks. I grin. "Best distraction ever." I go in for another peck, but Aiden bites my bottom lip, pulling me in for something rougher.
"Fuck, baby," he groans, pressing himself against me. "You make me feel like a fourteen-year-old horny teenager who's never had his dick wet before." I burst out laughing, shaking my head.
"I would offer to help," I tease, "but considering our families are inside, I don't think that's the best idea."
Aiden groans, gripping me tighter. "You're evil."
"Think about your grandma naked," I suggest, "or Roman crying." His eyes snap open.

"Yep. That did it." I chuckle, wrapping a hand around his bicep.

"Let's go back inside?"

He nods, pulling me toward the door. The warmth inside the house is a stark contrast to the cold I just escaped. As soon as I step back in, I spot Alina across the room and immediately make my way toward her, wrapping my arms around her.

"Hi, bestie," she whispers, hugging me tightly. Alina told me yesterday that after the semester ends, she's flying back to Russia for the next six to eight months. She needs a break—to spend time with her grandma, to breathe, and away from Roman.

I know the real reason, though. She's hurting. She doesn't want to keep begging Roman to love her, and I get it. I understand more than I wish I did. Roman is a good guy— he really is—but the two of them are horrible at communicating. They keep hurting each other in ways that can't be undone. When she told me her plan, I agreed that the break was a good idea. That no matter what, we'd all be here when she came back. Well, almost all of us. I graduate at the end of next year, and my goal is the Olympics. I don't know where life will take me after that.

"Are you okay?" I ask, brushing her blonde hair out of her
face.

Alina exhales shakily. "No. I love you, but I really don't want to be here. I keep seeing him, and it feels like my heart is going to give out. I love him, Kat, but he will never love me like that." I pull her in tighter as her eyes fill with tears.

"Listen to me," I whisper, my voice firm. "You are the strongest person I know. And one day, you'll find someone who loves you as madly as you love them.

Someone clingy, possessive, jealous—all the things you say you hate but secretly love." I smirk, making her chuckle through her tears. "If Roman isn't that person, then someone else will be."

She nods, laughing softly. "I'm so lucky to have you in my life. How will I survive six months without you?" I grin, linking my arm through hers as we head toward Alexei.

"Well, that's what Face-Time is for." Alina nods but suddenly stops, and stares at something near my head. "Why is there snow in your hair?" she asks, frowning. I glare across the room at Aiden. He smirks, winking at me. Alina chuckles, shaking her head.

"You two are menaces."

"Are you guys ready for the Omega Phi Christmas Bash?" she asks, abruptly changing the subject. I frown. "I was not informed about a bash."

"Apparently, it's supposed to be the biggest party of the year. Everyone is going," Alexei chimes in, giving us his best puppy- dog eyes.

"I need to get wasted and dance," Maddie says as she joins us. "If Maddie's going, so are we," Alina declares, pointing

between herself and me. I sigh. The things I do for my friends.

"It's already eleven," Alexei says. "Parents are about to leave. The second they go, we get ready and head out." I nod, pressing my lips together before glancing at Aiden, who's deep in conversation with my dad. As if he feels me staring, he turns, and the second his eyes lock onto mine, my heart leaps out of my chest. He grins.

I wink before turning back to Alexei.

"Stop eye-fucking each other across the room and just get a damn room," Alexei mutters. I slap his chest, irritated at his comment.

Just as predicted, the parents leave fifteen minutes later, and we all race upstairs to get ready.

Since my hair and makeup are already done, all I have to do is find an outfit. I settle on a blue jean mini skirt—folding the zipper for an even shorter fit—a black short-sleeve crop top, and black knee-high leather boots. I refresh my red lipstick, drown myself in perfume, grab my black fluffy coat, and head downstairs.

"Why are you always trying to send me to jail?" I look up from my phone and grin at Aiden.

"Gotta keep you on your toes somehow." He chuckles, pulling me into his arms.

"Fuck, you look so beautiful, angel." I smile, pulling away.

"Kit Kat, you're gonna give my brother a heart attack," Will says, laughing as he walks past. I watch him disappear upstairs sighing.

"I miss Will. I feel like I haven't spent any time with him lately. He's like the big brother I never had." Aiden places a soft kiss on top of my head.

"I'll plan something for all of us next week. I haven't seen him

much either. And I don't know if you noticed, but he barely spoke to Maddie tonight." I nod, my heart sinking for them both.

"Let's go, bitches," Alexei calls, coming down the stairs hand- in-hand with Graysen. I smile, clapping my hands together as we all head out

It takes twenty minutes to find parking, and by the time we step inside the massive frat house, Bad Bunny is booming through the speakers. I hand my coat to Aiden and rush to the dance floor, squealing when I see Maddie and Alina already dancing.

"You look gorgeous, oh my God," Maddie exclaims, spinning me around.

"So do you guys!" I grin, pointing at their outfits.

Aiden appears a second later, handing me two shots. I chug them both and kiss him right after.

Then, he heads toward the kitchen where Will and Roman are, while I stay on the dance floor with my girls.

Alina notices Roman watching us and flips him off. I press my lips together to hold in my laughter, but she giggles, and I can't help but join in. After a while, we take a break and head to the kitchen for more shots and that's when I see it.

A blonde girl's, touching Aidens arm, laughing at whatever he just said.

And the worst part? Aiden is laughing too. I will fucking kill him.

Alina's eyes glaze over when she sees Roman with another blonde wrapped around his waist. I clench my jaw and march straight toward Aiden.

"Shot, please, babe," I say, holding out my cup. Aiden glances between her and me.

The blonde has the nerve to snap her fingers in front of my face.

"Excuse me? Don't you see we're talking?" I ignore her. I only look at Aiden, daring him to try.

"Sure," he says, filling my cup with tequila. The blonde pouts. "Aiden, is she your girlfriend?" He hesitates. Looks at me. Then back at her. And shakes his head. "No, but-"

The words barely leave his mouth before my drink flies into his fucking face.

I don't wait for his reaction. I turn and walk away.
"Fucking asshole!" I mutter under my breath.
"WHAT THE FUCK WAS THAT?" Maddie demands as she pulls me into a hug. I scoff. "Apparently, all it takes is one blonde bitch for Aiden to forget I exist." I see him walking toward me. "Nope," I tell Maddie. "I don't want to talk to him. Let's go dance."
The music pulses through my veins as another Latin remix starts playing, the beat sinking into my bones. Alina, Maddie, and I move in perfect rhythm, our hips swaying in sync. At one point, we all move to the beat at the same time, and we squeal in excitement, grinning like idiots. I fucking love dancing.
Alina and I always joked that if ice skating didn't work out, we'd become professional dancers instead. Right now, I believe it.
A pair of hands settle on my hips, pulling me back against a solid chest. I let it happen, because fuck Aiden. No man will ever make me feel small. No man will ever make me feel like I don't matter.
The guy behind me grips my waist firmly, his body pressing against mine as we move together. I let my head fall back slightly, pretending—just for a second—that I don't care. That I'm not seething inside.
A hand yanks my wrist, pulling me away from the guy so fast I nearly stumble.
"What are you doing?" Aiden growls, his voice sharp, furious.
I scoff, wrenching my wrist free. "Fuck off, Aiden. Go back to your blonde bitch."
His tongue pokes at the corner of his mouth, his jaw flexing. Then—he laughs.
It's a dark, low chuckle. One that makes my pulse spike. I know that laugh.

"Are you with him? Is he bothering you?" the guy asks, eyeing Aiden warily.

I chuckle, my tone sharp and unforgiving. "No, I'm not. He's nothing to me."

Aiden flinches. Just barely. But I catch it. I don't give either of them a chance to respond before I turn and walk away. I need to find Alexei. I need to get the fuck out of here.

"Kat, wait," Aiden calls, his voice laced with frustration. "Katerina, I said fucking wait."

I grit my teeth, my hands shaking. "Fuck off, Aiden." I don't stop. I don't want to hear whatever excuse he's about to throw at me. But I don't make it two more steps before his strong hands wrap around my wrist, pulling me into his chest. He doesn't let me go. Instead, he drags me toward an empty room, shoving the door closed behind us before locking it.

"Just listen to me, please," he says, his voice tight. "I'm not losing you over something fucking stupid." I cross my arms, glaring at him. "Then maybe you should have thought about that before saying I wasn't yours." His hands run through his hair, his frustration evident.

"The only reason I said that is because she asked if you're my girlfriend. Which technically you are not. But you are my girl and she means nothing to me. It's just Molly, she's an old friend." I scoff, shaking my head.

"Do you think I'm five, Aiden? Do you really think she wanted to be just your friends. She was rubbing her hands all over you and you let her." His lips press into a thin line, and then he nods.

"I'm sorry! I didn't realise her intentions were different from mine. I was just talking to her as an old friend. I didn't touch her. I would never risk what we have.

Never!" I turn away, inhaling sharply. Don't fold, Kat. Don't fold.
But then he says the one thing that makes my heart stop.
"I was going to ask you to be my girlfriend on New Year's. I had it all planned out."
I whip around, my breath catching. "You were?" He nods. "You can ask the guys."
The silence between us is thick. Heavy. The only thing we hear is the muffled music outside.
Aiden takes a slow step toward me. "Hearing you say it… I hated it. So I know how you felt."
He moves closer, and my heartbeat thunders in my chest. "Will you please be my girlfriend?" His voice drops, almost
pleading. "Because I can't do this anymore." I let out a slow breath before nodding, a small smile tugging at my lips. "Yes."
Relief floods his face.
"But if you ever pull that shit again," I add, "I will kill you." Aiden laughs, nodding quickly. "Never. You're mine, baby. "
"Good," I murmur, stepping closer. "Now kiss me. I've been trying to keep my hands to myself all night, but fuck, you look so fucking hot." Aiden smirks, sliding my hands under his shirt, my fingers tracing along his abs. His muscles flex under my touch as he pulls me closer, his lips crashing against mine.
"You drive me fucking mad, Katerina," he growls against my lips.
"All day, I feel this need to mark you permanently. You were made to be mine, baby. Only mine." A moan escapes me as his hands grip my ass, his touch possessive, desperate.
I hear a sharp knock at the door and we both groan.

Aiden sighs, pressing his forehead against mine for a second before pulling away. He strides toward the door and yanks it open. Standing there, looking way too hopeful, is the blonde bitch. "Aiden—" She stops mid-sentence, her eyes landing on me standing behind him. I smirk.

"Let's go, babe," I say, grabbing Aiden's hand.

Her face drops. "B-but she threw a drink at you! And you still want her?" I bite my lip, trying to hold back my laughter.

Aiden shrugs, his grip on my waist tightening. "Her crazy matches mine. I'll always want her." I wave at Blondie as Aiden leads me downstairs. "Stop gloating," Aiden mutters, shaking his head with a smirk.

"I can't help it," I laugh. "Did you see her face?" Aiden chuckles,

pulling me close enough to press a quick kiss to my lips.

"You are such a bully," he murmurs, his lips brushing my jaw.

"Only when it comes to you," I tease as Aiden grins, nipping at my

bottom lip.

"I fucking love it when you get jealous."

"Only for you. I told you once—I don't share. And I stand by it."

Aiden groans, squeezing my ass. "Neither do I, angel face. You are mine and mine only. I will beat the shit out of any guy who even looks at you." I roll my eyes but can't stop the smile tugging at my lips.

"Let's get out of here," I whisper. Aiden nods, grabbing my hand as we head toward the door. And as I glance up at him, his jaw sharp under the dim lighting, his possessive grip around my waist, his entire being wrapped around me—

I know.
I know I'm so fucking whipped for this man. And I don't even care.

CHAPTER FORTY - ONE

KATERINA

We are one day away from school starting again. Today, we all decided to go snowboarding. By we, I mean Aiden, me, Alexei, Grayson, Will, and Maddie. I know damn well Alina and Roman weren't actually busy—
they just didn't want to see each other.
I've been snowboarding my entire life, but no one else—aside from Grayson—has, so today is going to be hilarious. I'm fully prepared to watch my friends eat shit on the trails.
I pull on my black leggings and layer them with tan sweat-
pants. Two pairs of thick, fluffy socks follow, along with my Skims tight crew neck. Then, I grab my black

snow overalls, zip them up, and add a beanie over my braided hair.

Once I'm bundled up, I grab the rest of my gear and head downstairs.

"I'm not excited for this," Alexei groans as he descends the stairs.

"Baby, I'll teach you," Grayson reassures him. "I told you to stop worrying, or you'll get wrinkles." I add making Alexei gasps

"Don't say that to me! My anxiety is already through the roof." Aiden and I burst out laughing at them. They are the perfect balance together. Alexei is crazy and outgoing while Graysen is mellow and a homebody. They balance each other out.

"Let's head out," Will says, grabbing his keys. "I didn't pack lunch, so we can just eat something up there." We all nod in agreement, grabbing our gears and heading out of the house.

Since it's snowing, we take two cars—my Jeep and Will's truck. We don't want to risk it with the others. Alexei and Grayson ride with Aiden and me, while Will and Maddie take his truck. "Oh God, babe, we should've gone with Will instead," Alexei complains as we pull out of the driveway. "I can't do two hours of Taylor Swift or Cigarettes After Sex." I cackle, holding my stomach.

"Funny, Alexei," I say dryly. "It won't be two hours of Taylor.

SZA dropped her new album, and I'm trying to listen to that."

Alexei lets out a dramatic sigh of relief, and I pout, crossing my arms.

"You like Tay-Tay. I'm not talking to you until you take it back." Alexei scoffs, turning to stare out the window like a petulant child.

Aiden places his hand on my thigh, giving it a squeeze and my vagina flutters.

My mind flashes back to last night, and I swear I can't get enough of this man.

Is it normal to have sex three rounds a night? No, right? That's what I thought.

I swat Aiden's hand away, and he glances at me, then at the road, then back again—repeating it a few times.

"Don't touch me. I took an oath to be celibate for the rest of the week," I announce.

Aiden laughs, keeping his eyes on the road. "When did you do that?"

"Just now," I say matter-of-factly. "I can't think around you, and my lady parts seem to only think about you all day, so it's a problem."

Aiden smirks, placing his hand right back on my thigh. "Well, my man parts think about you all day too, so it's not a problem."

I groan, covering my face with my hands. "It's okay, baby," Aiden teases. "It's normal." No, it's fucking not. "One week, Aiden. You can do it." I pat his shoulder in encouragement.

Aiden glares at me while I grin at him.

Two hours later, we finally arrive at the resort. Aiden parks, and we all get out, grabbing our gear from the trunk.

I put on my snow boots, zip up my jacket, and adjust my gloves while Aiden secures my helmet and goggles. He leans down, kissing my lips softly before I finish getting ready.

Everyone else gets their gear on, and we grab our snowboards before heading to get our passes. Aiden scans the QR code from his email, and five minutes later, we're officially set.

"Let's start at the bunny hill," I suggest. "We need to see how much work we're going to have on our hands."
Everyone nods in agreement, and we make our way over.

I sit down and teach them how to strap their boots into their snowboards while Grayson explains the heel edge and toe edge techniques. Then, I go over how to get off the ski lift, which— knowing this group—will be the first disaster.

Twenty minutes later, we're on the lift.

I sit next to Aiden, who looks… nervous as hell.

"Don't be nervous, babe," I say, squeezing his hand.

"I'll hold your hand going down."

Aiden nods as we near the top.

"Remember—move toward the edge of the seat, hold onto the railing, and face your snowboard ahead. Don't hit me. Let the board touch the ground before you step on it."

He nods again, and we do just that.

Aiden almost makes it but falls at the very end. I start laughing

but help him up, strapping his other boot in.

One by one, the others make it off. Alexei screams but somehow stays on his feet.

Will and Maddie, though? They both eat shit, and I lose it.

We spend the next few hours teaching them how to balance, shift their weight, and—most importantly—fall without breaking anything. Aiden catches on surprisingly fast, and by the third run, he actually makes it down the hill without falling.

"You killed that, baby!" I yell as I reach the bottom.

Aiden grins, a little too proud of himself.

"Naturally."

I roll my eyes, as I glance back at the hill for Will and Maddie. Will, on the other hand…? He sucks at snowboarding.

After lunch, we move to a bigger hill. Everything's going great—until we see a crowd of people and paramedics gathering at the bottom.

Aiden and I snowboard closer. And that's when we see Will. "Oh my God," I whisper. The paramedics are surrounding him, and I push my way through until I reach Maddie.

"What happened?" I demand. Maddie's pale as snow sitting next to Will, holding his hand on hers.

"His board got stuck in the snow, and he tumbled down the hill." I wince, turning to Will.

"Will, are you okay?" He shakes his head no, his jaw clenched in pain. They decide to airlift him, which means Will gets his first helicopter ride. Maddie goes with him while the rest of us make it down the hill and drive straight to the hospital.

By the time we arrive, Will's foot is in a cast, and Maddie is feeding him grapes.

"Life's sweet, huh?" Alexei asks with a smirks. "I can't believe you fell like that."

Grayson slaps Will's shoulder. "Dumbass."

"Hey, at least I have a cool memory for my first time snow- boarding," Will says.

Aiden glares at him, not finding it funny.

"It's just a sprain," Will reassures. "They said the cast will help stabilize it faster."

Aiden nods, but I can tell he's still mad. I wrap my arm around him, leaning into his warmth.

"I'm sorry, Will. We shouldn't have done this today."

Will immediately shakes his head. "Not your fault, Kit Kat. I thought I had it and went too fast." I nod, giving him a side hug.

Maddie stays with Will while we head back into town. The rest of us drive home together, leaving Will's car for Maddie to bring back tomorrow.

"God, it's almost 4 p.m. We have our evening ice skating class today," Aiden says as we pull into the driveway.

"Sophia is going to be at this one," he adds, and I smile at the thought of seeing her.

We rush inside, and I quickly change into another pair of leggings, grab my gloves, my thick Columbia jacket, and my ice skating bag.

I hop into Aiden's car, and we head toward campus. Fifteen minutes later, we pull up at the arena.

The moment I step inside, my heart warms at the sight of all the little ones lacing up their skates. Aiden's auntie Maria, is sitting on the bench tying Sophia's skates, and as soon as Aiden walks over, Sophia lets out a squeal, throwing her tiny arms around his waist.

I crouch down to help one of the younger skaters tie their laces when I hear my name being called. I glance up and see Maria waving at me with a warm grin. I wave back but gesture toward the kids, silently telling her I'll meet her after. She smiles, understanding, before stepping off the rink. A few seconds later, I hear the sound of tiny skates gliding toward me.

"Kit Kat! I missed you so much!" Sophia squeals, wrapping
her arms around me.

I chuckle, hugging her tightly. "Sophia girl, I missed you more, princess! Look how big you're getting!" She spins around excitedly, showing off her braids, and I clap my hands in approval.

"You look beautiful, Soph." She blushes, ducking behind Aiden's legs.

"Okay, class, let's gather around," I call out. "As always, boys with Aiden and girls with me!" Everyone follows the routine, and we start today's lesson. I teach the girls how to do jumps and how to spin in one spot. Sophia is definitely having fun, and every time she laughs, it makes my heart swell.

"Miss Hart, I want to be an Olympic champion like you," one of the little girls, Sariah, says, wrapping her arms around my legs in a hug. I chuckle, kneeling to her level.

"Thank you, Sariah. I'm not a champion yet, but hopefully soon." The girls nod enthusiastically, and Sophia claps her hands together.

"She will be one! And my brothers and I will be there to cheer her on!" I grin, nodding at her. "That's all the support I need."

The rest of practice flies by. By the time we're finished, Aiden has already put away the equipment, and Sophia and I head toward my car. I buckle her up in the back, and we drive to Aiden's actual house, to drop her off with her nanny. Before leaving, she gives me the biggest hug, making me promise that we'll have a girls' day soon.

Aiden and I drive home in comfortable silence, both exhausted from the day.

The second we step inside, I head straight upstairs to Aiden's room—which, let's be honest, has basically become my room. Without a second thought, I walk into his bathroom, peel off my clothes, and step into the shower. The warm water cascades over me, relaxing my tired muscles.

Fifteen seconds later, I hear the shower door open, Aiden steps in behind me, his hands resting on my waist—his skin cold from the air outside makes me shudder at the contact.

"I'm still mad at you," he murmurs.

I raise an eyebrow, wrapping my arms around his neck. "And what, my handsome boyfriend, are you mad at me for?" I bat my lashes innocently.

"You haven't let me touch you all day," he groans, his voice low. "It's driving me insane. I need you close to me."

I bite my lip, trying not to smirk. "Well, I took a celibacy oath for the rest of the week."

Aiden laughs, shaking his head, bringing me closer to him.

"My brain does not function properly around you, and my body is on its own personal mission to think about you all damn day, so I'm sticking to my decision."

Aiden's smirk grows as he presses himself against me, his lips hovering near my ear. "Well, my body thinks about you all day too," he whispers.

"So I don't see the problem." A breath hitches in my throat. Damn him.

I take a slow step back until my back is flush against the cool shower wall.

His hands trail up my sides, and goosebumps rise on my skin—despite the warmth of the water.

"Break your oath," he murmurs, his lips brushing against my temple. I swallow hard, tilting my head to look at him. His deep brown eyes are clouded with heat, and there's something about the way he's looking at me—like I belong to him—that makes my whole body ache. I grip the back of his neck, pulling him down so our lips almost touch.

"Make me," I whisper in his ear, bitting his earlobe. Aiden's
eyes darken full of lust, as he squeezes both of my breasts, one on each hand. I slam my lips on his and he bites my bottom one, pulling me closer to him. His cock

pokes my stomach and I groan, wrapping my right hand around it, stroking him as he plays with my breasts.

"Fuck baby." Aiden moans groaning on my mouth. He slams my back in the shower wall and lifts me by my thighs, as I wrap my legs around his waist.

One of his hands intertwines with mine and he holds it above my head as he trails kisses along my neck.

The tip of his cock aligns with my entrance and in one swift stroke he slides inside me. My lips part as I moan his name.

"Aiden." He thrusts in and pulls out slowly, thrusting in over and over again, while I'm in cloud nine.

"God baby, look at me." He grips my chin with his right hand to look at me and i moan bitting my lower lip. Aiden brings his lips on mine and I wrap my arms around his neck as he grips his hands under my thighs, sliding me up and down his dick while he thrusts in and out of me in deep strokes.

"You take me so well Katerina. You were made for me baby." I gasp as he starts to fuck me harder, squealing his name in pleasure.

"Look at my dick baby. Look how good your tight little pussy takes me." Those words were my undoing as my vision black out. I shudder holding into Aiden for dead life as i ride out my orgasm. Aiden leaves kisses on my neck, but then he starts sucking under my ear and god i want more. I know he will leave hickeys but it's okay.

"Fuck me harder." I manage to say between breaths. Aiden does just that and in seconds he is grunting as he comes inside me at the same time I orgasm for the second time.

"There goes my oath." I whisper and Aiden laughs as I join..

"Fuck your oath. Nothing can keep me away from you," Aiden murmurs, his voice rough with certainty. I chuckle softly as he finally sets me down, my feet meeting the cool shower tiles, a stark contrast to the warmth still lingering between us. We take our time washing each other, our touches softer now, more intimate in their tenderness. No rush, no urgency—just us.

Once we're done, I step out and wrap myself in a towel before
grabbing one of Aiden's oversized shirts, slipping it on. It drapes over me comfortably, smelling like him.
I climb into his bed, my body already sinking into the familiar
warmth of the sheets. Aiden joins me moments later, pulling me into his arms without hesitation.
His embrace is firm, reassuring—like home.
And just like that, sleep finds us easily, wrapped up in each other.

CHAPTER FORTY - TWO

KATERINA

The ice is gleaming under the bright overhead lights. The sound of blades slicing across the surface echoes around us as competitors warm up, coaches whisper last- minute advice, and the announcer calls for the next pair to take the ice.

This is it—our last qualifier, our last chance to prove we belong in the Olympics. Every gruelling practice, every moment of pain, every sacrifice—it all comes down to this.

I worked my ass off after my injury, training harder than ever. I had to. But now, standing here again, moments away from another performance—the performance—I feel like I can't breathe. I thought I was over my PTSD, but ever since he who shall not be named dropped me on purpose, a part of me is always on guard, always preparing for the worst.

Alexei is not him.

Alexei is like a brother. He values our safety too much to ever let something like that happen.

But I'm still scared. The competition is taking place at our arena today, and I'm a nervous wreck.

Everyone is coming—our families, our friends. Aiden's auntie Maria and Sophia will be here, and letting down that little girl would destroy me.

"If you keep frowning like that, you'll get forehead wrinkles,"

Alexei teases, smirking. I glare at him. He thinks he's so funny. He's just being petty because I told him the same thing the other day.

"Are you nervous?" I ask, and Alexei nods.

"Good, because I'm also shitting bricks."

He chuckles, and I join in before taking a deep breath.

"We'll smash this," he says confidently. "The song is amazing,

the choreography is phenomenal, and don't even get me started

on our costumes."

I nod, still overthinking everything. I always do that when I'm nervous. It's not that I doubt our ability—it's just… I guess I'm scared of failure. That all this work will be for nothing.

"Stop overthinking," Alexei says, rubbing my arms to comfort

me. "Your boyfriend will be here, his family, your dad, plus all our friends."

I hesitate. I wish my mom was here. Unfortunately, flight tickets are expensive, flying back and forth from Russia, costs a leg and an arm.

I send a quick text to Aiden, asking if he's here yet. It doesn't deliver.
I frown but shake it off. His phone is probably dead. He'll be here. He knows how much this means to me. Coach grins at Alexei and me, giving us a thumbs-up as she
talks to Alina.
Her qualifier is tomorrow, and I know she'll make it. The way Alina skates, is magical. Anyone who watches her is hypnotized. I glance toward the stands and spot my dad. He's talking to Aiden's mom while Sophia keeps glancing around the rink, searching for me.
"Sophia!" I call, lifting my hand to wave. The moment her eyes land on me, she grins and starts jumping up and down, waving excitedly. I chuckle, blowing her a kiss.
"Ladies and gentlemen, welcome to the last pre-Olympic qualifier of the year. Please take your seats, as our program will start shortly."
I inhale sharply, steadying myself as the announcement ends. Alexei nudges me, and I force a smile at him. My grin drops immediately when I see Max and his partner enter the arena. Fuck. I forgot that motherfucker is still in the game. I can't wait to see his face when we take home gold today.
"Kat, we're number fourteen," Alexei reminds me, rubbing
his hands together for warmth. I nod, rubbing my own hands
as I steal another glance at the stands. Still no Aiden. No Will. No Roman or Grayson.
Where the fuck are they?
"Where are the boys?" I ask, trying to keep my voice casual, but Alexei sees right through me. He shrugs. "I

don't know. Grayson hasn't answered my texts either. I'm sure they'll be here on time."
I nod, forcing myself to stay positive.

'He's not coming, Kat.
He doesn't care about you.
I keep telling you, only I will love you.'

Max's voice echoes in my mind, his smirk flashing behind my eyes like a haunting memory. Get the fuck out of my head, Max.
GET THE FUCK OUT!
I shut my eyes tightly, counting to ten as I take slow, deep breaths.
It helps—kind of.
But the ache in my chest won't go away.
He isn't here. He knows how much this means to me. And he isn't here.
He lied.
I watch pair after pair go before us, their performances a blur. Then, before I know it, our names are called.
Alexei holds my hand as we skate on the ice, moving toward the center of the rink. I try to smile, but it feels forced. The disappointment weighing me down is suffocating.
Reflections by The Neighbourhood starts playing, and we move— fluid, synchronized, precise. I push through the routine, refusing to let my emotions ruin this.
Alexei spins me, releases me, and I launch into a quadruple jump—
I land perfectly.
The crowd erupts into cheers. We continue skating, moving effortlessly. The rhythm carries us, our movements smooth, powerful. Alexei wraps his leg

around mine as we spin in place, then lifts me high into the air.

For a split second, I glance toward the stands— And my stomach drops.

His seat is still empty. He didn't come.

Alexei reaches for me, but I falter. I roll out of his arm too

soon, miss his hand— And fall.

The gasps from the crowd pierce through me like knives. Tears sting my eyes as I scramble to finish the routine, every step feeling heavier, every movement drenched in the weight of my mistake. We hit our final pose, the music fading. Applause erupts around us, but I barely hear it.

The moment we step off the ice, I run. I explode into tears the second I reach the locker room.

"I'm so sorry, Alexei!" I sob, my voice breaking. "I ruined our future for a stupid guy who didn't even care enough to be here for me." Alexei pulls me into a hug, his arms tight around me. "It's okay, Kat. I know you really wanted him here. It's okay.

We'll have another chance." But I shake my head, tears streaming down my cheeks. There won't be another chance.

We graduate next semester. There won't be another chance. And I fucking ruined it.

Coach Camilla walks into the room, wrapping her arms around both of us.

"I don't want to say I told you so," she sighs, "but, there's a reason feelings stay out of competitions. Now let's go. We have to make our appearance for the points." I wipe my tears, nodding, trying to pull myself together.

"I'm just glad you're okay," she adds softly, wrapping an arm around my shoulders. I lean into her. We sit in the podium area, waiting for our score.

I try to smile, but the tears won't stop. Like a dam has broken loose.

The man I loved bailed on me tonight, and because of my feelings for him, I fucked up my dreams.

We score 98 points—enough for bronze.

Max smirks at me from across the podium, gold hanging around his neck. His expression is mocking, dripping with satisfaction. It makes me want to punch him.

The second the medal ceremony ends, I get off the podium and head straight to the locker room. I change into my clothes as fast as I can, my hands shaking as I grab my phone. I start to text Alina, asking if I can crash at her place, but before I can send it—

The door slams open and Alina rushes in, immediately wrapping her arms around me.

And I break again.

I sob into her shoulder, her hands rubbing my back, whispering, "I'm here, I'm here."

"He didn't come, Ali," I choke out. "The only reason I fell is because I looked at the stands and saw his seat empty."

Alina hugs me tighter. "I'm sorry, my love. There should be a proper reason why. You know Aiden cares about you."

I lift my head, my vision blurry from crying, and see my dad standing in the doorway.

I let go of Alina and run straight into his arms.

"I'm so sorry, Dad," I whisper. "I tried, but I let everyone down." He strokes my hair, his arms strong and safe around me. "It's okay, honey. You still have the championship. And I know you'll win big." I nod, swallowing back more tears as he pulls away, wiping my face gently.

"Thanks for being here," I whisper.

He smiles, hugging me again. "I'll always be here for you."

Thirty minutes later, I'm in Alina's car, heading toward the figure skating house. I asked my dad to tell Aiden's auntie that I wasn't feeling well, but that I was grateful she came. I really am. But I don't want to see her. I can't face Sophia after failing. As soon as we walk inside the figure skating house, my phone starts ringing. I don't even need to check. I know it's him. A surge of rage

burns through me as I hit decline.

Text after text pops up, but it doesn't matter. Nothing he says will fix this. I don't want anything to do with him. The one man I ever loved forgot about me tonight. And I'm done.

I turn off my phone and hand it to Alina. I don't have to say anything. She understands, and I'm grateful beyond words to have her in my life. Alina is hurting too. But she's still here for me.

She's always there for me.

I change into the pyjamas she gives me and slide into the right side of her bed. A few minutes later, she joins me with a sigh.

"I don't know why he didn't show up," she murmurs. "But I know Aiden loves you, Kat. He's crazy about you." I shake my head, shutting my eyes tightly.

"It doesn't matter anymore, Ali. I almost ruined my future for a guy. For a guy who couldn't even be here for me." My voice wavers, but I force myself to finish. "I'm never doing that again." Alina gulps, watching me. "I know you don't mean that. You're hurt because you love him." I stare at the ceiling, forcing back the tears.

"It doesn't matter anymore," I whisper. Because figure skating is my life.

And Aiden is not part of it.

CHAPTER FORTY - THREE

KATERINA

The figure skating house is quiet. It's the kind of silence that should feel peaceful, should make me feel at home—but it doesn't. Because no matter how many times I try to tell myself this is where I belong, no matter how much I remind myself that skating is my priority, that I can't afford distractions—I still feel wrong.

I stare at my phone for the hundredth time, my thumb hovering over Aiden's name.

36 Missed Calls

15 New Messages

I squeeze my eyes shut, taking a deep breath. I can't talk to him. I won't talk to him. I need to clear my head. I need to focus.

So why does it feel like I can't breathe without him? A soft knock at my door pulls me from my thoughts. I already know who it is before I open it.

Alina stands there, arms crossed, one brow arched. "Are we going to talk about it?"

I sigh, stepping aside so she can come in. She closes the door behind her and sits on my bed, watching me carefully. "Kat, you've been avoiding him."

"I'm not—" She glares.

I groan, rubbing my temple. "Fine. I am."

Alina leans forward. "He's worried, you know." I swallow hard. "He'll be fine."

She scoffs. "Yeah? And what about you? Because from where I'm sitting, you look miserable."

I am miserable. But I don't say that. Instead, I shake my head. "I just need time."

Alina studies me for a long moment, then exhales. "You're

scared."

I stiffen. "No, I'm focused."

She tilts her head. "Focused on what? Running away? Pushing him away?"

I flinch, but she doesn't stop. "You think if you avoid him, you'll suddenly forget what he means to you? That it'll make everything easier?"

My throat tightens. "Alina—"

"You love him, Kat." My breath catches. The words sting—not because they're wrong, but because they're too right. And I hate it.

"I can't," I whisper. "I can't afford to love him."

Alina's expression softens. "Why? Because you fell once?"

I clench my fists. "Because if I let myself have him, I'll lose

everything else."

She shakes her head. "No, Kat. You're just scared of choosing him."

Tears burn behind my eyes, and I look away. "I need to focus on skating."

She sighs, standing up. "Skating is your dream. But Aiden? He's part of your life. You don't have to choose."

I don't say anything, and after a long pause, Alina steps toward the door.

"At some point," she says softly, "you're going to have to stop running. I love you but i have to start getting ready for the competition." I nod as she places a kiss on top of my head. Ali stands up and walks out of the room, leaving me alone with my thoughts. And for the first time since I left the hockey house—I start to wonder if I made the biggest mistake of my life.

After grabbing lunch, we all get ready for Alina's and Maddie's qualifier tonight. I put on a pair of black Lululemon leggings, white socks, and an oversized black sweater. I add my thick brown coat, a black beanie, and slide my feet into my beige Tasman Ugg slippers.

Grabbing my phone, I head downstairs, where Alexei is running a lint roller over Grayson's back.

They both turn toward me the moment they see me.

"Hey, Kat," Graysen says, wrapping his arms around me. I hesitate, but Alexei glares at me, so I hug him back.

"I love you, but sometimes you're dumb." I roll my eyes at Alexei's Russian words as he wraps his arms around me and kisses the top of my head.

"You broke his heart." He continues in Russian. I frown, my heartbeat accelerating in fear. Grayson kisses Alexei's cheek and runs outside to his car.

"Is Aiden okay?" I ask, panic creeping in. Alexei sighs, shaking his head.

"Grayson said he started trashing his room and then ran out. He won't answer anyone's calls." I rub my chest as a panic attack creeps in. My breathing fastens, and Alexei shakes his head.

"Hey, you're fine. He will be fine." I nod. Alexei's right. He will be fine. Fuck.

I should've just talked to him. Fuck, fuck, fuck. God, why am I so stupid? He loves me.

"Stop overthinking. We need to be there for Alina and Maddie tonight." I nod, closing my hands into fists, feeling the tips of my nails dig into my skin, anchoring me to the real world.

The four of us get into Grayson's car, and fifteen minutes later, we arrive at the arena. Maddie and Alina run inside to grab their numbers, while I tag along behind with Grayson and Alexei.

We check in and take our seats as the figure skaters warm up on the ice.

I scan the arena, and my eyes land on Roman tucked in the back. I tell Alexei I'll be back and make my way toward him.

"Hey, stranger," I say, taking the seat next to him. Roman looks at me but doesn't say anything.

"Does she know you're here?" Roman shakes his head, biting his bottom lip as his right leg bounces up and down.

He's nervous for her.

"You love her, don't you?" Roman looks at me, and I understand. He loves her, but he doesn't know how to love her right.

My heart hurts for my best friends.

"Well, if it makes you feel better, I also suck at this shit." I turn my head to face the ice again.

"No, you don't." My eyes scan the arena, and they land on Aiden's warm honey eyes. My heart skips a beat as we stare at each other. He doesn't move, and neither do I.

We just stare at each other. I want to scream and ask him, why he bailed on me. Why he didn't even bother to send me a text? I was to scream and yell at him.

"I don't know why you won't talk to him, because anyone with two eyes in their head can see how much you both love each other." I gulp, glancing back at Aiden, who's still looking at me.

"Brotherly advice: Stop self-sabotaging. Yes, figure skating means a lot, but having someone who loves you like that? It won't come again." I nod as my eyes leave Aiden's when the presenter starts welcoming us and reads the order of performances.

Alina is fifth, and Maddie is ninth. I sigh, rubbing my hands together, trying to calm my anxiety. I see Will walk in, and the moment he sees me and Roman, he takes a seat next to him.

Aiden stands up from his seat, but I get distracted and lose sight of him when Alexei yells out my name. He flips us off and gets up with Grayson following behind him.

They sit behind us as Alexei complains about having to move. I turn around and glare at him, telling him to stop talking before we get kicked out of the arena. Alexei huffs, crossing his arms over his chest, but nods, rolling his eyes. I smile and blow him a kiss. Someone sits next to me, and my heart jumps out of my chest when I turn around and see who it is.

Aiden.

He sits there, his body tense, staring straight ahead, not even bothering to look at me. I flinch when I feel Roman pinch my thigh. "You've been staring at him for the last two minutes. Just trying to help you not look crazy." I lean into Roman in disbelief.

"It's real? He's sitting next to me?" Roman nods, and I lean back in my seat.

I thought my mind was playing tricks on me.

After the first four performances, the presenter says Alina's name, and we all stand up, cheering for her. Alina skates into the middle of the arena as the lights dim. I move to the edge of my seat, nervous as hell for my best friend. "Work Song" by Hozier starts playing, and my throat closes up. I can feel Aiden's body heat, even though there is no part of him touching me.

Ali glides around the rink with such poise and perfect movements. My best friend was born to be a figure skater. The class and gentleness in every move hypnotize not just me but everyone in the audience. She jumps into a quad toe and lands it perfectly. I stand up, screaming and cheering for her as I clap my hands. My best friend grabs the edge of her blade and spins around.

If Roman didn't love her before, he definitely does now.

Alina skates around and then jumps again, my jaw falling open when she lands a quad axel perfectly. Alexei stands up, screaming as I try to gather my thoughts.

"Oh my god, oh my god," I shout, grabbing Roman's and Aiden's arms.

"She landed a fucking quad axel. Oh my god." Roman grins at me as he claps for the love of his life.

I turn toward Aiden, who is staring at my hand wrapped around his bicep. I remove it quickly, muttering an apology under my breath, and clear my throat, looking straight ahead.

I can feel his eyes on me but I refuse to look at him.

Alina finishes her routine, and the arena erupts in cheers. Alina waves at us, but her smile drops when she sees who is next to me.

"Fuck, I should have not come." Roman whispers as he sits down. I pat his back.

"It's okay Roman. Just keep trying." Roman nods, running a hand over his face in frustration.

Soon, it's Maddie's turn, and we all cheer for her as she takes her spot in the middle of the rink.

"Salvatore" by Lana Del Rey starts playing, and our best friend begins her routine. My eyes follow Maddie's every move as she glides gracefully on the ice. She jumps into a triple quad, and we all stand to cheer as she lands it perfectly.

When the final results are announced, Alina wins gold, and Maddie wins silver. We all jump and cheer, hugging each other, celebrating our friends wins.

I turn to my left, but the seat is empty. He left. I get up and run toward the exit.

Maybe I'll catch him. Maybe I can tell him I want to hear why he didn't show up, but when I step outside, he's gone. No cars moving. Nobody on sight.

I bite back a cry, lifting my hands to my head. How am i going to fix this?

CHAPTER FORTY - FOUR

KATERINA

I don't want to see him today. There are days when my heart wins over my head. Days when my heart is begging for me to hear him out so we don't lose him. And there are days like today. My brain has taken control over my heart and refuses to talk to Aiden, or listen to him. The house is quiet when I step inside. Too quiet. I don't know what I expected. I had timed it carefully, knowing the guys would still be at practice. I just needed to grab a few things—clothes, toiletries, anything I had left behind. In and out. No distractions. No conversations I wasn't ready for.
Not him.
But as I push my bedroom door open, the air shifts. I can feel someone watching me, and then I hear the door click shut behind me.

I spin around, my breath catching, as my eyes land on a very
tired Aiden. Aiden.
Leaning against the door like he's been waiting for this. Like he knew I would come back eventually, and he just had to wait long enough for me to walk right into his trap.
His eyes—stormy, unreadable, too much—lock onto mine, and the room feels smaller, the air thicker.
I swallow hard. "Move."
He doesn't.
I shift, trying to step past him, but he pushes off the door, blocking my way with nothing but his body, presence, and everything.
"You don't get to run from me," he says, his voice low, rough,
broken.
I flinch from the pain in his voice. "I'm not—"
"Yes, you are." His jaw clenches, his hands curling into fists at his sides. "And I let you. I let you walk away. I let you pretend like this—we—didn't matter."
His voice drops even lower, something dangerous laced in the way he steps closer. "But it does, Kat. And I'm done pretending it doesn't."
I hate the way my chest tightens at his words. Hate the way my fingers itch to reach for him, to pull him close, to fall into him like I always do.
But I can't. I won't." I really tried to be there, Kat." He whispers, eyes full of pain.
"Aiden, you didn't come." My voice shakes, but I keep my eyes on him. " I fell and almost lost my dream because I was so desperate to have you there, I kept glancing at the stands for you, so, please. Don't make up some excuse."

He shakes his head, stepping toward me. "Kat, I'm not making it up."

I cross my arms. "You disappeared. That's all I know."

He exhales hard. "A freshman pulled a prank on Westbridge. Coach found out right before practice and lost it. Had all of us in the weight room for three hours. No breaks. Nobody was allowed to leave or even get into the locker room."

I blink. That's... insane. But I don't say anything.

"I wanted to be there," he says. "I kept looking at the clock, thinking about you. But Coach was losing it. If anyone tried to leave, he threatened to bench us for the season. I didn't have my phone. I couldn't get to it."

My chest tightens, but I keep my expression flat. "You still didn't show up."

"I know." His voice cracks a little. "But I swear, it wasn't because I didn't want to. I just couldn't."

I square my shoulders. "Aiden, I—"

"I hated you."

The words hit like a blow, sharp and unexpected, and I go still. Aiden's breathing is uneven, his eyes burning into mine as if he's ripping himself open, raw and unfiltered, right in front of
me.

"God, I hated you so much when we first met," he murmurs, voice rough like he's been holding this in for too long. "You were everything I wasn't. Sharp edges and perfect grace. You made it look easy, and all I could do was crash and burn. You were fire, and I wanted to drown you out."

He takes a step closer, skates biting into the ice of my mind, forcing me back until my spine presses against the wall.

"But I couldn't stop watching you." His breath hitches. "Even when I told myself you were my enemy, I still watched you. Every turn. Every jump. Every stupid little smile you gave when you landed something clean. It drove me insane because I didn't understand it. I didn't want to."

I open my mouth, but nothing comes out because he's not done.

"And then you started watching me back." His voice is softer now but no less intense. "Not with hate. Not even with anger. Just… with this look, like you saw something in me I couldn't even see myself. And I knew I was screwed."

My chest tightens.

"I spent so much time trying to beat you at something— anything—just so I could feel like I mattered here." His fingers twitch like he wants to reach for me, but he doesn't. "But the truth is… you weren't the problem. You were just the only person I couldn't lie to. Every time you looked at me, it was like you knew. You saw all the cracks in me I didn't want anyone to see."

The air between us is razor-thin now.

"I don't know a lot of things," He exhales, eyes never leaving mine. "But all I know is, somewhere between wanting to be better than you and wanting to break you, I started wanting you. And it's terrifying because you deserve someone who's effortless and graceful and everything I'm not."

My breath is coming too fast, my heart hammering, my hands

shaking. And he sees it. I inhale sharply, but he keeps going.

"Do you know what you are to me?" His fingers graze my wrist, feather-light, but I feel it everywhere.

"You're a storm— the kind that drowns everything in its path. I thought if I hated you enough, I could hold myself above it. But you pulled me under. And now I'm choking on you."

My lips part, but no sound comes out.

"I can't stand the way you make beauty look effortless like you've never once doubted yourself." A shadow crosses his face. "Because I doubt everything. Every shift of my weight, every pass, every goddamn second I spend chasing a puck across this frozen hell."

He exhales, something breaking in his eyes. "I love you, and I hate how much it hurts."

My stomach plummets.

"I love you like a bruise loves bone—too deep to heal clean. I love you like a body hitting the boards—all impact and no grace. And if you walk away right now, I swear I'll hate you all over again." His voice cracks. "But it won't matter. Because I'll still love you under all of it."

The silence suffocates us.

"You're the one I keep loving, with fear of not being loved back. They are telling me to let go, but it feels as if I'm cheating on my own heart if I do. You are what home feels like, and my heart takes comfort in you. So how am I supposed to change the way I love and keep coming back to you if nothing can change the way I see you?"

God, why is he so perfect? I break, bringing him down to me, and slam my mouth on his, getting one last taste before I let him go.

A minute later, I pull away, regretting what I just did. The air between us is thick—heavy with the remnants of what just happened, of what we just did, of what I just let happen. And it's dangerous because of the way Aiden is looking at me right now. Like I'm the only thing holding him together? It's going to ruin me, and I'm going to ruin him.

I step back. Just an inch. Just enough to make space between us, to get my breathing under control, to ignore the way my lips still burn from his kiss.
His brows furrow. "Kat—"
"No." My voice comes out sharper than I intended. I clear my throat, clenching my fists at my sides.
"This—" I motion between us, between whatever the hell just happened—"was a mistake."
Aiden's entire body locks up. His expression shifts, morphing into something unreadable, but I see the way his fingers twitch at his sides, the way his jaw tightens like he's bracing for impact.
"A mistake," he repeats, voice flat.
I swallow the lump in my throat, ignoring the way my stomach knots. "Yeah."
His eyes darken. "That's bullshit."
"It's not," I snap, forcing myself to stay steady, to lie. "You need to get over this—over me."
A muscle jumps in his jaw. "Don't do that."
"Do what?" I huff. "Tell you the truth?" His expression hardens.
"No." snaps, eyes begging with mine." Lie to me."
My breath catches. He knows. Of course, he knows. Aiden Knight isn't stupid. He's always seen through me in ways no one else ever has, cutting through my walls like they're made of glass. But I can't let him see this. I won't. So I lift my chin, steel my spine, and say the one thing that will finally break him.
"I don't love you, Aiden." Silence.
A wreckage of silence, sharp and suffocating, stretching between us like the aftermath of a storm. Aiden doesn't move. Doesn't blink. Just stares at me, his face unreadable, his entire body so still it's terrifying.
He lets out a breath. Slow. Controlled. But his hands curl

into fists like he's trying to hold himself together, like if he lets go for even a second, he'll fall apart.
I bite the inside of my cheek, willing myself to stay steady. To keep my face blank. To pretend this doesn't hurt like hell.
Because it does, it kills me. But I don't say another word.
Aiden inhales deeply, running a hand through his hair, before finally stepping back.
His voice is quiet when he speaks, rough at the edges.
"Okay." I don't breathe.
"I won't bother you anymore," he adds, and the way he says it— the finality, the sheer emptiness in his tone— makes something shatter inside me.
I force myself to nod. "Good."
Aiden turns, his movements slow and deliberate, and walks out the door. The second it clicks shut behind him, I crumble.
My knees buckle, my hands flying to my face as I gasp for breath as I break in the safety of my empty room because I just lost him. I just lost the only thing that ever made me feel alive. And the worst part?
I did it to myself.

CHAPTER FORTY - FIVE

AIDEN

I don't remember walking out the door. All I remember is the sound of it clicking shut behind me. That tiny, final sound. Like a period at the end of a sentence you never wanted to read.

I don't remember how I got to the rink. Or to the locker room. Or why I'm still sitting here in full gear, soaked in sweat and heartbreak, long after practice ended.

I just know that when she said she didn't love me, something in me snapped—and then nothing. A whole lot of nothing.

Will's voice cuts through the static in my head. "You gonna sit there all night, man?"

I don't answer. Roman drops down onto the bench across from me, his expression unreadable but his eyes too damn knowing. "She said it, didn't she?"

I glance at him, jaw locked. He already knows. Of course he does.

"She said she doesn't love me."

Will winces. Roman swears under his breath. I laugh, but it's hollow. Bitter. "She kissed me like she meant it and said goodbye like she didn't. Then she looked me in the eye and ripped me apart like it was easy."

Silence stretches between the three of us.

"I thought I could handle it," I say, my voice cracking. "I thought if she didn't love me, I'd feel...angry. Numb. Something. But all I feel is empty. Like she reached in and took whatever was left of me with her."

Roman leans forward, elbows on his knees. "You don't believe her."

"Does it matter?" I whisper. "She said it. She meant for me to hear it. That has to count for something." I run a hand through my hair, exhaling hard as I lean back against the wall. My spine hits the cold surface, but I barely feel it. My mind's not here. It's somewhere else—locked in that night, stuck in the look on her face, the way everything shifted before I even understood what was happening.

"I fell in love with her that night, you know?" I say. My voice comes out quieter than I expect, almost like I'm admitting it to myself for the first time.

"The night she let me be there for her after her surgery." The truth tastes heavy in my mouth. "My mind has been a fucking mess ever since—filled with thoughts of only her and the way she looked at me."

Rome just shakes his head and lets out a soft chuckle. But he doesn't get it. Not really. He wasn't there. He didn't feel it snap into place.

"You don't get it," I say, because I have to say it. "It wasn't just attraction, it wasn't just some fleeting moment. It was her—every part of her."

I grip my hockey stick in my hand a little tighter. My fingers are tense, aching, but I can't let go. I suck in a breath, slower this time.

"The sound of her voice, the warmth of her skin… it became the only home I've ever known." I look down, almost ashamed of how real that still feels. "Because, somehow, I felt more at home in her arms than I ever did in my own damn house."

Will watches me, but he stays quiet. Maybe that's what I need. No advice. No comfort. Just space to say it out loud.

I let out a laugh, low and bitter, shaking my head like I can't believe it either. "I fell in love that night. The night she let me in—really let me in. When she was vulnerable and didn't try to hide the fucked up parts. And now?"

I pause. My chest feels too tight again. Like it's folding in on itself.

"I don't know how the hell I'm supposed to exist without her."

Will exhales, dragging a hand through his hair. "She's scared, man. You know that. She doesn't lie well, but she lies when she's terrified. You think she kissed you because she doesn't care?"

I drop my head into my hands. "I don't know what to think anymore."

Roman's voice softens. "What did she say exactly?"

I don't want to say it out loud again. But I do.

"She said this—us—was a mistake. That I need to get over her. That she doesn't love me."

Will lets out a low whistle. "Damn."

"She looked me right in the eye," I say, swallowing hard. "Like she wanted to believe it, too. Like she needed me to believe it."

"You think she was trying to protect herself?" Roman asks.

"Maybe. Or maybe she was trying to protect me."

"From what?" Will says. "From being loved by her?"

I laugh, but it's more of a choked sound. "From being wrecked by her. From being someone she can't fix. From being the reason she falls apart."

Roman shakes his head. "You've never been her downfall, Aiden. You're the only one who's ever kept her steady."

I stare at the floor, the weight of it all pressing down on me. "Then why does it feel like I'm the reason she's walking away?"

Neither of them answers. And maybe there is no answer.

A couple hours later, we end up at Maddie and Alina's. There's supposed to be some team movie night. Distraction. Noise. Something to keep my mind off the train wreck of my life. I'm doing fine. Or faking it well enough.

Until she walks in. Katerina Hart, has the kind of beauty that you appreciate, even from afar. She steps into the living room like she hasn't just shattered me into a thousand pieces. Like we're strangers again. She's wearing Alina's hoodie, hair up, no makeup, and she still looks like the most important thing in every room she enters.

And my heart? My heart does that stupid thing where it leaps. My hands clench and unclech, as anxiety starts creeping in. Will sees it. Roman sees it. I bet even the fucking couch sees it.

Kat freezes for a second when she sees me. And that second is everything. Because her mask slips. Her eyes go soft. Her lips part like she forgot how to breathe.

Then Maddie says something and the moment's gone.

Kat glances away and sits at the far end of the couch, like there aren't magnets under our skin pulling us back together.

I can't stop staring at her, but she won't look at me.

Roman elbows me. "Still think she doesn't love you?"

I don't answer. Because deep down, I already know she does.

She just doesn't know how to love me without setting herself on fire in the process.

And I don't know how to stop burning for her.

Will nudges me with a beer. "C'mon. You need to relax. Pretend she's not here for five minutes."

"Yeah, sure," I mutter. "I'll just ignore the girl who gutted me two hours ago. Easy."

Roman smirks. "We're not saying it's easy. We're saying you're spiraling and it's painful to watch."

I shoot him a glare, but it's weak. "Thanks, Doc."

"Anytime, heartbreak hotel."

We settle in for the movie. Sort of. I don't know what's playing. Some action thing. People are getting shot. Blown up. Whatever. Roman and Will are doing their best to keep things light. Roman keeps tossing popcorn at Will's face. Will's giving him shit about missing open nets last game. Everyone else is laughing.

Except me.

Except her.

Across the room, Kat's curled up next to Alina, legs tucked under her, eyes fixed on the screen but unfocused. She laughs at the right moments. Says the right things. But I can see it. She's not here either.
Halfway through the movie, I can't take it anymore. I get up, mutter something about needing air, and slip out onto the balcony. The night is cold, biting against my skin even through my hoodie. I lean on the railing, trying to breathe.
A minute later, the door slides open. Will steps out, handing me another drink.
"You're allowed to hurt," he says quietly.
"I don't want to hurt. I want to shut it off."
"Then go tell her how you feel."
"I already did."
"And?"
"She still walked away."
He shrugs. "Then maybe now it's her turn to come back."
I shake my head. "I'm tired of being the only one who shows up."
Roman joins us, holding out a pack of gum like it's a peace offering. "We're not letting you sulk all night. You either confront her or you do shots with us and talk shit until you feel human again."
"I'll take the shots."
We head back in, and the rest of the night blurs into something weirdly familiar—guys being guys, teasing, laughing too loud, talking trash over Mario Kart. And for a second, I forget how bad it hurts. Kat stays quiet, doesn't interact much, but I catch her watching me. Once. Twice. A third time when she thinks I'm not looking. And every single time, it wrecks me a little more.

At some point, Maddie declares it's time for board games. Roman talks me into playing. Kat ends up on the other team.
Our eyes meet when we sit across from each other. For one second, I forget how to breathe again. She looks away first.
The game goes on. Our friends are loud. A couple of shots in I'm laughing. I'm making jokes. I'm being the version of myself they expect.
But inside, I'm still stuck on that look. That moment. That one breath of vulnerability I saw in her eyes before she buried it.
Later, as people start to clear out, I help Will grab some trash bags. We're in the kitchen when Kat walks in to grab water. She doesn't notice me at first. Then she does. She freezes, and I do too. The silence stretches, thick and electric.
She doesn't say anything and Neither do I. But I want to. God, I want to ask her if she meant it. If she regrets it. If she even knows how hard it is to breathe when she's near and I can't touch her.
She grabs her water and turns to leave.
Right before she disappears, she pauses. Doesn't look back, but says, "You didn't deserve what I said."
Then she's gone.
And I'm left standing there, that one line echoing in my head like it means something.
Like maybe… just maybe… this isn't the end after all.

CHAPTER FORTY - SIX

KATERINA

I don't sleep. Let me correct that. I can't sleep, even if I wanted to. The second Aiden walked out of that door, it was like something inside me collapsed, a part of me breaking beyond repair. And now, I'm lying in this unfamiliar bed in the figure skating house, staring at the ceiling, my chest so tight it hurts to breathe.
I told him I didn't love him. I lied. And he believed me. I squeeze my eyes shut, trying to block out the memory of his face, the way he looked at me like I had gutted him. Like I had taken a blade and cut right through him. I roll over, pressing my face into the pillow, but the ache won't
leave. It's in my ribs, in my lungs, in every shallow breath I take. I told myself this was the right thing. That I needed to focus, that I couldn't afford to let myself get distracted.
But all I feel is empty. By the time morning comes, I force myself out of bed, dragging my feet through my routine. I barely register Alina when she joins me in the

kitchen, her eyes sharp as she watches me stir my untouched cup of coffee. "You look like hell," she finally says.

I scoff, but there's no heat to it. "Thanks."

Alina sets her mug down, leaning on the counter. "You wanna tell me what happened?"

I stare down at my coffee, my stomach twisting. "Nothing."

She huffs, crossing her arms. "Kat, I've known you long enough to know when you're full of shit."

I swallow hard, my fingers curling around my mug. "I told him I didn't love him."

Alina freezes. Her brows pull together, and then her mouth parts slightly, like she can't quite believe what she just heard. "You—" She exhales sharply, shaking her head. "Are you kidding me?" I flinch but stay silent. "Kat." Her voice is softer now, but still laced with frustration. "Why?"

I lift my shoulders, even though I already know the answer. Because I was scared. Because I thought pushing him away would make it easier. Because I thought if I severed the connection, I could breathe again. But I was wrong. And now it's too late.

Alina sighs, rubbing her temples. "You're an idiot." I let out a humorless laugh. "I know."

She shakes her head, muttering something in Russian before looking at me again.

"What are you going to do?"

I stare into my coffee, my chest tight. "Nothing."

Alina's eyes narrow. "So that's it? You're just going to let him think you don't care? That you never did?"

My throat closes up, my fingers tightening around the mug. "What else can I do?"

Alina sighs, standing up. "For someone who fights like hell on the ice, you're a coward when it comes to him."

The words hit deep, but I don't argue. Because she's right. I am a coward.

I go to the rink later that afternoon, but the second I step inside, I know I made a mistake. Because Aiden is there. And he's not alone.

He's standing by the boards, talking to a girl I vaguely recognize—one of the hockey groupies, the kind that flocks to the team after big games. She's laughing at something he said, reaching out to touch his arm, and he lets her.

He lets her.

One day! It took him one day to move on.

I don't realize I've stopped moving until Alexei steps up beside me, following my gaze. He exhales sharply.

"Kat—"

"I don't care," I say quickly, my voice clipped. I force my feet to move, heading toward the ice like I didn't just feel my stomach implode.

Alexei doesn't push, but I feel his gaze burning into me. The entire practice is a disaster. My jumps are shaky, my turns too stiff, my focus gone. Every time I try to get out of my head, my eyes betray me, flicking toward where Aiden is standing by the glass, completely unbothered, like I don't even exist. Good. That's what I wanted, right?

Then why does it feel like I can't breathe?

I push harder, throwing myself into a triple lutz, but my blade catches the ice wrong— And I fall.

Hard.

The impact rattles through me, knocking the wind from my lungs, pain flaring across my knee and wrist as I slide across the ice.

A rush of movement—voices, skates scraping to a stop—

Aiden is there before I even register the pain, his gloved hand reaching for me.

"Are you okay?"

His voice is tight, controlled, but his eyes—his eyes betray him. Because they're frantic, flickering over me, checking for injuries, for damage.

I hate it. I hate that he still cares.

So I push his hand away and pull myself up, forcing my expression blank.

"I'm fine." Aiden's jaw tightens.

"Kat—"

"I said I'm fine," I snap, brushing past him, skating back toward Alexei before I can break all over again. Aiden doesn't stop me and he doesn't call after me. He just watches me go and when I finally glance back, his expression is unreadable, his body rigid. I hurt him. And now he's hurting me back. The ache in my knee is nothing compared to the ache in my chest.

After practice I sit in the locker room, pressing an ice pack against my leg, staring at nothing in particular. The rink is empty now—everyone else has left. Even Alexei, after sending me a long, pointed look, decided not to push me further. But Aiden?

He hadn't said a word. Not when I fell. Not when I snapped at him. Not when I skated off without looking back. And for the first time in my life, I don't know what hurts more—the silence or the distance.

I go back to the figure skating house instead of the hockey house. It's safer there. Less reminders. Less temptation to go back to him. Alina isn't there when I arrive, which means I'm left alone with my thoughts, and I hate it. I busy myself, grabbing a sweatshirt and a pair of leggings before hopping in the shower, letting the scalding water burn away the tension in my muscles.

It doesn't help.

Because no matter how much I try to ignore it, my mind keeps replaying the moment I pushed Aiden's hand away. The flash of something raw in his eyes. The way he clenched his jaw, like he was barely holding himself together.

I did that.

I squeeze my eyes shut, pressing my forehead against the shower tile.

I thought pushing him away would make things easier. That if I kept running, I wouldn't have to deal with the weight of him—of us. But instead, it just feels like I'm drowning.

By the time night falls, Alina still isn't back, which means I have no one to stop me when I do something stupid. Like go back to the hockey house.

I tell myself I just need to grab the rest of my things. That I'm not looking for him. That I don't care. But the second I step inside, the air shifts.

Because he's there. Sitting on the couch, watching a game on mute, his body relaxed in a way that's too forced, too careful. I swallow hard, gripping the strap of my bag as I move toward the stairs. I don't look at him. I don't acknowledge him.

"Running away again?" His voice is quiet, but it hits.

I stop, my fingers tightening around the railing. "I'm not running."

Aiden scoffs, standing up. "Right. Because avoiding me at practice, moving out of the house, and refusing to even look at me isn't running."

I exhale sharply, turning to face him. "What do you want me to say, Aiden?"

His jaw clenches. "I want you to stop lying to me."

I lift my chin, trying to steady my breathing. "I'm not lying."

Aiden takes a step closer. "No? Then look me in the eye and tell me you don't love me."
My stomach twists violently. "Aiden—"
"Say it." His voice is rough, almost pleading. "Say it and I'll drop it. I'll leave you alone. You'll never have to deal with me again."
I open my mouth, but nothing comes out. Because I can't say it.
Aiden's gaze darkens, his fingers flexing at his sides. "That's what I thought."
I shake my head, my throat burning. "It doesn't matter."
His brows pull together. "How does it not matter?"
"Because love isn't enough!" I snap, my voice cracking. "Not for me! Not for you! Not for this!"
Silence.
Aiden exhales slowly, stepping even closer, his presence overwhelming. "That's the biggest load of bullshit I've ever heard." I shake my head, swallowing hard. "I can't lose skating."
"And you think you have to lose me to keep it?" His voice is softer now, raw at the edges. "That's not how this works, Kat."
I clench my jaw, looking away. "I don't know how else to do this."
Aiden lifts a hand, hesitating for a second before brushing his fingers against my cheek. "Then let me show you."
My breath catches, my heart slamming against my ribs. But before I can say anything—before I can think— Aiden leans in, his lips hovering just over mine, his breath warm against my skin.
"You can push me away all you want," he murmurs. "But I'm not going anywhere." Aiden steps back, leaving me standing there, breathless, heart aching, wanting more.

And I realize, with a sinking feeling in my chest— I might have already lost the battle.

CHAPTER FORTY - SEVEN

KATERINA

I wish I could say ignoring Aiden gets easier. It doesn't.
Every time I step into the rink, every time I pass him in the hallway, every time our eyes meet across the room—it's like
something inside me cracks. But I refuse to let it show, because this is what I chose, right? So I deal with it. I force myself to move on. To focus. To pretend.
Aiden, though? He doesn't pretend. He looks wrecked. His easy confidence? Gone. His sharp, cocky smirks? Nonexistent.
He's there, but it's like part of him isn't. Like the fight's been drained from him.
And the worst part? It's because of me.
When we're teaching, he doesn't interact with me, Aiden

grabs his little ones and goes on his side of the arena without sparring me a single glance.

At practice, I keep my head down, but I feel him watching me. His presence is a weight pressing against my skin, a shadow that won't leave. And when I stumble on a jump—not from lack of skill but because my mind won't stop racing—I hear him curse under his breath from the other side of the glass. I snap my head up, glaring at him, daring him to say something. But he just shakes his head and turns away.

After practice, I head straight for the locker room, hoping to

escape before I have to face him again. But the second I round the corner, I slam into a solid chest. Warm hands steady me before I can fall, but I jerk away before I register who it is.

Aiden.

His jaw tightens as I step back, my pulse pounding in my ears. I don't say anything. I don't move. Neither does he.

For a long moment, we just stare at each other, tension thick, suffocating. His eyes are dark, stormy, like he's barely holding himself together.

And then—

"Say it again."

My stomach twists. "What?"

Aiden exhales sharply, stepping closer. "Say you don't love me."

My throat goes dry. How many times does he want me to say it?

He shakes his head, his voice lower, rougher. "Look me in the eye and say it.

I can't.

I can't breathe, can't think, can't do anything but stand here, locked in this battle I know I'm losing.

Aiden scoffs, raking a hand through his hair. "Say it, so I can move on." My chest tightens. "It doesn't matter." I love you, I think to myself. I'm sorry for hurting you. His gaze sharpens. "It matters to me."
I press my lips together, forcing the words out before I can stop them. "Then that's your problem." Aiden's body locks up. His eyes darken, something breaking in them. For a second, I think he's going to say something, that he's going to fight for this. He steps back and nods, walking away. And this time, he doesn't look back. This time, I think I might have actually lost him. And this time, I don't know if I'll survive it. Aiden doesn't speak to me after that. Not at practice. Not at the rink. Not anywhere. And I tell myself it's a good thing. That this is what I wanted.
That this is better. But it's not. Because now, instead of lingering stares and sharp-edged words, there's nothing. And somehow, that's worse.

A week passes like this. A week of Aiden walking past me like I don't exist. Of watching him skate harder, push himself further, like he's trying to burn me out of his system.
Like I was never there to begin with. I should be relieved. I should be happy that he finally got the message. But all I feel is cold. Alina corners me after practice, slamming her locker shut with unnecessary force.
"Okay, enough."
I sigh, pulling off my skates. "I don't have the energy for this right now."

grabs his little ones and goes on his side of the arena without sparring me a single glance.

At practice, I keep my head down, but I feel him watching me. His presence is a weight pressing against my skin, a shadow that won't leave. And when I stumble on a jump—not from lack of skill but because my mind won't stop racing—I hear him curse under his breath from the other side of the glass. I snap my head up, glaring at him, daring him to say something. But he just shakes his head and turns away.

After practice, I head straight for the locker room, hoping to

escape before I have to face him again. But the second I round the corner, I slam into a solid chest. Warm hands steady me before I can fall, but I jerk away before I register who it is.

Aiden.

His jaw tightens as I step back, my pulse pounding in my ears. I don't say anything. I don't move. Neither does he.

For a long moment, we just stare at each other, tension thick, suffocating. His eyes are dark, stormy, like he's barely holding himself together.

And then—

"Say it again."

My stomach twists. "What?"

Aiden exhales sharply, stepping closer. "Say you don't love me."

My throat goes dry. How many times does he want me to say it?

He shakes his head, his voice lower, rougher. "Look me in the eye and say it.

I can't.

I can't breathe, can't think, can't do anything but stand here, locked in this battle I know I'm losing.

Aiden scoffs, raking a hand through his hair. "Say it, so I can move on." My chest tightens. "It doesn't matter."
I love you, I think to myself. I'm sorry for hurting you.
His gaze sharpens. "It matters to me."
I press my lips together, forcing the words out before I can stop them. "Then that's your problem." Aiden's body locks up. His eyes darken, something breaking in them. For a second, I think he's going to say something, that he's going to fight for this. He steps back and nods, walking away. And this time, he doesn't look back.
This time, I think I might have actually lost him. And this time, I don't know if I'll survive it. Aiden doesn't speak to me after that. Not at practice. Not at the rink. Not anywhere. And I tell myself it's a good thing. That this is what I wanted.
That this is better. But it's not. Because now, instead of lingering stares and sharp-edged words, there's nothing. And somehow, that's worse.

A week passes like this. A week of Aiden walking past me like I don't exist. Of watching him skate harder, push himself further, like he's trying to burn me out of his system.
Like I was never there to begin with. I should be relieved. I should be happy that he finally got the message. But all I feel is cold. Alina corners me after practice, slamming her locker shut with unnecessary force.
"Okay, enough."
I sigh, pulling off my skates. "I don't have the energy for this right now."

"Well, too bad, because I do." She crosses her arms, eyes flashing.

"What the hell is wrong with you?"

I glance up, my throat tightening. "Nothing."

She glares at me. "You've been a ghost for the past week. And Aiden?" Her voice softens. "Kat, he looks wrecked."

Something inside me twists, sharp and painful. But I force myself to keep my expression blank. "That's not my problem." Alina makes a sound of frustration.

"God, you're impossible." I don't respond. Just focus on untying my skates with fingers that suddenly feel too stiff.

After a long silence, she exhales. "You don't have to punish yourself, you know." I flinch.

"I'm not—"

"Yes, you are." She kneels beside me, her voice gentler now.

"You're scared. And instead of facing it, you're pushing away the one person who actually sees you."

I clench my jaw, staring down at my hands. "I don't know how to do this, Alina."

She nudges me. "Then let him teach you."

I shake my head, my throat burning. "I can't."

Alina sighs, her expression heavy with something I don't want to name.

"You're going to have to figure this out eventually, Kat. Before it's too late, because others would kill to have someone love them, the way Aiden loves you."

She leaves, and I sit there alone, the weight of her words pressing down on me. I know she is talking about herself.

That night, I make the mistake of checking my phone. There's nothing from Aiden, of course, but there is a picture of Aiden at a party.

He is in the background, standing next to some girl I don't recognize.
She's close—too close. Leaning into him, smiling up at him
like she already knows she has his attention.
And Aiden? He is smiling at her. My heart rate picks up and something sharp lodges in my chest.
I turn my phone off and toss it onto my bed, but the image
sticks.
He's moving on and maybe that's what I wanted, but seeing hime smiling at other girls, I realise that, that's not what i want. I don't want him to move on.
 I don't sleep. Not really. I stare at the ceiling, replaying every moment with Aiden. The way he looked at me. The way he used to see me. Now he's just gone. At some point, I do the only thing I can think of.
I call my mom, even though It's eleven pm in Russia, she answers after two rings, her voice soft with concern.
"Katerina?"
I exhale shakily. "Hey, Mom."
A pause. "Sweetheart, what's wrong?" I press my palm against my forehead. Where do I even start?
"I—" My voice cracks. "I hurt someone. And I think I hurt him badly."
My mother is quiet for a long moment. "Aiden?" Tears burn my eyes, but I refuse to let them fall.
"Yeah."
She exhales, her voice knowing. Too knowing. "And now you regret it."
I let out a strangled laugh. "That's the problem. I don't know." I close my eyes, my throat tight. "I don't know how to let someone stay, Mom. I don't know how to let someone close without waiting for them to leave."

My mother is quiet, and when she finally speaks, her voice is
softer than I've ever heard it.
"Katerina, baby… I know why you're scared."
I grip the blanket tighter, feeling like a child again.
"I know you're hurt from everything that has happened," she continues. "But you can't push people away just because you're scared they might leave or hurt you."
I swallow, the tears dangerously close now.
"I don't want to lose him," I whisper. "But I don't know how to keep him, either."
She sighs. "Then start small. Talk to him. Let him see that
you care. Even if it's scary."
I nod, even though she can't see me. "Okay."
The next morning, Alexei shows up at my door and he's not alone. He's holding a bag of croissants and two cups of coffee. I raise an eyebrow, but he just pushes past me into my apartment.
"You look like shit," he says cheerfully, setting the coffee on the counter.
I scowl. "Good morning to you, too." He flops onto my couch, kicking his feet up. "We're having a Kat Day." I blink at him. "A what?" Alexei grins. "A Kat Day. Where we do, everything you love. Movies. Junk food. Skating—if you want. No boys. No drama. Just you and me."
I stare at him, and something in my chest eases. Alexei knows. He sees me in a way I sometimes forget.
I sit down beside him, taking a sip of coffee. "Fine. But I get to pick the movie."
He smirks. "Go ahead, Malyshka. But I swear to God if you pick some depressing French indie film, I'm walking out." Somewhere between watching three

movies and eating way too much popcorn, I start to feel human again.
Alexei doesn't push. He doesn't ask about Aiden.
He just lets me exist.

CHAPTER FORTY - EIGHT

KATERINA

I tell myself I don't care. That the picture doesn't matter. That it's just a stupid party. That Aiden can do whatever the hell he wants because I made my choice. But when I walk into the rink the next day and see him actually
talking to her— My heart aches.
She's standing too close. Her hand brushes against his arm when she laughs, and I hate that I notice. I hate that I immediately compare myself to her—tall, blonde, model-pretty, exactly the kind of girl who wouldn't run from him, who wouldn't push him away at every turn. Aiden says something, and she laughs again, flipping her hair over her shoulder. Fucking hell. I slam my skates onto the bench harder than necessary.

Alina, who's lacing up next to me, raises an eyebrow. "Are you okay?"

"Fine," I mutter.

She follows my gaze, her lips twitching when she sees what I'm glaring at. "Ohhh. This is interesting."

"Shut up." Alina hums, clearly amused.

"You do realize you're the one who pushed him away, right?"

"I know," I grit out.

"And yet, you look about two seconds away from throwing her into the boards."

"Please, stop."

Alina snickers, but thankfully, she doesn't push it. Instead, she stands and stretches, glancing at Aiden again before smirking at me. "You should do something about it."

I scoff. "Like what?"

She grins. "I don't know. Maybe remind him why he was obsessed with you in the first place?"

I narrow my eyes at her. "That's a terrible idea."

She shrugs. "Maybe. But it'd be fun." I roll my eyes, but the idea sticks in my head. Because if Aiden wants to play this game, if he wants to act like I didn't rip him apart just a week ago—fine.

Two can play. I step onto the ice, sliding past Aiden without looking at him, but I know he sees me. I make sure he does.

Everything I do is sharper, more precise. Every spin, every jump—flawless. Because if he's going to entertain the idea of someone else, I want him to remember exactly what he had.

And it works.

I feel his gaze on me. I feel the tension every time I pass him, every time he tries to ignore me and fails and by the time practice ends, I can see the frustration brewing in him.

Good.

Let him burn.

But just as I start untying my skates, I hear her voice—her voice—again.

"You coming tonight, Aiden?" I don't know what pisses me off more—her confidence or the fact that he doesn't immediately say no. Something bitter rises in my chest. Before I can stop myself, I stand, grabbing my water bottle and tossing it onto the bench next to Aiden. Hard. His brows furrow as he looks up at me. I smile, sweet and fake.

"Don't stay out too late, Aidy." I say with a taunting smirk. He glances at me in disbelief but doesn't say anything. The girl glances between us, confused, but Aiden doesn't acknowledge her.

His attention is all on me.

Good. I grab my bag and leave, ignoring the way my heart is racing. Because if he thinks I'm just going to sit back and watch him move on—

He's out of his damn mind.

The party is suffocating. Music pounds through the walls, the bass thrumming in my veins, but it's not enough to drown out the thoughts screaming in my head. The ones that have been clawing at me since I walked away from Aiden at the rink.

I shouldn't have come. I knew he would be here. Knew that the second I saw him, I'd feel this unbearable pull all over again. And yet, I came anyway. Because I'm a masochist. Because I need to see him, even if it hurts.

And God, does it hurt. He's across the room, leaning against the kitchen counter, a drink in his hand, looking unfairly good in a fitted black shirt that clings to his arms. His jaw is sharp, lips pressed into a tight line, but his eyes—

His eyes are already on me.

Watching. Waiting. I swallow hard, tearing my gaze away, but it's useless. The tension crackles like a live wire, and I can feel the weight of him even from across the room. I try to ignore it. Try to pretend that it doesn't send heat rushing through my veins.

I fail. I make it all of twenty minutes before Aiden finds me. Or maybe I was waiting for him to. Either way, when I step into an empty hallway, desperate for air, he's suddenly there.

Blocking my exit. Trapping me between him and the wall like he's done so many times before.

I reach for the doorknob of the room next to me and exhale in relief when the door opens. I walk in and Aiden follows right behind me. He stares at me, really looks at me, but this time, there's no smirk. No teasing remarks. Just fire burning beneath his skin.

"You're jealous."

I flinch. "I'm not."

He tilts his head, stepping closer. "Liar."

I glare at him, hating how easily he sees through me. "I don't care who you spend your time with, Aiden."

His lips twitch, but it's not a smile. It's something darker. "Right. That's why you've been looking at me all night like you want to rip me apart."

I exhale sharply, pressing my hands against the wall behind me.

"You're imagining things."

Aiden leans in, voice dangerously low. "Say it again. Maybe you'll start believing it."

I hate how easily he undoes me. How I can't lie to him without him seeing right through it. I hate seeing girls around him but more than anything, I hate how scared I am to lose him,

"I can't do this anymore." My voice trembles, barely above a whisper, yet it shatters the silence between us. My hands curl into fists at my sides as I force myself to meet his eyes—those damn eyes that have been both my solace and my undoing.

"I can't keep pretending that I don't care. That I don't feel this… this unbearable pull toward you. It's exhausting, fighting something that's already consumed me whole."

I take a shaky breath, feeling the weight of every unsaid word pressing against my ribs.

"I've spent so long convincing myself that I was fine without you, that I didn't need anyone. That if I just kept my walls high enough, no one could hurt me. But then you came along and ruined that—ruined me."

"You made me feel things I didn't want to feel, and I hate you for it. I hate you because you made me want you. And God, I want you so much it scares me."

My eyes burn, but I refuse to let the tears fall. Not yet.

"You are the first person who's ever seen me—really seen me. And instead of running, instead of turning away from all my broken pieces, you stayed. No one's ever done that before." A bitter laugh escapes my lips. "I don't know how to love someone without destroying myself in the process, but if there's one person, I'd be willing to fall apart for, it's you."

I step closer now, my voice cracking, raw and unfiltered.

"I love you. I love you so much it hurts. And if you don't feel the same, if this—whatever this is—means nothing to you, if you already moved on, then tell me.

Lie to me if you have to. But if there's even the smallest part of you that feels this too… don't let me go." Tears run down my cheek, but Aiden doesn't speak. He just stares at me, like he's trying to commit every inch of me to memory, like he's making sure this isn't some cruel joke.

Then he takes three steps towards me, his hands tangling themselves in my hair.

One second, I'm standing there, heart racing in my throat, and the next, his lips crash into mine. The kiss is fire, desperate and raw, hands tangling in my hair, gripping me like he's afraid I'll disappear. I don't hold back. I can't. My fingers dig into his shirt, pulling him closer, as if I could fuse us together, as if I could make up for every second, I spent trying to push him away.

Aiden groans against my mouth, his hands sliding down my sides, gripping my waist, lifting me until my back is pressed against the wall.

I gasp against his lips, and he devours the sound, his body pressing flush against mine.

"I can't stand you," I whisper between kisses, my voice wrecked.

Aiden smirks against my mouth. "Yes, you can."

I bite his lip, just to prove a point, and he growls, pushing me harder against the wall, making my breath catch.

Heat flares between us, consuming, unbearable. I arch into him, needing more, needing everything.

His tongue slipped between my lips, tracing over my teeth,

teasing my tongue, and my brain stuttered into slow motion. I noticed everything— the scratch of his stubble against my cheek, the heat of his lips on mine, the taste of him. Mint and orange, like he'd chewed gum after downing a Fanta. It shouldn't have been so hot, but it was— the taste, the scent, the sensation of him pressed against me. It made a soft whimper rise in my throat.

"Are you okay?"

He pulled back just enough to search my face, his eyes dark with something I couldn't name, something cautious and consuming all at once. Later, I would think about how movies always show men taking without asking, and how that's supposed to be romantic. But this? This moment of checking, of knowing I wanted this too? It was more erotic than any frantic, desperate grab could ever be. How could i not love him? Not that I didn't want him desperate. I wanted him to lose himself in this, to take and to give, to press me so hard into the mattress that I'd feel it tomorrow. But knowing that he cared if I was okay— not just in general, but in this moment, right now— was powerful.

"More," I whispered.

He didn't hesitate this time. More kisses, more of his tongue sliding against mine, more of his lips moving across my jaw, my throat, my collarbone. His teeth closed gently over my earlobe, tugging, making me shudder. His hands, rough and searching, tangled in my hair, one at the back of my head, the other pressing into the small of my back, pulling me into him. His breathing quickened, deep and ragged, and I felt his groan vibrate against my skin. His body, firm and strong, molds with mine, his thighs bracketing my hips, his chest pressing against my breasts. And then, the hard length of him, hot and unyielding against my stomach.

I pull my small top over my head, giving him access to my chest.

"Bed," I gasped.

I back out of the door, keeping Aiden close, unwilling to let go, until the backs of my legs met the mattress and I let myself fall backward.

He follows, hovering over me as I scoot back, his weight pressing me into the bed. I arch up into him, needing the friction, needing him. He slides lower, his hands pushing my skirt up to my hips, fingertips tracing over the front of my panties. It had been so long since he had touched me like this, had wanted me like this. Electricity shot through me, pooling low in my stomach. I feel one of his fingers slide inside of me and I gasp.

"Oh my god." I whimper.

His other hand tugs at my bra, fingers bringing it down, freeing my breasts.

He leaned down, mouth warm and wet over my nipples, exposing me to his tongue, his teeth.

He sucks, licks, teases, and I gasp, my fingers threading into his hair, anchoring him to me. His legs shift, his knees pressing between mine, urging me open, making space for himself between my thighs.

"Please Aiden," I gasp, my hands fumbling with his belt, tugging, desperate. "I just… need… now. Please."

He understands. The urgency. The way waiting wasn't an option. He undoes his belt, shoves his jeans and boxers down just enough, then reaches between us, pushing my panties further aside.

"I love seeing you like this angel. Falling apart for me."

I gasp the moment his tip, pushes into me.

"I love you." I whisper, bringing his mouth into mine.

Aiden pushes into me, slow and careful. My legs wrap around his waist, heels digging into the back of his thighs, urging him deeper.

"I'm so sorry." I mutter panting, as Aiden slides in an out of me.

"I-I'm so sorry Aiden." I say again, slamming my lips into his.

"I love you." He whispers, leaving a trail of kisses on my neck.

"You were made for me Angel. No one else. Just me." Aiden says, and my heart swells at his words. I feel like I can breath again.

"Aiden," I gasp again.

My body adjusts, stretches around him, and then the rhythm changes— faster, harder. My moans turn into cries, my nails dragging down his back, the bed frame slamming into the wall in time with his thrusts.

The tension coiled inside me, tighter and tighter, until it snaps. I shatter around him, my body pulsing, my legs pulling him in as I gasp his name, desperate and lost. He follows suit, a rough, ragged shout as he buries himself deep, body shaking, collapsing against me as he comes undone.

We lay there, tangled, panting, our bodies still fused together. I feel him, still inside me, his breath slowing against my neck.

"I'm never letting you go again." I whisper, leaning my head on his chest. Content at having him next to me.

"I'm never letting you push me away again." He whispers, placing a sweet but innocent kiss on my forehead.

CHAPTER FORTY - NINE

KATERINA

For the first time in weeks, I wake up without the weight of denial crushing my chest.

Because this time, I wake up with him. Aiden's arms are wrapped around me, his body warm and solid against mine, his breath steady as he sleeps. The room is still dark, the world outside quiet, but in this moment, everything feels right. Like the battle we fought to get here—every push, every pull—was worth it.

I shift slightly, and almost instantly, his grip tightens, pulling me closer.

"Stay," he murmurs, his voice rough with sleep, his lips brushing the top of my head.

I smile against his chest, letting my fingers trace the lines of his muscles, memorizing the way he feels beneath my touch. "I'm not going anywhere."

He exhales deeply, like he's been holding onto something for far too long, like he finally believes me. Neither of us moves for a long time, content to just exist in this stolen moment, but eventually, my stomach betrays me, growling loud enough to make Aiden chuckle.

I groan, burying my face in his chest. "You better not say anything."

His laughter vibrates against my skin. "You're adorable when

you're embarrassed."

I smack his arm half-heartedly, but he just grabs my wrist, pressing a kiss to my palm before intertwining our fingers. My heart stutters.

God, I missed this. Him. Us.

I shift to look up at him, my fingers still tangled with his. "So… what now?"

Aiden's lips twitch, but there's something soft in his eyes. "You tell me, Angel Face."

I roll my eyes at the nickname, but the warmth spreading

through my chest is undeniable. "Well, I was thinking pancakes."

He huffs a laugh, pulling me on top of him effortlessly. "Not what I meant, but now that you mention it, I am starving."

I grin, poking his chest. "Fine. We'll discuss the meaning of life after pancakes."

The kitchen is warm, filled with the scent of coffee and vanilla as I flip pancakes onto a plate. Aiden leans against the counter, arms crossed, watching me with a look I can't quite place.

I raise an eyebrow. "Why are you staring at me like that?"

He smirks. "Just making sure you don't burn down the kitchen."

I toss a piece of pancake at him, which he catches effortlessly, popping it into his mouth. "Rude."

He grins, but then his expression softens, his fingers brushing against my waist as he pulls me closer. "You know I'm never letting you go again, right?"

I swallow, my hands resting against his chest. "Pretty sure you told me that last night, while you were ten inches deep in me."

He studies me for a beat with a smug grin, then dips his head, kissing me slow and deep, like he's sealing a promise neither of us is willing to break.

And for the first time in a long time, I don't feel the need to run.

Because I am home. And home is him. Happiness feels foreign.

Like something I'm still getting used to. Like something I'm scared might slip through my fingers if I hold onto it too tightly. But Aiden? He doesn't let me doubt it. Doesn't let me question it. He just stays—unwavering, steady, constant. And every time I catch him looking at me like I hung the stars, I start to believe that maybe, just maybe, this is real.

The first test comes when we walk into the rink together the next morning. Eyes snap to us instantly, whispers already forming in the air. I don't know what they expected—that we'd pretend last night didn't happen? That I'd keep pushing him away, keep running from the inevitable? Not anymore.

Aiden's hand stays on my waist as we make our way inside, his grip firm, as if daring anyone to question this. And I should feel self-conscious, I should feel overwhelmed by the attention, but instead, I just feel… light. Like nothing else matters. Like he is all that matters.

Alexei skates up to us, crossing his arms with a knowing
smirk. "Finally. Thought I was going to have to lock you two in a room to figure your shit out."

I roll my eyes, but Aiden just shrugs. "Wouldn't have worked. She's too stubborn."

Alexei snickers. "And you're not?"

"Fair point."

Alina appears beside Alexei, her gaze flicking between me and Aiden before she beams. "Oh, thank God. If I had to watch you two be miserable for another week, I was going to start throwing things." I huff a laugh, shaking my head.

"So much for subtlety." Alina waves me off, looping her arm
through mine.

"Please, everyone knew you two were inevitable. It was just a matter of when."

Aiden smirks. "Took her long enough."

I smack his arm, but he just grins, catching my hand in his and pressing a kiss to my knuckles.

Alina pretends to gag. "Gross."

Alexei nudges her. "You're just bitter because your love life is a disaster."

Her expression darkens. "Don't start, Romanov."

I glance at her sharply, catching the way she tenses, the way her expression shutters just a little and suddenly, I know exactly what she's talking about.

Roman.

Aiden must notice too because his grip on my waist tightens, his voice dropping into something more serious. "Are you okay?"

Alina forces a smile, but it doesn't quite reach her eyes. "I'm fine."

I know she's not. But I don't push. Not yet. Instead, I squeeze her hand, offering silent reassurance before turning back to the ice. Because for the first time in a long time, I'm okay, and I refuse to let anything take that from me. Last night while we were tangled in the sheets, he asked me to be his girlfriend again. The words still feel strange on my tongue.

Girlfriend. It feels different. It feels real now that we have come clean about our feelings.

After practice, Aiden doesn't tell me where we're going. He just shows up at my door with that stupid cocky smirk and a hand outstretched toward me like it's the easiest thing in the world.

"Come on, Angel Face. Let's go." I narrow my eyes at him, arms crossed. "Where?"

He just grins. "You'll see."

I pretend to be annoyed, but there's no stopping the warmth spreading through my chest. So, I roll my eyes, grab my jacket, and let him take my hand.

The drive is quiet, but not uncomfortable. His fingers tap absently against the steering wheel, his free hand resting on my knee, tracing absentminded circles through my leggings. I hate how much I like it. The casual intimacy. The way he just does things without thinking, like it's second nature. Like touching me is a habit he never wants to break.

We drive for about thirty minutes before I realize where we're headed. The lake.

My heart does something stupid in my chest.

Aiden parks near the edge, the water reflecting the city lights in the distance, shimmering under the early evening sky. There's a blanket already laid out a small picnic set up with takeout containers from my favourite restaurant.

My throat tightens. "You planned this?"

Aiden shrugs, but there's something almost shy in the way he looks at me. "Figured we've never had an actual date before."

I bite my lip, trying and failing to keep my heart from soaring.

"You didn't have to do all this."

He steps closer, fingers tilting my chin up so I'm forced to meet his gaze. "I wanted to."

I swallow hard. "Why?"

His brows furrow slightly, like he can't believe I even asked that. "Because you're mine, Kat." His voice drops lower, rougher. "And I want to do this right."

My breath catches. Because God, I want that too.

Aiden smirks like he knows exactly what I'm thinking, then pulls me toward the blanket, making me sit before handing me a takeout box. "Eat. Before you start overthinking and ruin the moment."

I scoff but take the food, digging in while he does the same. We sit in silence for a while, the only sound the soft lapping of the water against the shore. It's peaceful. But of course, Aiden can't let that last for long.

"So," he says, wiping his mouth. "How does it feel to be my girlfriend?"

I nearly choke on my food. "You're so annoying." He grins. "But you love me."

I glare at him, but the warmth in my chest betrays me. "Unfortunately."

Aiden chuckles, leaning in to kiss my cheek, his lips lingering for just a second too long. "Lucky me."

I shake my head, rolling my eyes, but my stomach won't stop flipping.
Because yeah.
Lucky him.
But also…. Lucky me.

CHAPTER FIFTY

KATERINA

The arena is crowded to the brim. The crowd roars, the ice glows under the bright lights, and every muscle in my body is wired with tension as I watch Aidenfly across the rink. He moves like he owns it. Like the ice was made for him. Every sharp turn, every pass, every shot—it's flawless.

I'm vibrating with nerves, my breath trapped in my throat. The final period is down to the last minute. The scoreboard is tied. The tension is suffocating.

"Come on, Aidy," I whisper, gripping the sleeve of Alina's jacket.

She squeezes my hand, her expression tight with anticipation. Aiden steals the puck. The crowd erupts as he takes off, weaving through defenders like they're nothing, like this is his moment and no one's going to take it from him. He shoots—

Time slows.

The puck sails through the air— And hits the back of the net.
Goal. The stadium explodes.
Aiden skates toward his teammates, his arms raised, his entire body radiating triumph as they pile onto him, shouts of victory ringing through the ice. They won. They fucking won.
I don't think. I move.
Before I know it, I'm pushing through the crowd, slipping past security, Aiden turns—
And his eyes go soft. His teammates are still cheering, still celebrating, but Aiden?
He only sees me and I don't hesitate. The moment he skates towards me, I launch myself at him, arms wrapping around his neck as he manages to catch me effortlessly, spinning us on the ice as I press my lips to his.
"I'm so proud of you." I say between kisses, my cheeks in pain from grinning.
The kiss is fire, desperate and triumphant, all our emotions
crashing into each other at once. He grins against my lips, his arms tightening around me.
"I fucking love you," he mutters, voice husky.
I smirk, brushing my nose against his. "Yeah? You sure?" He growls, kissing me again, and I giggle, feeling the weight of the moment settle in my chest. Aiden's hand cups my cheek, his thumb brushing over my skin, his lips lingering on mine, like he's afraid to let go. His voice is quieter this time,
raw.
"I've never been more sure of anything in my life."
My breath catches, because I believe him.Because for the first time in forever, I let myself believe in something good. "I love you to baby." I whisper,

tugging him tighter. The crowd is losing it, but I don't care, cause all i'm looking at is him. The boy who drives me crazy. The boy who knows exactly how to push my buttons.
The boy who never backed down when I pushed him away.
I was so scared. So convinced that loving someone meant losing them.
But when I kiss Aiden, when he whispers I love you like it's something he's known since the beginning, I realize, that I already lost myself to him.

The team throws a party back at the hockey house, and for the first time in weeks, everything feels right. The music is loud, the house is packed, and people keep shoving drinks into my hands. Aiden is glued to my side, his arm resting casually around my waist, but his fingers trace circles against my skin, like he can't stop touching me. Maddie and Will are arguing over who gets the last slice of pizza, Grayson is dancing like a lunatic, and Alexei is grinning at me from across the room.
But then I see her, my beautiful best friend. She laughs when she's supposed to, drinks when someone hands her one, but there's something hollow in her eyes and I know what it is.
Roman.
She hasn't talked about it, hasn't mentioned him, but I see it. The way she glances toward the door like she's expecting him to walk in. The way she grips her cup a little too tightly whenever his name is brought up. And

when midnight rolls around and he still hasn't shown, she stands abruptly. "I'm heading out."

I frown. "Alina—"

"I'm fine," she says, forcing a smile. "Really." She's lying.

I don't let her leave alone.

Instead, I pull her back to the house with me, and we crawl into my bed, like we used to when we were kids, whispering about stupid things to distract from the things that actually hurt. She stares at the ceiling, her voice quiet. "I don't know what I'm supposed to do." I reach for her hand, squeezing gently.

"You don't have to figure it out tonight." She nods, but the sadness lingers. And as I hold her hand in the dark, I hate that I can't fix this for her. But I'll be here. Just like she's always been here for me.

At some point, Alina falls asleep, and I slip out of bed, making my way to the kitchen.

Aiden is already there, leaning against the counter, arms crossed.

I stop breathing for a second. Because he's watching me with relief in his brown eyes. He doesn't speak at first. Just studies me.

Finally, he tilts his head. "You okay?"

I exhale. "Yeah." Aiden doesn't believe me. He pushes off the counter, stepping closer, his hand sliding up my arm, his touch warm, grounding.

"She's not alone baby." I swallow, my throat tight. "I know."

And I do."I feel bad for her. She is my best friend, my sister." Aiden nods as i step closer. Aiden's hand cups my jaw, his thumb brushing over my cheek. His voice is soft. "You scared me tonight."

I frown. "Why?"

"When i couldn't find you downstairs, I thought—" He sighs, shaking his head. "I thought you changed your mind."

My heart clenches. I reach up, wrapping my fingers around
his wrist.

"I'm not going anywhere. I love you."

Aiden's breath catches, his eyes darkening and then he kisses me. This time, it's slower, more deliberate, like he's memorizing me. Like he's trying to hold onto this moment forever.

And I let him.

Because I'm done being scared.

CHAPTER FIFTY - ONE

KATERINA

The days leading up to Worlds pass in a blur of training, nerves, and stolen moments with Aiden. But before I board my flight to the biggest competition of my career, there's someone I need to see. Sophia.
She's waiting for me in her hospital room, grinning from ear to ear the moment I step inside. "Kat!"
I barely have time to brace myself before she throws herself into my arms, giggling as I spin her around. She's still tiny in my hold, but there's more colour in her cheeks, more life in her voice. Her numbers are up, and the doctors are optimistic. Aiden told me he's been sleeping better since the news, even if he'd never admit just how scared he was before.
I set her down on the bed, ruffling her scarf-covered head. "Miss me, princess?"
She nods, swinging her legs. "Aidy said you were too busy training to come see me, but I told him you'd visit."
I smirk. "You know me too well."

She beams, then pulls something from under her blanket. "I made you a good luck charm!"

It's a tiny bracelet, woven in blue and white threads. I stare at it, my heart squeezing in my chest.

"Do you like it?" she asks, suddenly unsure.

I slide it onto my wrist immediately. "I love it, Soph."

She claps her hands together, satisfied. "Now you have to win."

I laugh, pressing a kiss to her forehead. "I'll do my best."

I spend the next hour with Soph. Her asking me about our final choreography and why mint chocolate chip ice cream, is the best.

I left her room a converted woman.

World Championships are chaos. The moment Alexei and I land, we're thrown into nonstop training, press conferences, and the heavy weight of expectation. This is our moment. Our last shot before the Olympics team is finalized. And I refuse to let it slip through my fingers.

Alexei meets my gaze across the rink as we step onto the ice for the free skate, his expression determined. "You ready, Malyshka?"

I take a deep breath. "Let's do this."

I tighten my grip on Alexei's hand as we step onto the ice. The crowd is deafening, but in this moment, it's just us. My best friend. My partner. We take our positions, facing each other. A single breath passes between us. I nod and he nods back.

The music begins. Soft, delicate piano notes ripple through the arena, weaving through the tension in the air. We push off together, our blades carving perfectly synchronized arcs into the ice. Every movement is second nature. Every step, a heartbeat.

I exhale sharply, preparing for our first pass. We gather speed, skating in perfect symmetry toward our first element—side-by- side triple axels.

I take off, then—I land. Clean. Effortless.

Alexei lands half a second later, perfectly in sync, like he's been doing this with me his entire life.

Alexei reaches for me. Without a shred of hesitation, I jump into his hands, and he lifts me into a soaring quad twist. The world tilts as I spin, his strength keeping me aloft. I spot the ice, knowing exactly when to prepare for the landing. Alexei's hands catch me like I'm weightless, lowering me smoothly to the ice. The roar of the crowd spikes. But I don't hear it. I only hear the music, the sharp glide of our skates, the familiar rhythm of us.

We build speed into our side-by-side triple lutz, landing in

perfect unison.

Alexei's grip on my waist tightens. My body tenses. He throws me into the air. I twist.

One. Two. Three. Four.

I land. Solid. Unshaken. Perfect. The sound of the blades slicing across the ice is like music itself, smooth and endless. My heart slams against my ribs as I meet Alexei's eyes.

We did it.

My heart is racing as we glide into our last sequence— side- by-side biellmann spins.

We push off into our edges, arms stretching toward the sky, bodies arching into impossible curves, the world blurring around us. Our final pose—his hand gripping my waist, my fingers clutched around his wrist, our breathing ragged but victorious—feels like the culmination of everything we've fought for.

The music ends and for a moment, there's nothing but silence.

The arena erupts.

I can hear my heartbeat pounding in my ears.

The scoreboard flashes, bright and undeniable. Highest score of the night. Gold.

My knees buckle. The roar of the arena is deafening, the weight of the moment slamming into me all at once. We did it. I did it.

I press my hand to my mouth, my breath coming in sharp, disbelieving gasps.

Alexei lets out a shout of triumph, lifting me clean off the
ice, spinning me in a tight hug. His laughter rings in my ears, giddy and victorious. "You did it, Katerina!" he yells, his arms strong around me.

I did it.

For a second, it doesn't feel real. The fear, the doubts, the years of clawing my way back—it all led to this moment. I hear the cheers, the cameras flashing, the rush of skaters and officials flooding the ice, but all I can do is clutch my best friend, my partner, the one who never let me fall. Tears blur my vision, but I don't care.

I hold onto Alexei, my body shaking with laughter, with disbelief, with something too big to put into words.

And then—I see him. My handsome boyfriend, standing at the rink barrier, hands gripping the railing, his eyes locked onto mine. Everything inside me stills. For a heartbeat, it's just him and me. Then I move.

I don't think. I sprint off towards him, still in my skates, nearly tripping as I leap toward him. Aiden catches me without hesitation, just like I knew he would.

His arms wrap around me tightly, lifting me against him, his face buried in my hair.

"You're incredible," he murmurs against my ear, his voice thick with emotion. My hands fist into the fabric of his jacket, my chest heaving.

"I can't believe it," I whisper, still trembling.

He pulls back just enough to look at me, his dark eyes searching mine.

"Believe it," he says, voice gruff and full of pride. I let out a breathless laugh, my forehead dropping against his. For years, I thought winning would be the thing that completed me.

But this moment, this man, his arms around me—this is the real gold. He cups my jaw, his thumb tracing my cheekbone. "You are—" He shakes his head, as if he can't find the words.

"I love you, Katerina."

The noise, the cameras, the world—it all fades away. I tighten my grip on him, my chest aching with something deep and certain.

"I love you too," I whisper and then his lips are on mine. The kiss is slow, deep, unshakably real. Not a victory kiss. Not a rush of adrenaline.

Something more, something that tells me he's here, always.

When I pull away from Aiden, my mom is there, staring at me with a proud look on her face. Tears are streaming down her face, but she's smiling.

"My baby," she breathes, pulling me into a tight hug, her hands shaking as they cup my face. I blink back my own tears, my throat tight.

For so long, I wanted to make her proud. To show her I could do this, that I could get back everything I lost. I don't have to ask. I see it in her eyes.
"I'm so proud of you," she whispers. "So, so proud." A choked laugh escapes me as I nod, pressing my forehead to hers. Then—a voice I wasn't sure I'd hear today.
"I knew you would do it."
I turn, my heart stopping. My father. I grin at him as he stands a few feet away, hands in his pockets, his expression unreadable. I walk toward him, my steps sure and when he hugs me, I let him.

The medal is heavy around my neck. The cameras are still flashing. Reporters are shouting questions, my coaches are crying, and Alexei is already talking about our next routine. But, all I can feel is this warmth inside me. Aiden is here. My mom is here and even my father is here.
For so long, I thought I had to win alone, that to be strong, I had to stand on my own.
But I was wrong, because this moment? It's not just mine. It belongs to everyone who never stopped believing in me. To Aiden, who saw past my walls, to Alina, my sister in every way that matters, to Alexei, my partner, my best friend. To my mother, who fought battles I never even saw. Even to my father, who, in his own way, came back. I have everything I ever wanted. And as I step onto the highest podium, lifting my face toward the ceiling, letting the weight of gold press against my skin—
I close my eyes.

And I breathe it all in. This is it.
This is happiness.

EPILOGUE

KATERINA

The first snowfall of the season drapes the campus in white, and for once, life feels light.

No pressure. No uncertainty. Just happiness.

I stand by the rink, watching Aiden skate circles around the empty ice, his movements effortless. He's showing off, smirking at me every time he pulls off a sharp stop or sends ice flying in my direction.

"Are you trying to impress me?" I call, wrapping my coat tighter around me.

He skates toward me, stopping just short of the boards, leaning over them with that familiar cocky grin. "Is it working?"

I pretend to consider. "Hmm. I don't know. I think I'm more impressed when you win championships."

His smirk deepens. "Oh, you love when I win championships." I roll my eyes, but my smile betrays me. "Shut up and kiss me,

Knight."

He doesn't hesitate.

Aiden tugs me forward, pressing his lips to mine, soft but sure. I melt into him, my fingers gripping his jacket, his arms wrapping around my waist, holding me like he never intends to let go.

When we finally break apart, I press my forehead against his. "I love you."

The words come easily now, without hesitation, without fear. Because I do. I love him in a way that is undeniable, unshakable.

Aiden brushes a thumb over my cheek, his gaze filled with

something deep and endless. "I love you too, Angel Face."

I breathe him in, letting myself get lost in this moment, in

him.

The Olympics are just around the corner. Our futures are wide open. But right here, right now, none of that matters.

All that matters is us. Happily. In love. Together.

And for the first time in my life, I know I'm exactly where I'm

meant to be. The cheers are deafening. The weight of the medal around my neck is familiar, but this time—it means everything.

A year later…. Olympic gold.

I close my eyes, inhaling the moment, letting the rush of victory sink into my bones. I did it. After years of pain, after pushing my body past its limits, after nearly losing it all—I stand here, an Olympic champion.

And when I step off the podium, the first person I see is him. Aiden pushes past the barriers, past security, past every single person trying to keep him back. And then he's there, lifting me off the ground, spinning me until I can't breathe, pressing his

lips to mine as if he's been waiting his whole life to do it.

"You did it, Angel Face," he murmurs against my lips, his voice hoarse with emotion.

I smile, brushing my nose against his. "So did you, NHL

superstar."

He smirks, but there's something softer in his eyes. "Not as impressive as Olympic gold."

I scoff. "Please. You won the Stanley Cup last season."

"And I'd trade it in a second just to see you like this," he says, voice serious, gaze steady. "Happy. Unstoppable."

I don't think I'll ever stop falling for him.

The End

Breaking The Ice (Again)
Pleasant Oaks University Book Two

Sneak Peak

PROLOGUE

ROMAN

The world ended on a rainy Thursday night.
I don't remember the crash. Not really. Just headlights screaming toward us, Maddie's sharp gasp, and the sickening crunch of metal collapsing. Then blackness.
When I woke up, everything was too bright. Too white. A sterile smell clung to my nose, and there was an IV taped to my arm. For a few seconds, I thought it had been a nightmare. That Maddie would be beside me, cracking some stupid joke about how I looked like hell. But then my father's voice cut through the fog.
"She's gone, Roman."
I think my soul ripped apart in that moment.
I don't remember much after that. I must have screamed because my throat was raw when I woke up again. Will was there, sitting in the chair beside my hospital bed, staring at the floor like if he looked up, he might shatter. His hands were clenched, knuckles white. His voice was hollow when he finally spoke.
"She was everything to me."
I wanted to tell him I knew. That she was everything to me too. But the words wouldn't come.

Maddie's funeral was two days later. The sky was a dull, heavy gray, thick with the kind of storm that never quite breaks. I stood in the front, my body stiff in a black suit that felt too tight, too suffocating. The casket was closed. They wouldn't let us see her. Not after what the crash had done.

Will stood beside me, his shoulders shaking, silent tears streaking his face. He hadn't spoken all morning.

Graysen was next to him, his usually sharp expression hollowed out. Aiden and Kat held hands tightly, as if letting go would pull them under. Alexei stood behind them, his face unreadable, but his eyes were red.

Alina wasn't there.

She hadn't answered a single call, hadn't shown up at the hospital, hadn't been here now. I wanted to be angry, to curse her name for not saying goodbye to the person who loved her like a sister. But all I felt was numb.

The priest spoke in a low voice, but I barely heard him. My hands were clenched into fists, nails biting into my palms. This wasn't real. It couldn't be. Maddie was too loud, too wild, too alive to be lying in that box.

Then they started lowering her into the ground, and Will broke. A choked, gut-wrenching sob ripped from him as he fell to his knees. He pressed a hand to his face, shaking so hard that Graysen had to grab his arm to steady him. I turned away, because if I looked at him for another second, I would shatter too.

Kat was crying into Aiden's chest, her small frame trembling. Alexei just stood there, silent, but his jaw was clenched like he was holding back something too dangerous to let loose.

And then there was me.

Standing there, feeling like my insides had been hollowed out, like I was nothing but an empty body walking through a life that didn't belong to me anymore. Maddie had been my little sister. My only sibling. And now she was just a name on a gravestone.

The priest finished speaking. People began to leave. But I stayed. I stood there, staring at the fresh dirt covering my sister, and realized something terrifying.
I couldn't remember the sound of her laugh.

I don't know how long I stood there after everyone left. The cemetery had emptied, the sun slipping lower, but I couldn't move. My hands were shaking at my sides, nails digging into my palms so hard they might draw blood. The air was thick with the scent of damp earth, of flowers that would wilt in a matter of days.
Will had been the last to go. He had stayed kneeling by her grave long after everyone else had left, his fingers pressed against the cold dirt like he could still reach her. When Graysen finally convinced him to stand, he looked at me, his eyes hollow.
"She was supposed to be my forever," he whispered. His voice was wrecked, torn apart. "I was supposed to marry her."
I couldn't answer.
Because I knew. I had seen it in the way he looked at her, the way she had looked back. Maddie had been his whole world. And now that world was gone.
I let him leave. Let him break somewhere else because I couldn't bear to see it anymore. But I stayed. Alone with the silence, with the fresh grave, with the overwhelming weight pressing down on my chest.
A cold wind cut through the cemetery, rattling the branches of the bare trees above. I barely felt it.
I swallowed hard and dropped to my knees, pressing my forehead against the damp ground.
"I'm so sorry, Maddie," I whispered. My voice cracked. "I was supposed to protect you."

She had been in the passenger seat. I had been driving. That much, I knew. But the rest was a blur of screeching tires and shattering glass. The doctors told me there was nothing I could've done, that the other car had come out of nowhere, that the impact had been too sudden, too violent.

But none of that mattered. She had been with me, and now she was gone.

I stayed until my hands were numb, until my suit was soaked from kneeling in the damp grass. Until the world grew dark around me.

Then I felt a presence behind me.

I turned sharply, my pulse hammering, but it was only Alexei. He stood a few feet away, his expression unreadable, his dark coat blending into the shadows. He didn't say anything at first, just watched me.

"I knew you'd still be here," he finally said.

I swallowed against the lump in my throat. "She's gone, Alexei." The words barely came out.

He nodded once, like he understood. Maybe he did. He walked closer, his movements slow, careful, like he thought I might break. "You should come back."

"I can't."

He sighed, shoving his hands into his coat pockets. "Then I'll wait."

He sat down a few feet away, staring at the grave. Neither of us spoke. There was nothing to say.

I don't know how much time passed, but at some point, I closed my eyes, exhaustion weighing me down. I thought maybe, just maybe, Maddie's voice would come back to me. That I would hear her laugh, remember the way she used to tease me, hear the way she said my name.

But there was nothing. Just silence.

CHAPTER ONE

ALINA

"I can't believe you're leaving me Kat." i groan as I lay in Kat's bed. She smiles and drops the shirt she was folding, walks towards her bed, laying down with me. "I'm sorry Ali. Aiden's new team starts their training camp next week. I'm trying to spend as much time as I can, before our intense Olympic training starts. " I groan wrapping my arms around her. Who am I going to annoy at two am. Whose bed am I going to crawl when my heart hearts?
"Won't you miss Michigan though? And your dad?" Maddie nods but manages to give me a tight lipped smile.
"I will, but it's not like I'll be gone forever. Plus, my dad can visit me all the time. I'll miss Will and Roman though. Since Maddie passed away both of them have given up and seem to have this don't give a fuck mentality." She says, worry written all over her face, my heart drops at the mention of Roman.
God knows how much i miss him, but he really hurt me by pushing me away. I deserve someone that will give me all of themselves not just small parts.
"He is okay. As okay ass he can be, given the circumstances. I noticed your Aura changed as soon as I mentioned him." I nod pressing my lips in a thin line. At least he is not here this semester.

"Just a warning you'll probably see him around campus." My head snapped toward Kat so fast i almost broke my neck.

"Why? Wasn't he supposed to graduate last semester?" Kat nods as she looks away from me.

"Why didn't he?" I ask, having a bad feeling.

Why the hell would he drop out of the semester and want to spend more time in college, instead of playing hockey with his best friend on NHL.

"Oh my god! Did he lose his spot of the NHL team?" I bring my hands to my mouth, flabbergasted at all the information thrown at me. I know he is really going through it after losing Maddie, did he throw away everything he worked for?

"I can't tell you why he dropped out, it's his secret to say, but no, he did not lose his spot. He will just start after he graduates." I take a deep breath in relief nodding my head.

At least there's that.

The door creaks open and our heads snap towards it.

"Ali, Kat, it's almost ten pm. We all want to leave together." I nod at Stass, standing up from Kat's bed and walking towards the door.

"Ali" Kat calls, making me halt in my steps.

"For what it's worth, he still cares about you. Very much so." My heart skips a couple beats as it hammers out of my chest, but all I do is nod and walk out of the room following Stassie to her room.

"What are you wearing?" I ask as Stass opens her closet. She shrugs as she looks through her closet. Stassie, is short for Anastasia, my cousin. During my break semester, I was in Russia for about a month and then flew to Spain where I spent the rest of the summer with my mom's grandparents and Stassie's family.

Somehow I convinced my uncle to let Stassie come to the US and train as a figure skater and dancer here, at one of the best universities.

I love my cousin, but she has no filter and most of the time, she gets herself in trouble non stop.

"I'm all ready, are you guys almost done?" I glance at our roommate Talai and smile.

"Lai-lai, you look so pretty." I say pointing at her up and down.

Talai, is part of our figure skating team and she also dances with me. She is the sweetest human you will ever find.

Her outfit definitely slays. She has on a pair of high waisted shorts with a pair of black cowboy boots and a black corset top. Her hair is pinned straight and she has minimal makeup on but a bright red lipstick on.

"God damn girl." Stassie says clapping.

"Enough about me, it's your guys turn. Stass, find what you're wearing and Alina, go to your room and finish getting ready." I chuckle but get up nodding.

"Yes mom, I'll be out in fifteen." I walk out of their rooms and into mine across the hall.

Excitement floats through me at the thought of seeing Roman again, but I'm also scared and anxious.

God I'm going to throw up.

I walk inside my walk-in closet and skim through my clothes until I find the perfect outfit.

I put on this white tube bra top, with my beige jean mini skirt. A pair of knee-high maroon boots and an over sight maroon leather jacket. I add some cream to my hair, to refresh my curly hair, some blush on my cheeks and a layer of my fav maroon lipstick.

I smack my lips as I look at myself in the mirror and nod spraying my signature perfume, KAYALI vanilla.

Everyone always asks me what perfume I'm wearing wherever I go.

Grabbing my phone and making sure my ID is on the back of my case, I walk out of my room and make my way downstairs.

"God damn cousin. Who will be the lucky man tonight?" Stassie asks as she grabs my right hand and spins me around.

"Hopefully my other bestie," Kat says walking out of her room." my cheeks flush as I shake my head no.

"Are you coming with us?" Talai asks Kat, but she shakes her head no.

"No i have to get everything ready before I leave tomorrow." I nod as she walks into our kitchen and turn my attention to Stassie. Her outfit it cute. She has a white lace bralette on, a black mini skirt, black boots and cropped black leather jacket.

"No drama tonight." I say pointing at Stassie. She rolls her eyes and raises her hands up.

Stassie is such a trouble maker. I know there will be drama tonight and my cousin will be the center of it.

We walk out of the house and get into the Uber that was waiting for us. I need to make sure he gets a good tip. The guy confirms my name and starts driving towards the Hockey house.

After finding out Roman is here, my stomach keeps twisting and turning into backflips.

Nothing a drink can't fix Alina. He hurt you and you left. He hurt you by pushing you away.

It's his fault.

Fifteen minutes later the car stops in front of the familiar house.

I tip the driver and we all get out, walking towards the entrance hand in hand. The front door is open and you can hear the loud music outside.

The smell of alcohol surrounds u the moment we step inside the house and it's hot. Very hot.

Talai goes to grab a couple of drinks while Stassie and I hang out jackets into their closet.

Perks of having been at this house over and over before. Talai returns with our drinks and we gulp them all day, going for a second round and third.

Carry on from timberland and Justin Timberlake starts playing and Stassie screams, dragging us into the makeshift dance floor.

"Me, you, all night." Stassie screams moving her body. I laugh moving my hips down to the floor and then up again.

I grind into Talai who grinds into Stassie, all three of us moving our bodies together.

I spin around to face Talai but my eyes move behind her and catch the attention of the one person I was trying to avoid.

My smile drops and I stop dancing as I see Roman across the room, staring at me with the same intensity as he always would.

Is it possible for a guy to get hotter? This guy just gets hotter and hotter. The white tee he has on is a little loose on is body, but his biceps look like they are about to break the shirt.

Someone starts dancing behind me and I feel someones crotch in my back. I notice it's a guy by their arms and Talai starts clapping as the guy dances with me. Tries to dance cause I'm not moving,

I look back at Roman and he tightens his hold on his cup so much, that he breaks it and there is glass everywhere. I notice blood starts dripping from his hand, but all he does is stare at me.

Grayson says something to him and Roman nods, walking away and upstairs.

My god, he is dripping blood everywhere. Is he okay?"
Will he pass out? What if he passes out?
"I'll be right back." I say stepping away and making my way through the crowd and walk upstairs towards Romans room.
I knock but I get no reply. I turn the doorknob and open the door, making my way inside. I hear water running so he must be trying to clean his wound.
I stop by his bathroom door and take a deep breath, as I see him by the sink, trying to remove glass with tweezers not even noticing I'm here.
"That seems painful." I say crossing my arms and leaning into the bathroom door.
Roman turns to face me looking shocked that I'm in his room. God he is so handsome. How can I ever move on when he looks at me like I'm the only girl in the world.
"You're here." He mutters. I nod taking a couple steps towards him and grabbing his hand into mine, bringing it up so I can inspect the cut.
I grab the tweezers from his other hand and nod towards the counter. He sits on it opening his legs and my traitor body moves in between them. I remove glass piece, after glass piece until there is nothing left. Roman says nothing, just stares at me.
I rinse his hand with water and damp a cloth in alcohol dabbing it in his cuts. For the last step, I grab a gauze and tape and wrap it around his hand. When I'm done I take a step back but Romans hands wrap around my waist, stopping me from moving any further.
"You are actually here." He whispers as he moves a piece of my hair behind my ear.
"You look beautiful Solnyshka. I love the pink hair." Blush creeps on my cheeks and all I can do is look down at the floor.

He loves calling me that, his own sunshine. When we first meet he would ask me what sunshine was in Russian. I would lie to him, but then the bastard googled it and kept calling me it.

I pretended to hate it, but it's now my favourite word.

"Why are you here?" I ask with a frown. "You were supposed to graduate last semester and be with your team." Roman laughs and for a second I think he has lost it.

"Long story, but i promise you there is no other place I'd rather be than here." Roman hand goes under my chin and he lift it up. I look at him and he takes a deep breath, his green eyes roaming my face, as if he is trying to memorize every tiny detail about me.

"God Alina, how do you go from beautiful to breathtaking in a couple of months?" his thumb, pulls my lower lip and he lets go, my lower lip bouncing back in it's place.

"Roman, I need some help with- "Aliiiii" Will runs towards me engulfing me into a big hug.

"I missed you so much. Thank god you are back, I have no one to talk to about my shit, this dumbass doesn't care and Kat and Aiden are leaving me." I chuckle as he wraps his arms around my shoulder and pulls me towards the door.

"Let's grab a drink. I'm so happy you're back." I nod at Will but glance at Roman one more time, who is looking at us amused.

We make our way downstairs, with Roman following behind us.

"There you are. We were looking everywhere for you." Stassie says lacing her hand with mine.

"Excuse me, can you take your hands of my cousin, before I cut them off of you?" Will scoffs pulling me more towards him.

"Try me hot stuff. I just got Ali back who are you to tell me to get my hands off her?" Will shouts at Stassie who looks like she will explode.

"I'm her cousin you dickhead, who the fuck are you?" Stass asks as she wraps her left arm around my shoulders pulling me towards her.

"I'm her best friend you crazy." I chuckle pulling away from both of them.

"Okay enough, I'm not a rag doll. Will, this is my cousin Anastasia and that's our friend Talai. Stass, this is William one of my best guy friends." Stass nods as she glares at Will and then looks behind him.

"Who the hell is that?" I press my lips into a thin line and point at Roman. "This is Roman."

I say Romans name fast but Stassie understands me and smirks. "That's Roman? God damn, good choice cuz." she whispers in my ear but I push her away.

"Either way, we were leaving. We've been here long enough," I add quickly, hoping to avoid any more awkward exchanges. My head is spinning from the alcohol and the sight of Roman, and I'm not sure how much more I can handle tonight.

"Leaving? We just got here!" Will groans, but Talai nods, picking up on the tension hanging in the air.

"Ali's right. We've had enough fun for one night," Talai says, her tone softer, as if she senses the turmoil brewing inside me.

Stassie raises an eyebrow but doesn't argue, for once. "Fine. Let's bounce before I cause a scene."

I breathe a sigh of relief and turn to grab my jacket. But just as I'm about to move, I feel a hand gently wrap around my wrist.

"Ali," Roman says softly, his touch sending shivers up my spine. I freeze, not turning around.

"Please, just... one minute," his voice is barely above a whisper, but I hear the ache in it.

I swallow hard, my throat suddenly dry. I know if I look at him, I'm done for. But against my better judgment, I turn.

"Roman—"

"Just... let me explain. Not here. Not tonight. But soon," his green eyes search mine, filled with something I can't decipher. Hope? Regret? I don't know.

I shake my head, pulling my hand back gently.

"Roman... I can't do this again. Not right now."

His jaw clenches, but he nods. "I get it. But I'm not giving up on you, Alina. I never did."

His words hit me harder than I expect, and for a second, I almost let my guard down. Almost.

"Let's go," I murmur, forcing my feet to move before I get trapped in his orbit again.

Stassie, Talai, and Will follow me out of the house, the cool night air hitting me like a wave of reality.

"Well, that was... intense," Stassie mutters as we make our way toward the street.

"Are you okay?" Talai asks, concern etched on her face.

"I will be," I lie, my stomach still twisted in knots.

"That's the famous Roman, huh?" Stassie pipes up, smirking. "No wonder you're messed up over him. That man is fine."

"Stass, not helping," I mumble, running a hand through my hair.

"Sorry, sorry," she says, but I catch the playful glint in her eye.

"Do you want to talk about it?" Talai asks gently, her voice more understanding.

"Not tonight," I whisper. "I just need to clear my head."

Will wraps an arm around me, giving me a comforting squeeze. "You know I'm always here, Ali. Whatever you need."

I lean into him for a moment, grateful for his steady presence.

As we wait for our Uber, my mind drifts back to Roman's words.

I'm not giving up on you.

God help me. Because I'm not sure I'm strong enough to keep pushing him away.

ACKNOWLEDGMENTS

There are moments in life that feel like turning points. For me, this book is one of them.

Publishing this story—Aiden and Kat's story—is something I've dreamed about for as long as I can remember. Since I was little, I've been scribbling short stories in notebooks, filling pages with characters and feelings I never quite had the courage to share. I kept those stories close, never thinking they'd one day lead me here. But here I am, and I didn't get here alone.

To my family—thank you for always believing in me, even during the times I doubted myself. Your love and support have been the foundation I've leaned on through every step of this journey.

To my husband—thank you for your patience, your constant encouragement, and your unwavering belief in my dream. You saw this version of me before I did. To my sweet three-year-old son—you might be too young to understand this now, but you inspire me in ways you can't imagine. You remind me daily of the kind of strength, joy, and love that fuels everything I write.

To my mom, my sister —your faith in me has meant the world. You never let me forget that I'm capable, even on the days when self-doubt shouted the loudest. You pushed me, supported me, and reminded me why I started writing in the first place.

To finally be able to say, "I published my book," still feels surreal. It took courage I didn't think I had—but I found it, with the help of every single person who stood beside me.

To my beta readers—thank you for taking the time to read, question, and guide this story into what it is now.

Nicoletta and Chassidy, your insights were thoughtful, honest, and so incredibly helpful. You didn't just read this book—you helped shape it, and I'm so grateful.

To my formatting team—thank you for bringing polish and professionalism to the final product. You helped me take this across the finish line with confidence. And Farisai—thank you for helping me bring my vision of Katerina and Aiden to life. It's stunning, and it captures the soul of this book in a way I didn't think was possible.

To my ARC team—thank you for being excited to dive into Aiden and Kat's journey before the rest of the world got the chance. Your support, your kind words, and your willingness to take a chance on a debut author means more than you know.

This book started as a quiet dream. Today, it's real. And it's because of all of you.

From the bottom of my heart—thank you.

To my readers—thank you for picking up this story and spending time with these characters. Whether you laughed, cried, or stayed up way too late reading, just know: you made this journey worthwhile. I hope Aiden and Kat's story touched you in some way, big or small. And if you're someone out there holding onto a dream, afraid to share it—this is your sign.

"There is no greater agony than bearing an untold story inside you." —Maya Angelou

Keep writing. Keep dreaming. Keep going.

With love,
    A.C. MOTUGA

www.ingramcontent.com/pod-product-compliance
Lightning Source LLC
LaVergne TN
LVHW041738060526
838201LV00046B/849